The ThinkTank Book

The ThinkTank™ Book

Jonathan Kamin

Berkeley • Paris • Düsseldorf • London

Cover design by Sharon Leong
Book design by Lisa Amon

ISBN 0-89588-224-8
Manufactured in the United States of America
Printed by Haddon Craftsmen
10 9 8 7 6 5 4 3 2

TO ESTELLE AND HENRY KAMIN,
my parents—
whose unwavering faith and support
made possible the circumstances
in which to write this book.

I could rule the world,
If I could only get the parts.

—The Waitresses, 1983

ACKNOWLEDGEMENTS

This book would not have been possible without the contributions of many others. First and foremost, I owe a debt of immense gratitude to David Greene. David helped introduce me to computers, gave me my first exposure to ThinkTank, helped me out of assorted technical jams, and discussed many of the ideas presented in this book with me when they were in their formative stages. A great deal of the material in Chapter 10 in particular is based on David's thinking on the subject.

Many people at Living Videotext, Inc., publishers of ThinkTank, went out of their way to help me in this project. Two in particular deserve special note: David Winer, president of Living Videotext, provided me with information available nowhere else, and arranged for the use of a computer on which to test the program and create the manuscript; Mary Cadloni lent a sympathetic ear when I ran into problems, gave me a great deal of help and advice, and took an active interest in the project as it progressed, Scott Love went over the manuscript carefully and offered helpful suggestions.

Of no less importance are many members of the staff of SYBEX. Carole Alden, editor extraordinaire, did her utmost to squeeze every obscurity and ambiguity out of the text, and is largely responsible for whatever style and grace it may have. Rudy Langer supported the project from the beginning. Paul Panish and Lorraine Aochi took an active part in the manuscript's development. Joel Kreisman tested all my examples, to ensure their accuracy. Kathy Jones, Barbara Wetzel, and Wally Rutherford discussed the ideas presented in Chapter 6 with me, and helped steer me in fruitful directions. Doug Mosher, an avid ThinkTank user, was always ready to share his insights into the program's workings, and provided me with the results of his research on file sizes, which are presented in Chapter 9. Special thanks are also due to Valerie Robbins, who word-processed the manuscript under great pressure, to Sarah Seaver, who did a masterful job on the index, to Bonnie Gruen who added editorial assistance, and to the members of the SYBEX Production Department, who gave it its present form: Lisa Amon, design and paste-up, Donna Scanlon, typesetting, and Dawn Amsberry, proofreading.

Before I began the actual manuscript, many ThinkTank users were kind enough to share their ideas concerning what would be useful to have in a book such as this one. For these efforts, I thank Mike McKeon, Bernie DeKoven, Don Decker, Rachel Carter, Steven Berman, G. C. Jernstedt, Bill Langenes, David Glaser, James G. Loofbourrow, and Philip S. Magee. I hope this book meets all of your needs.

Finally, thanks to my wife Nancy, for her patience.

TABLE OF CONTENTS

3 The Grand Tour   29

6 From an Idea to a Master Plan   113

7 Using the Paragraph Editor   131

8 Printing a Document   167

9 Managing Your Files and Working around Bugs 195

10 Thinking about Thinking 217

INTRODUCTION

This book will help you get a handle on ThinkTank, whether you are a person who is just starting out or an experienced user. If you are a novice, you will find it helpful to begin by reading *The ThinkTank User's Manual* and then read the book from start to finish, trying out all of the examples, as many of the chapters are primarily tutorial in nature. On the other hand, if you are an experienced user, you can use the many tables as reference material, so the book will remain useful long after you have mastered the basics.

All levels of users will find a great deal to learn from *The ThinkTank Book.* It is not uncommon for someone to use this program for some time quite effectively, while gradually realizing that it has many more potential uses. The manual that is included with the software package explains all of ThinkTank's commands and modes, but it does not go into detail about *how* to use them.

I have attempted to go beyond these limits in several ways. First, I have provided projects to demonstrate the effects of every mode. Second, I have organized the projects in ways that require the use of several modes in the course of a task, so you can learn both the relationships between the modes and the most efficient ways of accomplishing various recurring tasks. Third, I have provided projects that suggest applications for the program that you may not have discovered for yourself. ThinkTank is quite open-ended in the variety of uses to which it can be put. When you have finished this book, you may find yourself both using the program for new purposes and using it more efficiently for your original purposes.

HOW THIS BOOK IS ORGANIZED

In the course of this book, the capabilities of ThinkTank will be demonstrated through a series of projects. You may choose to type in the examples exactly as they are presented in text. However, the selection of projects is varied enough to suggest parallel examples from your own projects. Feel free to type in your own information and to read only the sections that apply to your interests. Be sure to follow along with ThinkTank up and running on your computer, so you can try out combinations of keystrokes and observe their effects.

Let's take a brief tour through the book. **Chapter 1, "What is ThinkTank?"** introduces the program, gives a brief description of its structure, and suggests some of its many uses.

Chapter 2, "Setting up ThinkTank," is designed to get the package up and running. It explains the uses of the various programs on the ThinkTank Program Disk, and the types of files that ThinkTank can create. If you are an old hand at ThinkTank, you may safely skip this chapter, although you might find new and better ways to set up your work. If you are new to the package, however, I suggest you read this chapter carefully. It will help you avoid some of the pitfalls of using this software package for the first time.

If you are new to your computer, or if you have not run software that requires the use of the Disk Operating System (DOS) directly, at this point you may want to refer to **Appendix B.** Unlike many popular software packages that automatically activate whatever is needed from DOS, ThinkTank requires the user to interact with DOS. Appendix B will teach you enough of the basics of DOS to be able to use the program efficiently.

In **Chapter 3, "The Grand Tour,"** you are guided through all of ThinkTank's modes of operation. The tour starts with opening and closing files, so you can start a new file to work with. Next, you will learn to create and edit a simple outline, so you have some material on which to try out various other modes of operation. The INSERT mode, the Headline Editor, and the FILES mode are thoroughly explained in this chapter, while all the other modes are introduced briefly.

Chapter 4, "From a List to a Reuseable Calendar," takes you through a more complex exercise, to give you an idea of how ThinkTank can transform ideas. Starting with a simple list of things to do, you will learn how ThinkTank can reorganize it into a calendar. Next, you will use a technique called *templating* to create sets of headlines you will use repeatedly.

Chapter 5, "Creating Templates," shows you even more complex uses of templating. You will look over the shoulder of a salesman as he creates a system for logging sales calls, and follow him as he uses it. You will also follow a market researcher as he creates a system for keeping his resume up-to-date. As we watch, all the necessary keystrokes to accomplish these tasks—or equivalent tasks of your own—are introduced on the way. ThinkTank's word processor is also introduced briefly. By the time you finish this chapter, you should have a clear idea of how to use templating in your own work.

By the time you get to **Chapter 6, "From an Idea to a Master Plan,"** you will be familiar with the major aspects of the program, except for word processing and printing. At this point, we turn away from the details to get a larger view. In order to demonstrate how the many capabilities of ThinkTank can simplify and reorganize facets of a large problem, you will observe a mythical solar-heating company, Sky High Technologies, Inc., which has just developed a cost-effective, reasonably priced home solar heating/generating system. We will follow a marketing manager as she researches the market, gathers information, and puts together a final plan. In the course of this chapter, you will see ThinkTank used for brainstorming and organizing new ideas, creating and filling in the details of a plan, planning projects, scheduling, and a few other broad-scale purposes. These organizational principles will apply equally well to problems as diverse as developing a product plan, developing a grant proposal, setting up a new business, managing an office, or writing a book.

Chapter 7, "Using the Paragraph Editor," will show you the uses of the Paragraph Editor—ThinkTank's word processor. You will look at all the tricks to using the word processor effectively, many of which are barely mentioned in the *User's Manual*.

Chapter 8, "Printing a Document," explains the print formatting options. You will learn what they do and how to use them in combination to get the kind of printed output you want. You will also learn how to make the most effective use of ThinkTank prior to sending a file to WordStar, if ThinkTank's options cannot produce the results you desire.

In **Chapter 9, "Managing Your Files and Working Around Bugs,"** you will find out how to deal with problems like crashed files, files that are too long, and errors. In addition, you will create and transfer files with the PORT menu. In this chapter, you will also find many hints and tricks that will allow you to accomplish various tasks which you might have thought impossible in ThinkTank. Finally, a few miscellaneous commands are introduced.

Chapter 10, "Thinking about Thinking," concludes the exploration of ThinkTank with a brief review. This chapter also considers the implications of using an idea-processing software package.

Three appendices are included for reference. **Appendix A** is a reference table of all the ThinkTank commands, explained and listed alphabetically. **Appendix B** introduces the elements of the IBM Personal Computer Disk Operating System. If you have a computer that uses Microsoft's MS-DOS instead of PC-DOS, most of this appendix will be equally applicable to your computer. **Appendix C** is another reference table, explaining the effects of the escape key in ThinkTank's various modes.

TYPOGRAPHICAL CONVENTIONS

this type style   Anything that appears on the computer screen, whether generated by the computer or the program, or typed in by a user. Also used for DOS commands and prompts.

ALL CAPITALS   ThinkTank commands.

P T S S   Keys to be pressed in sequence by the user to enter commands.

Ctrl-Home   Keys to be pressed in combination by the user to enter commands.

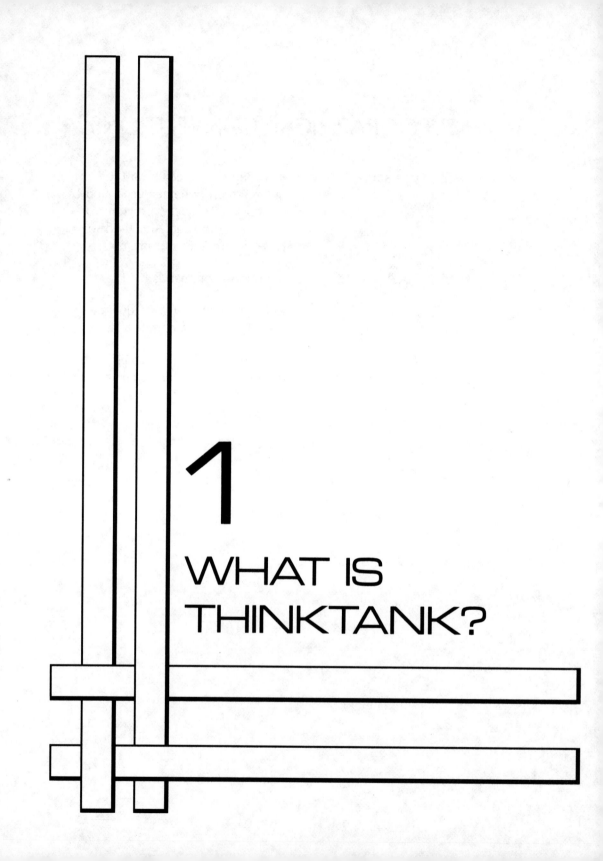

1

WHAT IS
THINKTANK?

ThinkTank is an entirely new type of software. At first glance, it shows some resemblance to a data base manager and to a word processor. When you start using ThinkTank, however, you will get the impression that its primary function is generating outlines. But it can do much more.

Most computer software is designed to speed up the accomplishment of specific tasks. Indeed, the best software seems designed to make a task one already knows faster and more efficient. A spreadsheet, for example, gives you a traditional format— a grid of numbers—to work with. Unlike a grid on paper, however, a spreadsheet program instantaneously makes changes throughout the grid when a single value changes, so you don't have to recalculate each value by hand. Similarly, a word processor is a transformation of the conventional typewriter. With a word processor, you can edit and format text before printing it on paper, eliminating tedious cutting, pasting, and retyping.

You can also look at ThinkTank as a program that simplifies a familiar task, creating outlines. ThinkTank is to hierarchical structures what a spreadsheet is to a grid of numbers. ThinkTank does allow you to create and maintain outlines to a high degree of complexity, and to change them easily without starting over from scratch.

However, ThinkTank has two characteristics that take it well beyond the limitations implied by the term "outline generator." First, it has been billed as "the first idea processor," and, properly used, it lives up to this billing. First, it simultaneously generates outlines, keeps files, and functions as a word processor, while it allows you to plan, manage, and organize all your projects *in multiple forms* at any stage of development. Second, ThinkTank's flexible structure lets you shift instantly from the big picture to any level of detail and back again. Because of this feature, you can use it to deal with problems involving more information than you could normally handle, without confusing your mind in the process.

To begin our exploration, let's look at the outline generating capacity of this unique package.

OUTLINES

No doubt, ever since you were in fifth grade, teachers have told you of the importance of outlines. Outlines will help you organize your thoughts, they said. Some of them may even have asked you to submit outlines along with your papers. But there's one thing they didn't tell you: outlines are very hard to maintain. Every time you want to add a new idea, your outline has to be redone. If a new idea changes the organization of your work, it's back to the drawing board. ThinkTank changes all that. You can insert new ideas where appropriate and move entire sections of outlines in a few keystrokes.

There's something else your teachers didn't tell you, probably because they didn't understand it fully: you can't organize your thoughts before you have had them. I can recall numerous occasions from my student days when I needed to bounce my thoughts off someone else. Until I had externalized my ideas, I couldn't really understand their implications and relationships. If I went to a teacher, I was asked for an outline, with the argument that if I couldn't outline my idea, I didn't understand it.

But I knew from personal experience that I could not create an outline of a project or a paper before I had both bounced my ideas off someone and done a substantial amount of background research. Only then would I understand my idea well enough to outline it. At this early stage, I just wanted to find out if my ideas had enough substance to merit proceeding with the background work.

In part, my predicament was a consequence of the nature of creative thinking itself. Rarely does an idea arrive fully formed, resplendent with detail. Mozart said his symphonies came to him this way, and he had but to copy them to score paper. But more commonly, creativity starts with a germ of an idea whose implications are not clear. As you start to toy with your idea, you may find yourself going in either of two directions, or perhaps both of them at once.

As you move in one direction, your idea may bear forth another little idea, which in turn produces others, and so on into the night. Later, you can look at your notes, if you're lucky enough to have taken any, and see how your thoughts fall together, rearrange some, discard others, and build on what you've got. Eventually, this process bears fruit in some form of finished product—the solution to a knotty technical problem that's been keeping you awake, or the conclusion that all your notes are pointing to that's been invisibly staring you in the face for days.

Research on creative thought has revealed that a basic principle of creativity is a deliberate alternation between two types of thought processes. At one time, a creative thinker lets the imagination flow freely, suspending all judgment. Later, critical thought is brought to bear on the products of the imagination. Scientific tests have shown that people who temporarily suppress their critical faculties generate almost twice as many effective ideas as those who permit their critical faculties to interfere with their imagination. As Friedrich von Schiller put it, "It hinders the creative mind if the intellect examines too closely the ideas as they pour in."

ThinkTank is an ideal tool for encouraging the separation of these two aspects of thought. When you are in the brainstorming stage, ThinkTank's flexibility allows you to enter ideas at random. When the time comes to assess and organize your thoughts, ThinkTank's hierarchical structure makes it easy to put them into some kind of useful and comprehensible order.

On the other hand, sometimes creativity proceeds in the opposite direction. You come up with an idea that obviously has far-reaching implications—the classic light-bulb-over-the-head exerience: a new product, the perfect research plan, or a new way of doing business. The goal is immediately clear, but how to get there is not quite so obvious. So you have to break your idea down into its component parts, and then translate the components into a series of steps to be carried out. ThinkTank is an excellent tool for this type of idea generation as well. You can place your main idea at the top of an outline, insert its component parts at a subordinate level, and then work on one component at a time, ignoring the others until you are ready to deal with them.

As you work on a problem, you may find both processes occurring at once. While plotting out the steps to achieve one of your intermediate goals, an unrelated, or even irrelevant, idea may come to your mind. You must record your thoughts as they come to you, or risk losing them forever. ThinkTank lets you move freely from one part of your outline to another, so you can capture those fleeting but useful thoughts while they are still fresh, and quickly return to where you left off. Later, when you have finished the task at hand, your fleeting thoughts will not have flown; they will be ready and waiting for you to use them.

The Structure of ThinkTank Outlines

An outline is a logical structure. In a well-structured outline, everything placed subordinate to a given heading is also *logically* subordinate to it. Therefore, if you know the overall structure of an outline, you should be able to deduce logically the headings superordinate to any given heading.

Although you can't see it in a traditional outline on paper, an outline is a *tree structure*. Let's look at a traditional paper outline, as illustrated in Figure 1.1.

This figure appears to be a simple series of steps. But if you go down the left margin, you will progressively encounter a number

<u>TITLE</u>

I. First Major Topic
   A. First Major Subhead
   B. Second Major Subhead
      1. First minor subhead to second major subhead
      2. Second minor subhead
         a. Sub-subhead
         b. Sub-subhead
            i. Detail
            ii. Detail
            iii. Detail
II. Second Major Topic
   A. First Major Subhead of Second Major Topic
III. Etc.

Figure 1.1: A typical outline structure.

of items (numbered I, II, and III) that are of equal importance. As you move to the right under one of these headings, you encounter another series of headings of equal importance (listed as A, B, and C), and so on. Figure 1.2 shows the same outline laid out as a tree. In Figure 1.2, you can follow any line upward and to the left to reach higher levels of generality.

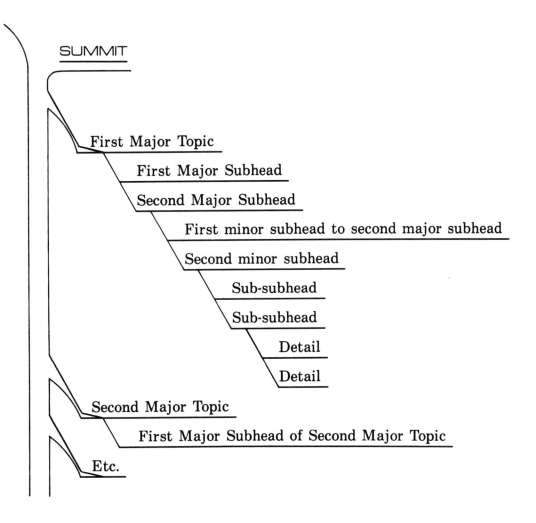

SUMMIT

First Major Topic

First Major Subhead

Second Major Subhead

First minor subhead to second major subhead

Second minor subhead

Sub-subhead

Sub-subhead

Detail

Detail

Second Major Topic

First Major Subhead of Second Major Topic

Etc.

Figure 1.2: A Typical outline shown as a tree structure.

ThinkTank takes advantage of the tree structure to allow for different kinds of organization. As you look at a ThinkTank outline on your computer screen you see, first, that everything is indented under the very top line (called *home* or the *summit* in ThinkTank). You also see the same indentations as in an outline on paper, with various items nested under others. But unlike a sheet of paper, ThinkTank lets you *expand* and *collapse* your outlines on the screen, so that you can look at any part of the structure you want to, with any degree of detail. If you collapse an outline and then expand it one degree, you will see only the major headings—the limbs of the tree whose root is at the top and whose trunk is the left margin of the screen. Expand one of the major headings, and you'll see the branches. Expand a branch, and you'll see the twigs, and so on. Each additional indentation corresponds to an additional level of detail in Figure 1.2. *And every heading has the potential for being the root of a similar logical structure.*

This is true because at any point in your outline, you can add levels of detail to a given heading, to a depth of 10,000 levels. Thus, every heading (called a *headline* in ThinkTank) is itself a potential outline.

Some headlines in a ThinkTank outline have plus signs to their left, and others have minus signs. The plus sign indicates the presence of additional detail under a headline. To see the additional detail, use the left-arrow and right-arrow keys on the numeric keypad to move the reverse-video highlight (called a *bar cursor* in ThinkTank) to the headline you want to examine, and press the + key to the right of the numeric keypad. If the details are not already visible, they will appear. (If they are already on the screen, the computer makes a sound and displays the message **fully expanded!**) When you are through examining the details, press the − key to the right of the numeric keypad to collapse the outline again. Thus, you can work with any degree of detail you need.

The Flexibility of ThinkTank Outlines

Although outlines are logical structures, we don't always think logically. Sometimes we completely change our perspective on a subject. ThinkTank not only allows you to build, expand and collapse outlines. It also allows you to rearrange them as the relationships between your ideas change.

If you discover that something you have nested in a subsection of a subsection is really your main idea, you can, with a minimum of effort, rearrange the entire structure to reflect your new perspective. If your headings appear to be in the wrong order, you can try them in new positions until the order looks right. If you find you have gone off on a tangent, you can move the tangental material to an appropriate spot in your outline. ThinkTank thus gives you access to the virtues of a paper outline without the restrictions it imposes.

ThinkTank's flexibility gives it other virtues as well. You can, in effect, have every part of your work, from in-basket to file cabinet, accessible on your computer at the same time. As you develop a new idea, you can throw in thoughts at random, and establish the relationships between them later. The ease with which you can make new entries encourages the free flow of ideas.

The Advantage of Modular Structure

ThinkTank treats all units of an outline at the same level of indentation as logically equal. Because of this fact, such units can be worked on independent of one another. They can also be moved within an outline without disturbing the relationship between the remaining units. As a result of these features, ThinkTank can be used for applications that require information organized in modules.

For example, a survey researcher might keep blocks of questions on specific topics—a set of demographic questions, a set of political-preference questions, a set of religious orientation questions, and a set of social-class determinants—each in a separate section of a ThinkTank outline. When she wants to construct a specific questionnaire, she simply opens up the appropriate section of her outline and pulls out the necessary questions each of which is a module at the same level as the others. She then can assemble them into their final form in a separate section of her outline.

Dan DeWitt, a management training consultant, also uses ThinkTank to manage modules of information in planning his training programs. "I teach from outlines," says Dan, "so of course, ThinkTank is useful for that. But even more important is how useful it is for training design. I can patch together parts of several training programs I've done before, and move modules around for maximum effectiveness. I can also use ThinkTank to create a 'boilerplate' that I can use for text for the trainees."

I have also talked to several software developers who say that they find ThinkTank a useful aid in creating structured code. They start with the goals of the program and enter a headline for each program module. Since all the modules are at the same level, it's relatively simple to keep rearranging them until the most efficient program design emerges. Working with each module independently, they then gradually add detail until the outline contains the complete pseudocode for a program.

BRAINSTORMING AND PLANNING

Another use for ThinkTank is brainstorming and project planning. With the help of ThinkTank, Sam Marino, an independent consultant, developed a plan for a product that he invented. He found the ease with which he could enter unstructured information in ThinkTank a great help in thinking through the ramifications of his idea. After brainstorming, he used ThinkTank's organizing power to sort his ideas into a plan—what the product would look like, what materials would be needed and how much they would cost, how to market it, and so on. Finally, he used ThinkTank to create a production schedule and keep track of his progress.

MAINTAINING FILES

ThinkTank's outline structure also lends itself to use as a data base manager. If you need to keep a number of similar records, e.g., phone logs, address entries, time sheets, or personnel records, you can set up a form, duplicate it any number of times, and move easily through the form, filling out each item in turn.

ThinkTank's sorting function can keep your records in alphabetical order, and its searching function can find any item in an outline.

Richard Wells, a salesman, uses ThinkTank to keep records of his sales calls. He has created a template (explained in Chapter 5), into which he inserts information about his clients. He also uses ThinkTank to keep track of the results of his sales calls and to keep his client lists in order.

Because ThinkTank will work with both headlines and complete paragraphs of text, and because all text must be created relative to a given headline, ThinkTank will also function as a data base system for storing, analyzing, and restructuring text. You can locate a paragraph by key words in its headline or let ThinkTank search for key words in the body of the text. You can move a paragraph, copy it, or add it to another paragraph, to see its relationship to your other ideas.

"Meetings, as you know, can be quite chaotic," points out Sarah Cantwell, secretary for a public organization, who finds this feature extremely helpful in preparing minutes for presentation. When she gets home after a meeting, Sarah enters all her notes, directly from her notepad, into a ThinkTank outline. Then she uses ThinkTank's organizational power to rearrange the information into meaningful groupings, so she can produce an orderly, comprehensible summary of what may have been quite disorderly proceedings.

THINKTANK AS A LEARNING TOOL

Students find ThinkTank invaluable for keeping notes on lectures and readings. ThinkTank's ability to restructure information allows learners to organize their new knowledge in an order that makes the most sense to them. Studies suggest that if a student rearranges newly learned material into a congenial form he or she learns that material more quickly and fully.

One such person is Susan Preston, an educational researcher, who kept all her notes from an anatomy and physiology course in a ThinkTank outline. Immediately after each lecture, she entered the notes into ThinkTank. As the course progressed, she found that she spent over 70 percent of her study time in ThinkTank. As she rearranged the information she had learned, she found that it became more comprehensible. She received an A in the course without any special preparation for the final exam.

CREATING TEXT

One of the reasons ThinkTank can perform such varied tasks successfully is that it contains a relatively powerful word processor. ThinkTank's Paragraph Editor has all the cursor-moving commands of WordStar, but since they are more logically defined, they are easier to learn. You can add, copy, or delete text anywhere in a paragraph, and you can make long documents by stringing paragraphs together. The ease with which you can move large blocks of text will be a pleasant surprise to anyone accustomed to the better-known word-processing programs.

ThinkTank will create files that can be read by WordStar, and by other word processing programs that use similarly structured files, so you can take your work up to the semifinal draft, transfer it to a word processor, and add the formatting before you print it.

Bob Langston, a professional writer, points out that "a word processor is relatively inefficient for outlining—it's not flexible enough. I like how easy it is to indent with ThinkTank, and to move things around." When Bob has all his ideas in their proper order, he uses ThinkTank's Paragraph Editor to write the first draft or two, and then transfers his file to WordStar for final polishing and formatting.

FREEDOM OF MOVEMENT

ThinkTank can thus be useful at many stages of your work. You can begin by roughing out and organizing your ideas. As your project develops, and you need to set up and coordinate schedules, lists of things needed and people to contact, ThinkTank will help you again. If you need to maintain files along the way, ThinkTank's data base characteristics come into play. When you are ready to make a verbal presentation to explain your work, ThinkTank will help you generate a compact outline from which to speak. If you want to supplement your talk with a written report, ThinkTank's Paragraph Editor will let you generate and organize that material, too, even if it's already embedded in your outline. You'll learn how to do all these things and more in the course of this book.

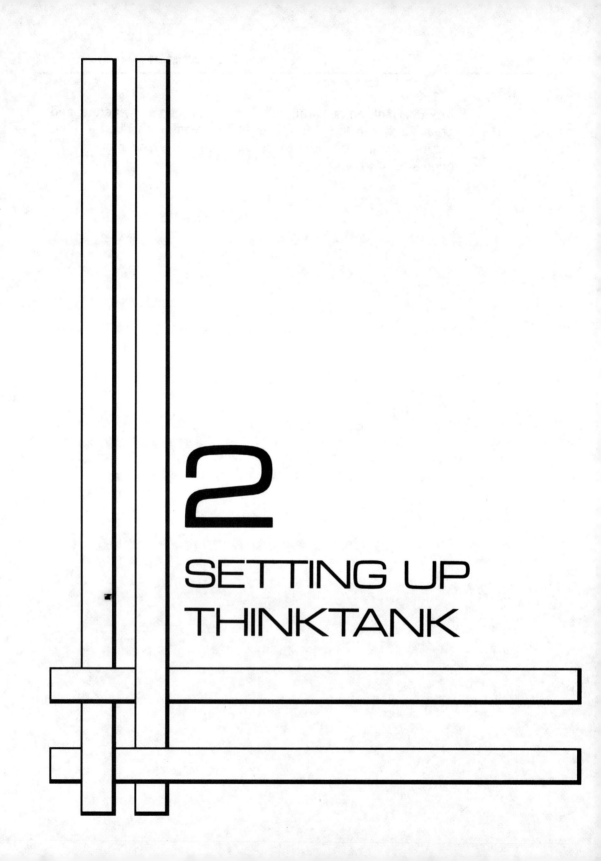

2
SETTING UP
THINKTANK

Before you start using ThinkTank, there are some things you should know about the way ThinkTank works in relationship to your computer. In this chapter, we will cover all these preliminaries. Although the information in this chapter is primarily background, please do not skip it—you will need it later, and it will make your use of ThinkTank flow more smoothly.

You will be introduced to all the files on the ThinkTank disk and what they are for, and you will learn how to customize ThinkTank for your computer system. You will also find out what kinds of files the program creates, and a bit about what they are good for. Finally, you will learn how to make backup copies of your files.

In order to make effective use of ThinkTank, you must understand something about your computer's Disk Operating System (DOS). If you are not familiar with DOS, please read Appendix B before going any further.

THINKTANK AND YOUR COMPUTER

Although ThinkTank will run on a variety of computers—the Apple II series and the Apple Macintosh, among others—this book deals with ThinkTank in its version for the IBM Personal Computer, and for such PC-compatibles as the Compaq and the Eagle. Users of the Apple II version of the program may find some of the applications useful, but the Apple II versions use entirely different keystrokes to enter the same commands, so if you are trying to adapt the content to one of those computers, be sure to have your manual handy.

To run ThinkTank on a PC or PC-compatible, your computer must have at least 256 kilobytes of random access memory (RAM). You will also need a monitor, your ThinkTank Program Disk, and a few blank disks formatted for your computer's operating system. If you are using an IBM-PC, you will need a version of the Personal Computer Disk Operating System (PC-DOS) numbered 2.0 or higher. If you are using a PC-compatible you must have the Microsoft Disk Operating System (MS-DOS), revision G or later.

GETTING STARTED

The very first thing you should do when you open the ThinkTank package is to *fill out and mail the warranty card*. When your card is received and processed, Living Videotext will send you a backup copy of the program disk.

You will also receive updated versions of the program as it is revised. If you still have version 1.000, for example, it is difficult to make the disk self-loading without destroying it, and you will probably encounter some errors that have since been corrected. If you have this version, and have filled out your warranty card, send your disk back to Living Videotext and ask for an update.

Backing up the Program Disk

The next thing to do is to make a backup copy of the disk. The disk is copy-protected, and copies will not run. However, if you run into trouble with any of the files on the ThinkTank Program Disk, you can remove the damaged files from the Program Disk and copy the backup copies back onto it. When you have completed these steps, the Program Disk should work properly again.

To make your backup copy, follow these steps:

Backing Up the Program Disk

KEYSTROKES	COMMANDS, ACTIONS, EFFECTS
	1. Insert yor DOS disk in drive A and turn on the computer.
Ctrl-Alt-Del	2. If the computer is already on, and you do not see an **A>** prompt, do a *warm boot*.
	3. Insert the Program Disk in drive A and a blank, formatted disk in drive B.
copy a:*.* b:/v ↵	4. Enter the DOS **COPY** command. The **/v** at the end of the command enters the DOS **VERIFY** command, which will generate an error message if the copy is not identical to the original.

erase b:*.* ↵

5. If you receive an error message, erase the disk to which you are copying the files, and repeat the procedure.

Configuring the Disk for Your System

If you don't have exactly two floppy disk drives, the next step is to run the **INSTALL** program. Follow the instructions in the next section where the programs and files on the program disk are described. Otherwise skip to the following section.

Making the Program Disk Self-Loading

The next step is to make the Program Disk self-loading. *Do not undertake this step unless you have received your backup disk from Living Videotext,* as there may be some risk to your program disk in the procedure. To make a disk self-loading, you must follow *exactly* the procedures outlined below. *Note:* If your computer is configured in a manner that requires a special DOS to make use of expanded memory or of a RAMdisk, skip this procedure, as you will always have to start up with your special DOS disk in any case, and you will get an error message when the disk tries to load itself.

Making the Program Disk Self-Loading

KEYSTROKES	COMMANDS, ACTIONS, EFFECTS
	1. Place the DOS disk in drive A of your computer.
	2. Turn on the computer.
Ctrl-Alt-Del	3. If it is already on, do a warm boot.
	4. When the **A >** prompt appears, place the Program Disk in drive B.
	5. Make sure you have made a backup copy of the files on the program disk.

erase b:*.*	6. Erase all the files on the program disk in drive B.
copy command.com b:/v	7. Copy the DOS **COMMAND.COM** file onto the Program Disk.
sys b:	8. Copy the DOS System Files onto the Program Disk.
	9. Remove the DOS disk from drive A, and insert your backup copy of the files from the Program Disk.
copy a:*.* b:/v	10. Copy the files from your backup copy back onto the program disk.

Your disk should now be self-loading. Be aware, however, that when you have made these changes, the Program Disk will be full. Adding anything to the sample outline on the program disk, or creating any new files on it, may make it impossible to load and run the program.

To load the program into your computer's memory and start it running, simply place the ThinkTank disk in drive A and press Ctrl-Alt-Del. The computer will display the system date (or the last date on which you used ThinkTank, whichever is later) and ask if you want to change it. Follow the screen prompts, and you can change the date using only the / key and the cursor-left and cursor-right keys.

You need not change the date, but *you must enter a date*. Also, *you must not remove the program disk* until the date is recorded and the red light on the drive goes out. Otherwise, you will see the message **thinktank program disk must be in drive a** and you will be returned to the operating system to start over. When you have entered a date, you are in ThinkTank, and can begin working.

THE FILES ON THE THINKTANK DISK

Besides the ThinkTank program, the Program Disk includes a number of other files and programs. You will encounter all of them at some time while using ThinkTank, so it's best to know what they do and how to use them effectively. When you look at the directory of your ThinkTank Program Disk, you will see the following file names:

> TANK.EXE
> TANKOPTS.DAT
> INSTALL.EXE
> AUTOEXEC.BAT
> TANK.DB
> TANK.SAV

You may not care what these various programs and files do, but if you have some understanding of their nature, you can reduce the likelihood of an unpleasant surprise considerably, so I'll go over them one by one. (If you don't know how to look at the disk directory, read Appendix B carefully.)

INSTALL.EXE

ThinkTank is initially set up for a computer with two disk drives for 5¼ floppy disks. If this is your configuration, you will not need the **INSTALL** program. Simply load the program following the procedures already described.

If you have a different number of drives, or hard disk drives, you must install ThinkTank for your system. The **INSTALL.EXE** program exists for this purpose. To run it, turn on your computer with your DOS System Disk in drive A. When the **A>** prompt appears on your screen, replace the DOS disk with the ThinkTank Program Disk, and type:

> install ⏎

Use the ↓ key on the numeric keypad (the cursor-down key) until the reverse-video highlight rests on the letter of the drive that you want to change. The space bar will move through your choices: **floppy drive, fixed drive,** and **no drive.** When the settings match the number and type of drives in your system, press Esc and then press Y. Your changes will be recorded on your disk, and you will be returned to the **A>** prompt.

If you have a hard disk drive, and want to copy ThinkTank onto it, see page 34 of the *ThinkTank User's Manual* for further instructions. If you have copied ThinkTank onto a hard disk, the loading instructions are slightly different. See page 35 of your *User's Manual* for details.

TANK.EXE

The TANK.EXE file is the ThinkTank program itself. You have already learned how to load it. To return to the operating system, simply press Esc Y while the Program Disk is in drive A. The rest of this book is devoted to how to use the program.

TANKOPTS.DAT

The **TANKOPTS.DAT** file keeps track of your drive configuration, the name of the outline file you last worked on, the date, and any formatting options you may have used for printing.

When you finish using ThinkTank, (*exit to the operating system* in computer jargon), the ThinkTank program always wants to record the status of the program and your most recent outline in the **TANKOPTS** file, and will look for that file in drive A (unless you have copied the program onto a hard disk, following the instructions in the manual). If the program is not present when you leave ThinkTank, you will see the error message **can't write to "options" file!,** and hear a mild alarm sound. You can avoid this either by making sure the **TANKOPTS** file is in drive A or by closing your outline before exiting to the operating system. The next time you use ThinkTank, it either will not open a file automatically, or it will open a file other than the last one you used. If you do close the file before exiting, the next time you use the program you will be in FILES mode, and no file will open automatically.

AUTOEXEC.BAT

The **AUTOEXEC.BAT** file loads the **TANK.EXE** program automatically, if you have copied the DOS **COMMAND.COM** program onto your program disk. Otherwise, it does nothing unless you modify it.

If you have a two-drive system and a parallel printer that requires no special setup routines, you can safely ignore this program. If your computer is configured in some other manner, however, you can edit this program in ways that will make it extremely useful.

TANK.DB

The **TANK.DB** file is the "Sample ThinkTank Outline" that you see when you load the ThinkTank program for the first time. The name of every ThinkTank outline includes the suffix **.DB** (*data base*). In this book, and in the *User's Manual,* you will find outline files alternatively referred to as data bases.

You do not need to append this suffix to the outline files you create because ThinkTank does it automatically. However, the **.DB** suffix does not automatically turn a file into a ThinkTank outline. If you use it on another type of file, and ask ThinkTank to open it, you will get the error message **can't open that outline!** On the other hand, you can prevent ThinkTank from opening a file by changing this suffix (also called an *extension*).

TANK.SAV

Any time you close a ThinkTank outline, ThinkTank creates an additional file with the same file name as the outline and the extension .SAV. This file tells ThinkTank exactly what the screen looked like when you last closed the outline, so that it can restore it to the exact point where you left off when you next open it. If you deliberately remove a .SAV file from a disk, its corresponding outline can still be opened, but only its first line will initially appear on your screen. The **TANK.SAV** file is the .SAV file for the "Sample ThinkTank outline."

SETTING UP

You already know how to load the ThinkTank program into your computer and get it running. But there are several ways you might want to organize your work to make it more efficient. Most of them require some familiarity with DOS. You will see many references to DOS in the following pages. If you are not familiar with PC-DOS, Appendix B will tell you what you need to know to get by. But DOS is a very powerful collection of programs, with many important functions. Although not necessary for running ThinkTank, it might be worth your while to study your DOS manual, or a book like *The IBM PC-DOS Handbook,* by Richard Allen King (SYBEX, 1983).

If your computer uses the MS-DOS operating system, most of the commands introduced in Appendix B still apply to your operating system. If the computer does not behave as expected when you use these commands, consult your system's DOS manual.

Let's look now at some of the ways you can organize your system.

Drive Priority

Your PC or PC-compatible computer always gives priority to drive A unless you specify otherwise.

ThinkTank also gives priority to drive A, so you must specify when you want to use another drive. To create your outlines on the data disk in drive B, place the program disk in drive A and a data disk in drive B, then specify that you want your outline to be on the B disk. If you put your outline files on the Program Disk in drive A, you will run out of space very quickly.

To specify that you want your .DB file in drive B, prefix the name of your file with **b:**. It doesn't matter whether the **b** is uppercase or lowercase. Do not leave a space after the colon. If you want ThinkTank to open an existing outline on a disk in drive B, you should also use the **b:** prefix.

There is another way to put your files on the disk in drive B: you can change the drive priority. Before you load ThinkTank, type

   b: ↵

when you see the **A>** prompt. That will change the priority to drive B. Now you will see a **B>** prompt instead of an **A>** prompt. To enter ThinkTank, you will have to type

   a:tank ↵

because the ThinkTank Program Disk must still be in drive A. But thereafter, all activity will take place on the disk in drive B. You will not have to specify the drive unless you want to work with a file on the disk in drive A. *Note:* ThinkTank normally displays the name of the file currently open at the bottom of the screen. When you have changed the priority to drive B, ThinkTank will only include a prefix in file names on drive A. To avoid confusion in this book, the drive priority will be drive A.

Single Disk Drive

You can also use ThinkTank with a single-disk drive. The computer loads the entire program into memory, so once you have entered the date, you can remove the Program Disk and insert a data disk. But you must make some changes first.

As mentioned, you should run the **INSTALL** program to set up ThinkTank for a single-drive system. Then use the DOS **COPY** command to copy the **TANKOPTS.DAT** file onto each of your data disks.

When you exit the program or close a file, the time and date of the exit will be written to the **TANKOPTS** file on your data disk, so you will avoid error messages at that time as well. You will also reduce the chances of losing data when you leave the program.

Normally, when you load ThinkTank, it sets up the screen exactly as it appeared the last time you exited the program. If a file was open, and that file is on one of the disks in the computer, it will open that file. If you are using a single-drive system, and don't put your files on the Program Disk, there will be no outline file in the computer once you remove the program disk. So you will start out in the FILES menu to choose an outline to work with. For more information on the FILES menu see Chapter 3.

Using Two Data Disks

You may find it convenient to work with two data disks, especially when you back up files or create other types of files available in ThinkTank. You will have no problems if you take these precautions first:

1. Use DOS to copy the **TANKOPTS.DAT** file onto any data disk that you might want to use in drive A (to be on the safe side, you might copy **TANKOPTS** onto all your data disks).

2. When you load ThinkTank into your computer, always set the date before you take out the Program Disk. ThinkTank will not load and run properly if you remove the disk before you have set the date. Wait until the red light goes out to remove the Program Disk and insert your second data disk. If you remove the Program Disk any sooner, you will be returned to the **A** prompt to start all over.

3. You *must* have a disk in drive A to close ThinkTank properly and return to the operating system. If you don't, you will get a disk error, and you will probably lose some data or have your outline hopelessly mangled. (If you find yourself in this situation, put the program disk back in drive A, and when the computer asks you **Abort, Retry, Ignore?**, press R for retry.)

You don't have to copy the **TANKOPTS** file on all your data disks, but if you don't, you may have problems leaving the program. You will get the error message **can't write to "options" file!** You may also have some difficulty using a printer, because ThinkTank includes many print formatting options whose settings are normally recorded in the **TANKOPTS** file. Without this file, you will have to reset these options every time you want to print, unless you wish to use the default settings. (See Chapter 8 for more information on print formatting options.)

Working with a RAMdisk

You can copy the **TANK.EXE** program into a RAMdisk, which leaves quite a bit more memory for your outlines. To do so, first fire up with DOS, then replace the DOS System Disk with the ThinkTank Program Disk and type:

      copy tank.exe=c: ↵

When you see the message 1 **file(s) copied,** type:

      c:tank ↵

The computer will then load ThinkTank from your RAMdisk, leaving the rest of its memory free. However, you still can't take the program disk out of drive A until after you have set the date. Follow the procedures described in the previous section if you want to use two data disks with your RAMdisk.

You may find it useful to reinsert your DOS disk after ThinkTank is up and running. Then you can access whatever DOS external commands you need relatively easily after closing ThinkTank. When you start up again, it is much quicker to reload ThinkTank from your RAMdisk than to load it from a floppy disk. Nevertheless, you must put the ThinkTank Program Disk back in drive A whenever you reload the program.

Other Disk Configurations

If you have any disk configuration other than those described, you must run the **INSTALL** program to tell ThinkTank how many and what kinds of disk drives you have. For instructions, see page 35 of the *User's Manual*. Page 34 contains additional instructions for using ThinkTank with a hard disk.

TYPES OF THINKTANK FILES

In addition to outlines, ThinkTank can create and read three types of DOS text files. They are called *structured text files, word-processor files* and *formatted text files*. ThinkTank can create these files from all or part of a ThinkTank outline file. To create text files, you must use ThinkTank's PORT command system. To see the PORT menu, press P. You will be given a choice between sending the data to a PRINTER (press P) or a TEXTFILE (press T). If you choose text file, you will be asked whether to SEND it (press S) or RECEIVE it into your current outline (press R). Press S to create a text file. You will then be given a choice between the three types of files, which are described below.

Structured Text Files

ThinkTank outline files store the outlines on disk exactly as they appear on the screen, including much of the "white space" that appears on the screen. Consequently, they use a great deal of storage space on the disk. ThinkTank therefore includes a type of file called a *structured text file*. Structured text files contain all the text of the outline file. However, instead of white space, ThinkTank inserts notes to itself explaining what goes where, so it can recreate an outline from a structured text file.

Structured text files take less than half the disk storage space of .DB (outline) files. They are therefore quite useful for making backup copies of your outlines.

You can also use structured text files to transfer information from one outline to another. A structured text file can be read into an outline file, and the transferred text will respond as expected to all of ThinkTank's commands. Structured text files, therefore, not only transfer information from one outline to another, but also allow you to share outlines with other ThinkTank users in a form in which they can be integrated into other users' files. Chapter 9 explains how to receive a structured text file into an outline.

Word-Processor Files

Because the Paragraph Editor—ThinkTank's word processor—does not have a full range of text-formatting features, ThinkTank includes the option of creating text files that can be read by the WordStar word-processing program, and by other word-processing programs that use similarly structured files. Word-processor files contain all the text of the ThinkTank outline—or the part of the ThinkTank outline—that you send to them.

However, to gain the advantages of a full-featured word processor, you must sacrifice some of the order provided by ThinkTank's hierarchical structure. While a ThinkTank outline may have many levels of indentation, reflecting the logical relationship of the various headlines to each other, word-processor files have all headlines printed flush left, followed by carriage returns. Paragraphs (created in the Paragraph Editor) are also followed by carriage returns. However, unless you have specifically inserted hard carriage returns into your paragraphs, ends of lines in paragraphs are terminated by soft carriage returns. Word-processor files are thus most useful for adding print formatting to outline files that include a great deal of text in paragraph form, rather than head-line form.

Word-processor files are discussed in more detail in Chapters 8 and 9.

Formatted Text Files

Formatted text files are used mainly for printing documents and outlines. You can use 17 print-formatting options, which we will explore in Chapter 8. Formatted text files may also be useful when you want other programs, which cannot accept files format-ted in the word processor style, to read your files. You may have to experiment a bit to find the format settings that are most com-patible with the receiving program. In Chapter 9, we will look at some specialized uses of formatted text files.

BACKING UP YOUR FILES

There are three ways to make backup copies of your outlines. First, you can use the DOS **DISKCOPY** program to make cop-ies of entire disks. Second, you can use the DOS **COPY** com-mand to make copies of a single file onto another disk, or onto the same disk under a different name. (If you are not familiar with these procedures, please see Appendix B.)

Third, you can back up files with structured text files. To do so, place the bar cursor at the summit of your outline, and then press P T S S, which enters the commands PORT TEXTFILE SEND STRUCTURED. (If you want to make a backup copy of only *part* of your outline, place the bar cursor on the superordinate head-line of the portion you want to copy, rather than at the summit.) You will then be asked for a file name. You can use any file name that DOS will accept, and an extension of your choice. ThinkTank gives all text files the extension **.TXT** if you do not enter an extension with the file name. Be sure to include the **b:** prefix if you want the text file to appear on the disk in drive B.

Once you have entered the file name, the text will scroll by as it goes into the file. If at any point you decide to stop—if you see errors, or if you have selected the wrong portion of your outline to send, for example—you can abort the process by pressing Esc. If you wish to start over with the same file name, ThinkTank will allow you to replace the existing file (the one that isn't complete) with a new one.

THINKTANK AND DOS

By now it should be clear that you will need DOS to manage your ThinkTank files. You must use DOS for renaming files, copying files and disks, seeing what files are on your disks, erasing files from disks, and for many other housekeeping chores. You can take care of these chores before loading ThinkTank or after you exit, but not while ThinkTank is running. To exit from ThinkTank and return to the operating system, pres Esc. ThinkTank always asks you, **call it a day?** and gives you a yes or no option, in case you hit the Esc key by mistake. Press Y to close your outline and exit ThinkTank.

You then have access to the DOS internal commands. If you need the external commands—to format a disk, copy a complete disk, or check the available memory, for example—you must insert your DOS System Disk in drive A before proceeding.

Now that you know how to set up ThinkTank, let's look at what ThinkTank can do. The following chapter gives you a grand tour of all of ThinkTank's modes of operation.

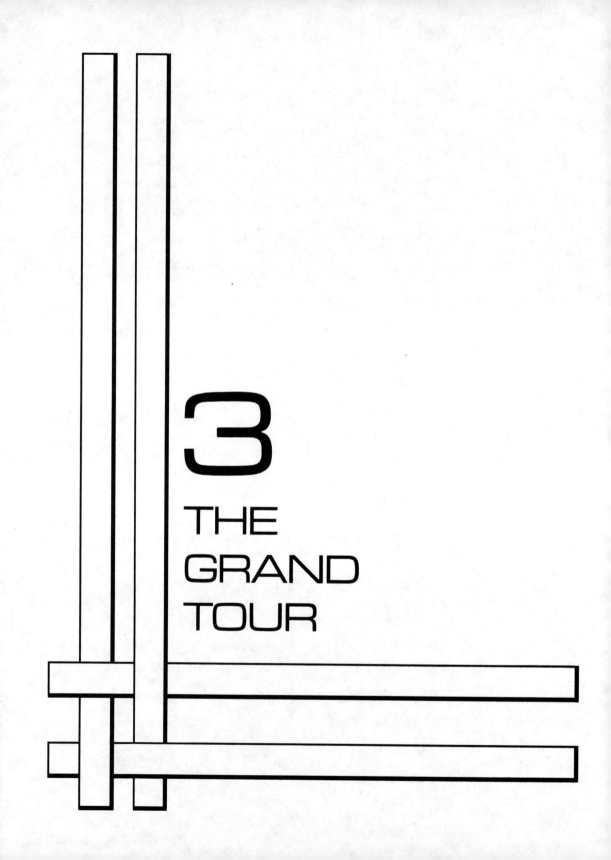

3
THE
GRAND
TOUR

This chapter will introduce you to all of ThinkTank's modes of operation. It will teach you how to:

- create a new outline;
- insert new headlines in an existing outline;
- open and close files;
- delete material from an outline;
- move material from one part of an outline to another;
- edit headlines that are already part of your outline.

There are many other operations you can perform, but they will be introduced only briefly, to give you an overview of the program's capabilities. They will be discussed more fully in later chapters.

If you are a new user, some of these operations will be unfamiliar to you, and you may want to read through the chapter twice, or return to it after you have had more experience using the program. If you have never run the ThinkTank program before, you might want to start by doing so now, following the instructions in the first 12 pages of the *User's Manual*.

After you load ThinkTank and set the date, one of two things will happen: if the program automatically opens an outline file you are at the *top level;* otherwise you have the choice of creating a new outline file or opening an old one, from the FILES mode. We will examine the top level first.

THE STRUCTURE OF THINKTANK

If an outline is displayed on the screen, you are at ThinkTank's top level. At the top level you can move around within an outline, expand an outline to see more detail, collapse it to see the overview, enter any of ThinkTank's modes of operation, and close the program for the day.

To envision the relationship of these modes to the top level, think of ThinkTank as having a *modular tree structure*. The top level is the root of the tree, and the various modes are the branches. Each mode allows you to perform a different task, such as opening a file or entering text. From the top level, you can enter most of the modes by a single keystroke.

Once you enter a mode, you are given a series of command options. Some of these options branch to further choices, which is the basis for the tree metaphor. Figure 3.1 is a graphic view of ThinkTank's tree structure, showing all the commands that can be executed from the top level. The branches are shown as well, except for the detailed structure of the program's two editing modes.

ThinkTank has three different cursors: a *bar cursor*, which is used to choose a part of your outline to work with, a *menu cursor*, which can be used to enter commands, and an *editing cursor*, for entering and editing text. The bar cursor, which you see at the top level, is represented by a reverse-video line highlighting one of the headlines. It is moved by pressing the arrow keys on the numeric keypad, which function exclusively as cursor-movement keys in ThinkTank. It is easiest to move the bar cursor with the cursor-right and cursor-left keys on the numeric keypad (the 6 and 4 keys, respectively).

If you don't have ThinkTank up on your screen, load it now. We're going to start a fresh outline. This is done from the FILES mode. If you already have an outline on display, you must press F to enter the FILES mode to close it.

A Detour Through the Menu

Every mode has a *command menu*. When you are at the top level, you will see the name of your outline and these messages: **arrow keys move bar cursor, use F10 for command menu,** and **(esc) to exit thinktank.** When you choose a mode, as you do when you press F, a command menu is displayed. You can select a command from this menu by using ThinkTank's second cursor, the *menu cursor*, which highlights a command in reverse video.

To select a command to execute, you can move the menu cursor left or right by using the cursor-left and cursor-right keys on the numeric keypad. When you get to the last one in either direction, the cursor will jump to the opposite end of the menu. The space bar will also move the menu cursor, but only to the right, although it, too, will send the cursor back to the left when it reaches the right end. (Additionally, the Home key will send the menu cursor to the leftmost command, and the End key to the rightmost command.) Menu cursor movement is summarized in Table 3.1.

MENU COMMANDS

Note: All cursor-movement keys are on the numeric keypad. The ← key is the ← key on the numeric keypad, not the backspace. The backspace key is above the ↵ key.

←	Moves cursor one command left. If already on leftmost command, moves cursor to rightmost command.
→	Moves cursor one command right. If already on rightmost command, moves cursor to leftmost command.
Home	Moves cursor to leftmost command.
End	Moves cursor to rightmost command.
Space Bar	Moves cursor one command right. If already on rightmost command, moves cursor to leftmost command.
↵	Enters the currently highlighted command.

Any command may be entered by pressing the key indicated on the lower menu bar when the command is highlighted.

Table 3.1: Menu cursor movement.

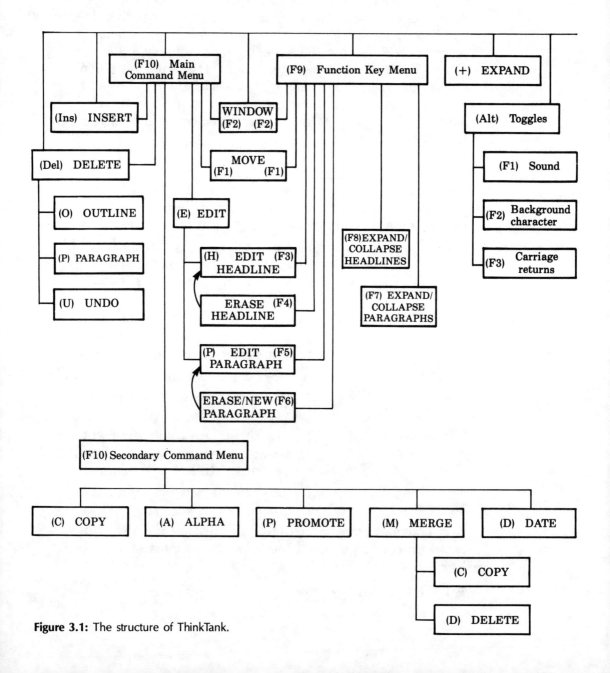

Figure 3.1: The structure of ThinkTank.

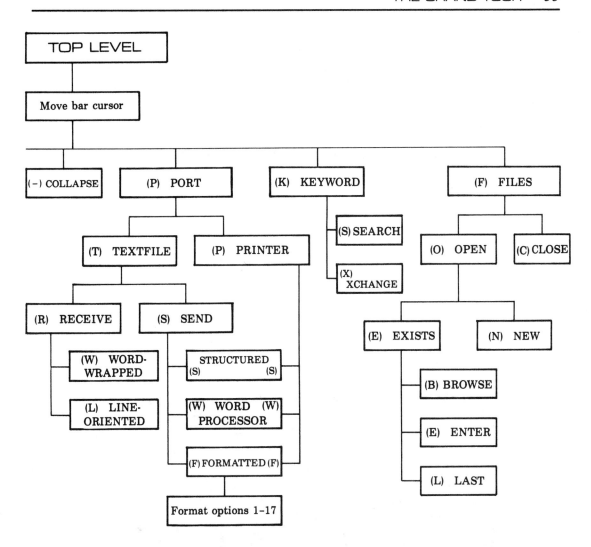

To execute a highlighted command, you can always press ↵
If you want to become more proficient in ThinkTank, use the
menus simply as a learning tool. Make it a habit to press the key
whose name is highlighted in the lower menu bar, rather than the
center key. This allows you to bypass the menus and enter the
commands directly. Unfortunately, many of the statements that
appear on the lower bar to explain the effects of commands are
somewhat cryptic. We'll explain the more obscure ones as we go
along.

THE FILES MODE

When you entered FILES mode, the Main Files Menu appeared.
As you can see from the menu, you have two options: to close the
currently open file, or to leave it open and return to the top level.
Close the file now, by pressing C. (If you don't want to close the file,
press Esc, and ThinkTank will return you to the exact spot where
you left off.) A new set of options will be displayed.

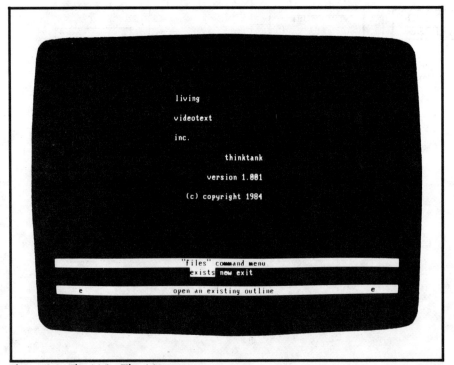

Figure 3.2: The Main Files Menu.

You are given three options: EXISTS, NEW, and EXIT. These options mean, briefly, to open an existing file, to start a new one, or to exit to the operating system. We'll look at the commands subsidiary to the EXISTS command shortly. For now, press N, because we are going to start a new file. ThinkTank won't let you enter any commands other than FILES mode commands until you have an outline opened. Figure 3.2 shows the Files Menu when there is no outline currently displayed, or open. You will be prompted for the name of your new outline. If your data disk is in drive B, begin the name of the outline with b:, since you don't want your new outline to be on your program disk. (If you have made your Program Disk self-loading, you *must* put your outline on a separate disk.)

For now call your outline file **b:exercise.** Don't use complex file names—you'll save yourself a lot of trouble in the long run if you use file names that you can remember. Just be sure that your file name is not longer than eight letters.

ThinkTank will then give you the message, **creating file "b:exercise.db"** (ThinkTank appends the extension **db** to all the outline files it creates), and after a bit of whirring and clicking, the work area of your screen will be blank, except for a line in the upper left corner of the screen, reading

– **Home**

You are now ready to begin a new outline.

Before we go any further, let's look at the rest of the FILES menu. First, close the file you just created (with only the word **Home** in it), by pressing F C again. After ThinkTank closes the file, press E, to display the Existing Files Menu, which is shown in Figure 3.3.

Browsing through the File Names

The first option is to browse through all the file names on both disks. To use the BROWSE command, press B, (or press ⏎ , because BROWSE is highlighted by the menu cursor) when the menu appears. When you choose to browse, a file name for an outline file appears in the top bar of the menu, while the first line of the outline appears in the menu space. You can move to the

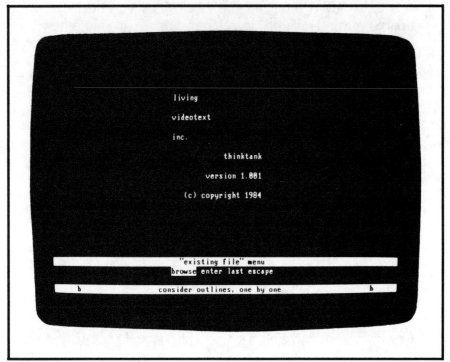

living

videotext

inc.

thinktank

version 1.001

(c) copyright 1984

"existing file" menu
browse enter last escape

b   consider outlines, one by one   b

Figure 3.3: The Existing Files Menu.

next file name by using the cursor-right key. You can bring back
the previously diplayed file name, with the cursor-left key. When
you see the name of the file you want to work with, simply
press ↵ , and ThinkTank will load the file and display it exactly
as it appeared when you last closed it.

Entering a File Name

If you know the name of the file you wish to work with, you
can use the ENTER command. First press Esc, to return to the
Main Files Menu. Press E (EXISTS), E (ENTER) again, and then type
in the file name (make sure you have used the **b:** prefix if it's on
the disk in drive B) and press ↵ . Although file names are stored
in capital letters on your disk, you can enter them using uppercase or lowercase letters.

This way of calling up a file is especially handy if you have many short ThinkTank files on a disk, since it is quicker than scanning through them all with the BROWSE command. In addition, you can press F4 to recall the last file name you entered. Just press E (ENTER), and then press F4, and the file name will appear in the menu space. If this isn't the file you want, press Esc instead of ↩ to return to the menu.

Reopening the LAST File

From the Existing Files Menu, the LAST command, chosen by pressing L, reopens the last file you had open. When you choose this option, ThinkTank reopens your previously open file with no further ado.

The ESCAPE Option

As you have seen, once you have chosen a method for opening an existing file, the Esc key will cancel the command and return you to the Existing Files Menu. If you decide you don't want to open an existing file, pressing Esc will return you to the NEW/EXISTS Menu, one step closer to the root of the tree. From there, you can either start a new outline, go back to the Existing Files Menu, or "call it a day," by pressing Esc Y. Table 3.2 summarizes all the commands in the FILES mode.

THE TOP LEVEL

Now you have an outline to work with. If it's not now on your screen, open it, and we'll explore in greater depth the modes available from the top level. Press F9 on the left side of the keyboard, and you will see a menu that tells what most of the other function keys do. (Presumably F10 is not included because its function is explained when you are at the top level.) Figure 3.4 illustrates the F9 menu of function keys.

You will notice that the upper bar of the menu tells you which menu or mode you are in, and the middle space lists your choices. The command on the far left (F1) is highlighted in

FILES MODE COMMANDS

Top-Level Commands

C	Closes currently open file.
R *or* Esc	Returns to current outline, at top level.

Main FILES Menu

N	Starts a new outline.
E	Opens an outline that already exists.
Esc Y	Exits to operating system ("call it a day").

Existing Files Menu

B	Browses through file names.
E	Enters files names from keyboard.
L	Reopens last file opened.
Esc	Returns to NEW/EXISTS menu.

Table 3.2: FILES Mode Commands

reverse video. The lower bar of the menu displays both the effect of the highlighted command and the name of the key that accesses the command. Take the time to browse through the Function Key Menu, then press Esc to return to the top level when you are finished.

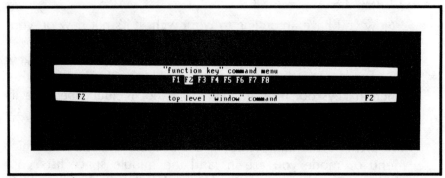

Figure 3.4: The Function Key Menu.

THE MAIN COMMAND MENU

At the top level, you will see the message, **use F10 for command menu.** To display the Main Command Menu, press F10. Figure 3.5 illustrates this menu. From it, you can choose most of ThinkTank's modes of operation. As with all the menus, you can browse through the available commands using the cursor keys or the space bar.

As you browse through this menu, you'll notice that many of the keys displayed on the Function Key Menu are also displayed here. Except for EXTRA, you can enter all of the modes listed on the menu by pressing a single key on the keyboard—the one highlighted in the lower menu bar when the menu cursor is on the command.

THE INSERT MODE

Press Esc to return to the top level, and we'll get to work. We are about to begin an exercise that we'll carry through several chapters, to introduce you briefly to all of ThinkTank's modes.

In the work area above the menu you should see only

     – **Home**

under the bar cursor. Press F4. The word **Home** disappears, and your flashing cursor is just to the right of the minus sign, ready to insert text in the headline. Press Esc. The word reappears. Try it

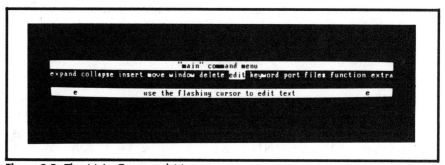

Figure 3.5: The Main Command Menu.

again. Type in your name. Press Esc. Once again, **Home** reappears. Now press F4, type in **ThinkTank Book Exercises,** and press ←┘ . Now your outline says:

      – **ThinkTank Book Exercises**

I put you in the Headline Editor first, so you could change the **Home** line. When you create a new outline, ThinkTank automatically starts it with the word **Home** at the summit (the first line of an outline file), to remind you that you can move there by pressing the Home key. Since the BROWSE command of the FILES mode always displays the summit line of an outline file, it's helpful to edit that line into something that will help you remember the contents of the file.

In the Headline editor the Esc key lets you return to the status quo ante. However, in most circumstances the Esc key completes a procedure. Appendix C lists all of the things the escape key does in the various command modes.

Now that you've edited the **Home** line, you can begin to create an outline, by inserting new headlines. Enter INSERT mode by pressing the Ins key, which is the 0 on the numeric keypad. When you enter INSERT mode from the summit, the bar cursor always jumps down a line, indents itself three spaces (which will henceforth be called a *degree* or *level* of indentation), and a question mark appears, followed by a single empty space and a flashing cursor. Now you can insert a new headline into your outline. Type in **PHONE LIST** and press ←┘ . It's easier to find first-level headings, if you use all caps, but it's not necessary . The new headline remains, and the cursor moves down a line. There is now a minus sign in front of **PHONE LIST,** where the question mark was, but a plus sign has appeared next to **ThinkTank Book Exercises.**

The plus sign indicates that there is information nested under a headline—that there is an outline present, so to speak. The minus sign indicates that there is no additional information under a headline.

Now press the cursor-right key. The question mark (and everything after it) moves one degree to the right and a plus sign appears next to **PHONE LIST,** where the minus sign was. Press the cursor-right key again. ThinkTank will sound its alarm, because its logical structure doesn't permit you to skip a level. Any headline can be subordinate only one degree to the previous headline, and ThinkTank represents subordination by a degree of indentation. Later, in Chapter 6, I'll show a trick to get around this restriction.

Now press the cursor-left key. The question mark moves back to the left, and the plus changes back to a minus. Move right again and make your first entry: a name, with last name first, and a phone number. Press ↩ to record the name, and enter a few more names and phone numbers, all at the same level of indentation. In other words, don't use the cursor keys. If you make a mistake while entering a name or number, you can backspace to the error with the backspace key above the ↩ key and correct it. If you try to get there with the cursor keys, you will only move the headline around, and you'll never get any closer. If you find that you've made mistakes after you've pressed ↩ , don't worry about it for now. We'll correct them when we get into the Headline Editor.

After you have entered a few names and phone numbers, press the Esc key to return to the top level. When you are in INSERT mode, either Esc or ↩ will enter the headline into your outline. But there is a difference. The ↩ key returns you to INSERT mode, so you can continue your entries, but the Esc key sends you back to the top level. If you press Esc by mistake when you meant to press ↩ , simply press Ins again, and you will return to INSERT mode.

However, if you get things hopelessly fouled up, and want to start over, press the Del key (below the numeric keypad) to delete the headline on which you are working and return you to the top level. You can then reenter INSERT mode with the Ins key if you wish.

Your outline should now look something like Figure 3.6. I lined up the phone numbers with the space bar to move to the columns where I wanted them before typing them in. If you want yours to line up, you can do so when the Headline Editor is discussed later in this chapter.

Adding to an Outline

Let's add some detail to the phone list. Press the Ins key. Your flashing cursor will appear directly below the previous position of

```
    +    ThinkTank Book Exercises
    +    PHONE LIST
         -   Franklin, Howard K.          (415) 555-2651
         -   Denton, Arthur               (209) 901-6027
         -   Brown, Clarence G.           (504) 201-1642
         -   Carter, Bennett              (201) 767-2212
         -   Summers, Scott               (907) 936-1111
         -   Darnell, August              (212) 112-0326
         -   Hernandez, Andrew            (212) 112-9009
         -   Weinberg, Dr. Morton         (415) 211-9803
```

Figure 3.6: A simple outline.

the bar cursor. Use the cursor-up key to move it directly below the first entry on your phone list. Next, press the cursor-right key to indent a degree, so that your outline looks like Figure 3.7.

Now type in the address of the person on your first entry, and press ← . The cursor will move down. Enter some other information that you might want to remember when calling that person, e.g., names of family members, or title and department. You can add both, on separate lines. Press ← after each entry.

When you are through with the first entry, press the cursor-down key (2 on the numeric keypad) to go to the next name. You'll get another alarm and an error message, **can't move cursor "down"**! That's because ThinkTank considers everything subordinate to a given headline as a unit. It will let you move to the next unit, but you have to do it consciously. First press the cursor-left key. Then your cursor will be at the same level of indentation as the headline below it, and you can jump over it with the cursor-down key. Next you'll want to move right with the cursor-right key, so the information under the second name will be subordinate to that name. Continue adding information to several entries. To preserve the logical structure of your list, be careful to indent your additions one and only one degree more than the name entry. When you have finished, press Esc.

If you want to add a greater degree of detail to your new entries, press Ins, and establish a new level of nesting, by pressing the cursor-right key. For example, the line **wish him a happy**

```
  +  ThinkTank Book Exercises
  +  PHONE LIST
     +  Franklin, Howard K.        (415) 555-2561
        ?
     -  Denton, Arthur             (209) 981-6827
     -  Brown, Clarence G.         (504) 281-1642
     -  Carter, Bennett            (201) 767-2212
     -  Summers, Scott             (987) 936-1111
     -  Darnell, August            (212) 112-0326
     -  Hernandez, Andrew          (212) 112-9009
     -  Weinberg, Dr. Morton       (415) 211-9803




             type new headline, then (escape)

      arrow keys re-position the bar cursor headline
              (backspace) erases last character
```

Figure 3.7: Adding new headlines to an outline.

birthday is indented under Arthur Denton's personal information, as it is secondary to that information. Similarly, his work address is secondary to the name of his place of business. With this structure, as we shall see, you can choose to look at the primary details without seeing the secondary details. (*Note:* If you press the cursor-right key when inserting under a collapsed headline, that headline will expand to show the next level of headlines below it, so you can choose your point of insertion.) Your outline should now look similar to Figure 3.8.

BASIC TOP-LEVEL COMMANDS

One of the features that gives ThinkTank so much power is the fact that you can look at only the portion of an outline you need to see. You can display every line of a portion of your outline,

```
+  ThinkTank Book Exercises
   +  PHONE LIST
      +  Franklin, Howard K.           (415) 555-2651
         -  2602 Regent Street, San Francisco, CA 94117
         +  Office: Compton, Alden, Weisberg & Scott   (415) 330-1111
            -  2 Embarcadero Center, Suite 4216, San Francisco, CA 94105
      +  Denton, Arthur                (209) 901-6027
         +  Sky High Technologies, Inc.
            -  11200 Dakota Av. W., Fresno, CA 94371
         +  Wife-Nancy, Son-Joe, 12, Daughter-Anita, 9
            -  wish him a happy birthday
      +  Brown, Clarence G.            (504) 201-1642
         -  3426 Perdido, New Orleans, LA 70119
         -  Travels to West Coast several times a year.
      +  Carter, Bennett               (201) 767-2212
         -  491 Somerville Road, Atco, NJ 07621
      +  Summers, Scott                (907) 936-1111
         +  12063 Huffman Road, Anchorage, AK 99516
         -  Newly married to Madelyne Pryor, professional pilot.
         -  Congratulations, Scott!
      +  Darnell, August               (212) 555-0326
         +  1567 E. 83rd St., New York, NY 10058
            -  Whaddya mean, "nowhere?"
      +  Hernandez, Andrew             (212) 112-9009
         -  1567 E. 83rd St., New York, NY 10058
      +  Weinberg, Dr. Morton          (415) 211-9803
         -  Laurel Medical Group
         +  5812 Laurel Street, Oakland, CA 94619
            -  Medical Insurance #603-801H-25G7
```

Figure 3.8: An outline with five levels of nesting.

while also being able to look at the most general headlines of the rest, so you can see the context into which your fully displayed portion fits.

You accomplish this by using the EXPAND and COLLAPSE commands on various parts of your outline. You select the portion to expand or collapse by moving the bar cursor to its superordinate headline. So you also have to know how to move the bar cursor. Now that you have an outline to work with, we'll explore the ways to move the cursor and to expand and collapse headlines. If you are still in INSERT mode (if you see a flashing cursor and a question mark), press Esc before you go on.

Moving the Bar Cursor

Every key on the numeric keypad (except the 5 key, which has no alternate designation), may be used to move the bar cursor

INSERT MODE COMMANDS

Cursor Movement

cursor-left	Moves point of entry one notch to the left. (If currently among a group of headlines at same level of indentation, moves point of entry to bottom of list.)
cursor-right	Moves point of entry one notch to the right. (If not already indented below headline immediately above. If indented, has no effect.)
cursor-up	Moves point of entry directly above next headline at current level of indentation above current cursor position (if there are no intervening superordinate headlines). If there are intervening superordinate headlines, has no effect.
cursor-down	Moves point of entry below next headline at current level of indentation (if there is one).

Other Commands

Ins	Puts ThinkTank in INSERT mode.
←	Enters headline, then returns to INSERT mode.
Esc	Enters headline, then returns to top level.
Del	Deletes current headline, then returns to top level.
Backspace	Deletes letter to left of cursor.

Table 3.3: Commands in INSERT Mode

through an outline. We'll look at the effects of each one in turn.

Using the Home Key to Move to the Next Higher Logical Level Press the Home key (7 on the numeric keypad). Your bar cursor will jump to the next superordinate headline—that is, the next headline above your present position that is one degree further to the left. Every time you press the Home key, the bar cursor jumps up to the next logical level. So if you forget how the part of your outline you are working on is related to the whole, you can always find out by pressing the Home key a few times. Each headline that it rests on will be more inclusive than the previous one, assuming that you have organized your outline logically.

There are several ways to use the Home key in conjunction with other keys to streamline your movement through an outline. We'll look at each of them. Begin by using the Home key to move to the summit of your outline. When you get there, press –, and then +. First, everything but **ThinkTank Book Exercises** will disappear, and then the words **PHONE LIST** will appear. Use the cursor-right key to move the bar cursor to **PHONE LIST,** and press the + key. Your original list of names and phone numbers will appear, while the details remain hidden. This allows you to get an overview of your outline, without distracting details.

Using the Cursor-up and Cursor-down Keys Use the cursor-right key to move down to the first entry in your phone list. Now press the cursor-down key (2 on the numeric keypad) several times. The bar cursor will move down from one headline to the next, just as it would if you pressed the cursor-right key. Move all the way to the bottom of your list. Now hold down the cursor-up key (8 on the numeric keypad). The bar cursor will move up to your first entry, and then the computer will beep to let you know the cursor has gone as far as it can. The cursor-up and -down keys will move only to headlines at the same logical level. This makes it easy to move around within a section, and avoid finding yourself in the middle of unrelated text. To see the advantage of this movement, move down through several entries with the cursor-right key and use the + key to expand every headline with a plus sign. (Holding down the ← key will have the same effect.) After you've expanded several headlines, press Home enough times to return to a line with a name and phone number. Now, when you use the cursor-up and -down keys, the bar cursor skips from one name to the next, without passing through all the details.

You can use these keys to move very quickly through even a long, fully detailed outline. Suppose, for example, that you are writing a book with ThinkTank. You are somewhere deep in the caverns of Chapter 7, and remember a fact you should have mentioned in Chapter 2. You press Home until you get to the headline Chapter 7, use the cursor-up key to move quickly (in six strokes) to Chapter 2, collapse Chapter 2 with the − key, expand it with the + key, and then use the cursor-right key, followed by the cursor-down key, to move to the subhead under which the information should be located. Expand that one, and you are ready to enter the missing fact.

Alternatively, while still in Chapter 7, you could press Home one more time to get to the book title, collapse the entire book and expand it to see the chapter headings. This would give you a much clearer picture of where you are going. Home − + is a combination of strokes you will find extremely useful.

Moving with PgUp, PgDn, and End

There are three more cursor-moving keys on the numeric keypad—PgUp, PgDn, and End. In a short outline such as this one, you won't have much use for them, but try them for practice. PgUp and PgDn move the cursor a "page" (21 lines) up and down, respectively. Since the work area has only 20 lines, your bar cursor will appear at the line just below the bottom of your previous screen when you page down, and at the line just above your previous screen when you page up, if the cursor is at the top of the screen. It is somewhat less predictable when you have paragraphs in your outline, however, as these keys always move the bar cursor to a headline.

When you want to scan through a large outline with lots of text, PgUp and PgDn are handy. They will move through large blocks of the outline, but they do not expand or collapse anything. When you use them, anything that has been expanded will be visible as you scan through.

On the other hand, the End key moves the cursor to the last headline in the outline under the bar cursor that is one level deeper than the current cursor position. It doesn't make any difference whether it is visible when you press the End key.

Let's see how this works. Move the bar cursor to a headline with a plus sign, and collapse the headline. Now press the End key. The outline under the headline on which you placed your bar cursor should now be expanded, exactly as if you had pressed the + key. However, the bar cursor will no longer be on the superordinate headline, where you had placed it when you pressed End. Instead, it will be on the last visible headline subordinate to the one you started on.

It doesn't matter whether the headline on which it now rests has a plus or a minus sign. Pressing the End key will not expand any additional levels. In other words, it won't move the bar cursor to the last headline under the bar cursor if the last headline is nested more than one level deeper than the superordinate headline. It will only expand the headline one degree, and then it will move the bar cursor to the last headline that becomes visible.

Collapsing an Outline

If the headline on which your bar cursor currently rests is preceded by a minus sign, press the cursor-left key. The bar cursor will move up one line. Keep pressing the cursor-left key until the bar cursor is on a headline with a plus sign. When there is a plus sign before your current headline, press the − key to the right of the numeric keypad. Everything indented under the bar cursor headline will disappear from view. If you press the − key when the bar cursor is on a headline with a minus sign, which means that nothing is nested under the headline under the bar cursor, nothing will happen.

Expanding an Outline

Now press the + key to the right of the numeric keypad. Everything under the bar cursor at the next logical level (one degree of indentation) will reappear. Some of the items that have reappeared may have plus signs. If you press the + key again, you hear the alarm and see the error message **fully expanded!**

(If you don't like ThinkTank's assorted beeps, clicks, and trills, you can turn them off (or on again) by pressing Alt-F1. Of course, with the sounds off, you may fail to notice an error message.)

This exercise illustrates two fundamental principles of ThinkTank's organization. Any ThinkTank command will act only on the range of the outline subordinate to the current position of the bar cursor, and ThinkTank commands act only on one logical level at a time, unless you specifically direct them to do otherwise, which you'll learn how to do shortly.

The + and − keys on the numeric keypad are the most basic ways of expanding and collapsing your outlines.

Expanding with the ← Key Let's explore some other ways to expand and collapse outlines. Keep pressing the cursor-left key until you are at the summit (where it says **ThinkTank Book Exercises**). Now press the − key. Everything disappears but the top line. Now hold down the ← key. As you hold it down, the bar cursor moves down, expanding every collapsed outline it passes. Everything under every headline with a plus sign—all your headlines and all your paragraphs—will be visible. You might thus consider the ← key a *read* key at the top level, because it allows you to read everything in your outline.

When your outlines get large, however, this method of expanding becomes very inefficient. You don't really know how many times the keyboard has entered the command, in rapid fire, into the computer's memory, and your outline will probably continue expanding well after you release the key, moving you too far down and expanding more than you want to see.

The F8 and F7 Keys The F8 key provides an alternate way of expanding outlines which is very useful when you have used the Paragraph Editor to insert paragraphs in your outline. It works just like the + key, except that the + key will expand paragraphs along with headlines, whereas the F8 key will expand only headlines. It accepts numeric and # command prefixes, so you can expose all levels of a complex outline to see the structure while keeping any paragraphs hidden. If you press F8 while the bar cursor is on an expanded headline, however, it will hide everything under the bar cursor, just as the − key will.

The F7 key functions like the F8 key, except that it works only on paragraphs, not headlines. If you have paragraphs in your outline and have expanded one level from the current bar cursor position, and only want to see the headlines, pressing F8 will hide the first paragraph, which will be the only one expanded. Conversely, it will expand a paragraph under the bar cursor without expanding any additional headlines.

Command Prefixes

ThinkTank allows you to expand the scope of some commands by using *command prefixes.* You enter a command prefix by pressing one of several designated keys, prior to, or in conjunction with, another command key. When a command's scope is expanded, it works on additional levels of the outline. A command prefix tells ThinkTank how many levels of your outline you want a command to work on.

Command prefixes affect most of the cursor keys at the top level, where they are most useful, and they also have some use in the MOVE mode and the Paragraph Editor. We'll examine the effect of the various types of command prefixes as they work at the top level.

The Ctrl Key   If you press Ctrl-Home, the bar cursor will jump to the summit of your outline. This is especially useful when you want to find something in another part of the outline, or examine the relationship between your current position and the entire outline. As with portions of the outline, you can press Ctrl-Home − + to get a quick view of the highest level of your outline.

Similarly, Ctrl-End will take you to the very last headline in your outline that is currently visible.

The # Key   The # key is an *infinity* key in ThinkTank. If you press # +, everything nested under the bar cursor, up to 10,000 levels deep (the highest number of levels ThinkTank allows) will be expanded. If you press # plus the cursor-right key, the bar cursor will move to the last visible headline in your outline. If you press # plus the cursor-left key, you will move the bar cursor to the summit.

Numeric Prefixes   If you want to extend the scope of a command to a more limited degree you can use numbers as command prefixes in a manner similar to the # key. Pressing 4 + will expand the outline under the bar cursor to its fourth level of nesting. Anything nested deeper than four levels will not be expanded. You can use numeric prefixes prior to any of the cursor-movement keys except End to increase the distance that the bar cursor moves. For example, 3 cursor-right will move the bar cursor to the third visible headline below its current position.

It is important to remember, however, that a prefix to a bar cursor command will act only on headlines that have been expanded. For example, if you press 5 cursor-right, and the headline under the bar cursor has, say, 15 subordinate headlines which are currently hidden, the cursor key will count the next *visible* headline as number two, and so on.

For reference, all the ways to move the bar cursor are summarized in Table 3.4.

BAR CURSOR MOVING COMMANDS

cursor-left	Moves cursor to next headline up or to the left.
cursor-right	Moves cursor to next headline down or to the right.
cursor-up	Moves cursor to next headline up, at same level of indentation; will not skip over a higher-level headline.
cursor-down	Moves cursor to next headline down, at same level of indentation; will not skip over a higher-level headline below it.
Home	Moves cursor to first superordinate headline above current position.
Ctrl-Home	Moves cursor to summit of outline.
End	Moves cursor to last headline below current cursor position, one level deeper.
Ctrl-End	Moves cursor to last headline currently not collapsed.

Table 3.4: Bar Cursor Moving Commands

⇧ -3 End	Moves cursor to last headline in file one level deeper than current position.
PgUp	Moves cursor 21 lines up. If that line is within an expanded paragraph, moves cursor to that paragraph's headline.
PgDn	Moves cursor 21 lines down. If that line is within an expanded paragraph, moves cursor to first headline following that paragraph.
NUMERIC PREFIXES	Before pressing Home, cursor-up, cursor-down, cursor-left, or cursor-right forces the command to act on the number of levels entered. For example, 3 Home will move the cursor to the next headline up that is three levels superordinate to the current position. 3 cursor-down will move the cursor to the third headline at the same level of indentation below the current postion. 3 cursor-left will move the cursor to the third headline above the current position, regardless of indentation.

Table 3.4: Bar Cursor Moving Commands (continued).

THE HEADLINE EDITOR

The Headline Editor is used only to make changes in existing headlines; it will not allow you to insert or move headlines. You can only insert or move in INSERT mode or MOVE mode.

Entering the Headline Editor

There are three ways to enter the Headline Editor. You can

press:

- F3
- the letters E H (EDIT HEADLINE)
- F4

Either of the first two ways of entering the Headline Editor will place a flashing cursor at the end of the headline that was highlighted by the bar cursor before you entered it.

The F4 key erases the headline under the bar cursor and positions the flashing cursor just after the minus or plus sign, so you can enter a completely different headline. You already used this key to change **Home** to **ThinkTank Book Exercises.**

If you enter the Headline Editor you can continue editing headlines anywhere in your outline without returning to the top level. You can move to any headline in your outline by using the cursor movement methods described below. If a headline you want to edit is currently hidden, you can expose it by pressing + when the flashing cursor is on its superordinate headline, without returning to the top level.

Moving the Headline Editor Cursor

Once you are in the Headline Editor, you can move the flashing cursor character by character, word by word, or line by line as shown in Table 3.5. The cursor-left and -right keys move the cursor left and right one letter, respectively. Ctrl-cursor-left will move the cursor to the last letter of the previous word. Similarly, Ctrl-cursor-right will move the cursor to the first letter of the next word. If you hold down the keys, all of these movements will repeat. Home will move the cursor to the very beginning of the headline on which it is currently located, and End to the end of it.

The cursor-up and -down keys will move the cursor to the next headline up and down, respectively. The only exception is that if the cursor is further to the right than the end of the headline you are moving to, a move up or down will move to the end of the headline to which you are moving. Otherwise, these keys move the cursor straight up and down.

As in the top level, the PgUp and PgDn keys will move across a substantial number of headlines, skipping over any paragraphs that may be present. You can move even further by using the Ctrl key. Ctrl-Home will move the cursor to the first headline in your outline, and Ctrl-End to the last.

Inserting Text in an Existing Headline

It is very easy to insert text in an existing headline. Simply move the cursor to the point at which you wish to begin inserting, and start typing. The Headline Editor is always in INSERT mode, so you can't type over existing headlines, except by using the F4 key (which erases the old one). For example, suppose you had a headline with errors, such as the following:

- Take it tothe cleanrs.

Here is how you would correct it. Move the bar cursor to that headline, and press E H to enter the Headline Editor. The flashing cursor is on the period. Press the cursor-left key twice to place the cursor on the **r** in **cleanrs.** Then simply type an **e** and the word will read **cleaners.** As with most word processors, insertion always occurs exactly where the cursor is currently located, moving the letter under it to the right. Finally, press Ctrl-cursor-left to move to the **e** in **tothe,** move back two more spaces to the **t** by pressing the cursor-left key twice, and hit the space bar. Now your headline says

- Take it to the cleaners.

Press ↵ , and you are back at the top level, with all the changes intact.

Now you are ready to line up the telephone numbers in the phone list you created earlier. Enter the Headline Editor (E H or F3), press Ctrl-cursor-left twice to get to the end of the first name, and press the space bar until the phone number is where you want it. Next, use the cursor-down key to get to the next entry down, press the cursor-right key a few times if you are in the middle of a name, and press the space bar until the second number is lined up beneath the first. Repeat this procedure until all the numbers are lined up, and then press ↵ . If by chance you insert too many spaces in a line, you can move the number to the left again by pressing the Del key.

Deleting Text

There are two ways to delete text from a headline. As in INSERT mode, the backspace key will delete a letter to the left of the cursor. If you hold it down, it will continue to delete letters up to the beginning of a headline.

The Del key below the numeric keypad will also delete text in the Headline Editor. It deletes the letter directly under the cursor, and if you hold it down, it will continue to delete letters to the right of the cursor.

Let's try deleting. Suppose now that your headline says

-**Takendrit to the cleantders.**

If you move the bar cursor to the **n** in **Takendrit,** you could press the Del key three times to get rid of the **ndr** and then add a space with the space bar. Alternatively, you could have moved to the **i** in the same word, and pressed the backspace key three times.

You can also get rid of **td** in **cleantders** by either moving to the **t** and using the Del key twice or by moving to the **e** and using the backspace key. The one you decide to use depends on where the cursor happens to be at the moment, and the location of the item you want to delete. As usual, to enter the changes you have made and return to the top level, press ←┘ .

Leaving the Headline Editor

There are two ways to exit the Headline Editor, regardless of how you entered it. Pressing ←┘ will save the changes you have made, while pressing Esc will restore the line *on which you are currently working* to its condition prior to editing. Remember, once you have changed one headline and moved on to another your changes are final. Pressing Esc will not change them back. Table 3.5 summarizes the Headline Editor commands.

OTHER TOP-LEVEL COMMANDS AND MODES

There are a few more top-level commands. The WINDOW command and the DELETE command will be discussed fully here.

The other top-level modes—the MOVE command, the Paragraph Editor, the KEYWORD command, and the PORT mode—are fairly complex, and will merely be introduced here for the sake of completeness. They will be discussed fully later.

HEADLINE EDITOR COMMANDS

Entering and Leaving

F3	Enters Headline Editor.
E H	Enters Headline Editor.
F4	Deletes current bar cursor headline for replacement. Remains in Headline Editor.
←	Enters current edited headline into memory, leaving intact changes to previously edited headlines, then returns to top level.
Esc	Restores current edited headline to its form before editing, leaving intact changes to previously edited headlines, then returns to top level.

Moving the Headline Editor Cursor

cursor-left	Moves cursor left one letter.
cursor-right	Moves cursor right one letter.
Ctrl-cursor-left	Moves cursor to last letter of previous word.
Ctrl-cursor-right	Moves cursor to fist letter of next word.
Home	Moves cursor to beginning of current line.
End	Moves cursor to end of current line.
PgUp	Moves cursor up one "page" (21 lines)

Table 3.5: Headline Editor Commands

PgDn	Moves cursor down one "page" (21 lines)
Ctrl-Home	Moves cursor to first letter of complete outline.
Ctrl-End	Moves cursor to last letter of complete outline.

Deleting Text

Backspace	Deletes letter to left of flashing cursor.
Del	Deletes letter directly under flashing cursor, moving subsequent letters one space to the left (continues to delete letters to right of flashing cursor).

Table 3.5: Headline Editor Commands (continued).

The WINDOW Command

You can think of your screen as a window moving over your outline. You can look into any portion of your outline that is currently expanded by moving the window over the portion you want to see. You can scroll this window left, right, up, or down using the WINDOW command. To enter this command, press F2. You can then use the cursor-up, -down, -left, and -right keys to move to the part of your outline that you want to see. As you press the cursor keys, the window will move over the outline. When you are through moving the window, press Esc, or F2 again, to return to the top level. Although the usefulness of this command may not be apparent when your outline is short, remember that headlines can be nested to a depth of 10,000 levels, and can be as long as 76 characters. If you have even four levels of nesting, and some of the headlines are maximum length, you may want to use the WINDOW command to view the right-hand end of some of your headlines.

There are a few minor hitches to using the WINDOW command. You can move any distance, but when you return to the top level, the bar cursor, which remains where it was before you pressed F2, must be on the screen. If you scroll so far that your bar cursor disappears (which you might do if, for example, you want to read a paragraph that's more than one screen long), the display will jump back to a point that includes the bar cursor when you return to the top level. If you have scrolled below the bar cursor, the bar cursor will be at the top left corner of the screen when you press Esc or F2. If you have scrolled above the bar cursor, it will reappear at the lower left corner of the workspace when you return to the top level.

Similarly, if you scroll so far to the left or right that part of the headline on which the bar cursor rests moves off the screen, when you return to the top level, the screen will readjust itself so that all of the bar cursor headline is visible, including the plus or minus sign.

You can also move the window by pressing the space bar at the top level. Each press of the space bar will move the display three spaces to the right until the right end of the bar cursor is at the right edge of the screen. Then it will move the window left until the bar cursor is at the left edge of the screen. If you hold the space bar down, the display will move continuously to the right until it reaches the right edge and then reverse direction.

The DELETE Mode

The DELETE mode will let you delete outlines (including empty outlines) and paragraphs. To enter DELETE mode, press the Del key. To leave it, press Esc.

Like all ThinkTank modes, DELETE mode displays a menu when you enter it. The menu will display three or four options. You can delete an outline, delete the paragraph under a headline (only if one is present), undo a deletion, which is discussed below, or return to the top level without deleting anything. Figure 3.9 shows the DELETE menu, and the commands are summarized in Table 3.6.

The bar cursor always jumps *up* to the next headline at the same level of indentation when a deletion is performed, unless it is already at the first headline at that level. So when deleting a number of successive headlines, take advantage of the bar cursor's normal movement. Start at the bottom rather than the top if

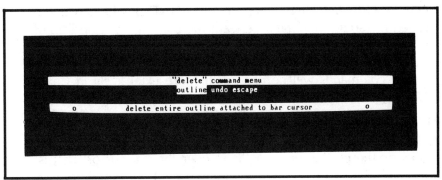

Figure 3.9: The DELETE Menu.

DELETE MENU COMMANDS

Del	Enters DELETE Mode
O	Deletes outline under and including current bar cursor headline.
P	Deletes paragraph (if present) directly beneath current bar cursor headline.
U	Undoes deletion—restores most recently deleted outline directly beneath bar cursor position.
Esc	Returns to top level without deleting anything.

Table 3.6: DELETE Menu Commands.

you want to save some of the headlines at the same level above the headline you are deleting, and start at the top if you want to save some headlines at the end. If you are deleting all of them, it doesn't matter where you start, because the cursor will not jump to a superordinate headline unless it has no place else to go.

You can also undo a deletion if you make a mistake. As we'll see later, this is also useful for moving things over large distances, because you can undo your deletion after you move your bar cursor elsewhere in your outline. Unlike similar commands in many word-processing programs, the UNDO will cause the deleted material to reappear beneath the bar cursor, regardless of the original location of the deleted material.

You cannot, however, undo the deletion of a paragraph. The DELETE commands will be dealt with more extensively in Chapters 5 and 7.

Using PROMOTE to Delete a Headline while Preserving Everything Subsidiary to It   DELETE, like all other ThinkTank modes, works on the portion of an outline under the bar cursor. That is, when you delete an outline, everything nested under the bar cursor headline, including the bar cursor headline itself, will be deleted. If you want to delete a headline, but preserve everything nested under it as part of your outline, you must first use the PROMOTE command from the Secondary Command Menu (press F10 F10 P). That will move all headlines below the bar cursor one degree to the left. Then your current headline will be empty, and you can delete it without losing the outlines that were previously nested beneath it. Let's look at an example. Suppose your outline looks like Figure 3.10.

Move the bar cursor to **I want to get rid of this headline.** Press F10 F10 P. After some whirring and clicking, your outline will look like Figure 3.11.

Now you can use DELETE mode. While your bar cursor is still on **I want to get rid of this headline.**, press the Del key. Then press O (OUTLINE) to delete it. The bar cursor will jump up to the next headline that is above **I want to keep this headline.** at the same level of indentation.

```
    +  I want to get rid of this headline.
       +  I want to keep this headline.
          -  It will be gone if I delete the one above it.
          -  So will this one.
       +  I want to keep this headline, too.
          -  It would disappear at the same time,
          -  because it's part of the same outline.
```

Figure 3.10: An outline prior to using PROMOTE and DELETE.

```
    -   I want to get rid of this headline.
    +   I want to keep this headline.
        -   It will be gone if I delete the one above it.
        -   So will this one.
    +   I want to keep this headline, too.
        -   It would disappear at the same time,
        -   because it's part of the same outline.
```

Figure 3.11: The effect of the PROMOTE command.

The MOVE Command

The F1 function key puts you in MOVE mode, which allows you to move an outline (a headline and everything nested under it) to any point in your file. Fundamentally, MOVE mode lets you place the bar cursor on a headline and then move that headline, including all subordinate material, with the cursor keys.

However, the movements are not the same as bar cursor movements at the top level. There are some complex tricks to using this command effectively. The complexities are designed to make sure that you do not destroy the logical structure of your outline when you move something into, or out of, a given section.

By way of introduction, first put the bar cursor on the headline you want to move, then use the cursor-up, down, left, and right keys to move that headline. *The movements of the bar cursor as you press these keys, however, are not like normal bar cursor movements; they are like their movements at the point of insertion in INSERT mode.* This means that your movements are subject to the same limitations that govern INSERT mode. You can't move directly up or down past a headline that's less indented, because you have to move left to get around it. You can't move anything more than one level of indentation to the right of the next headline above. Most importantly, you can't simply pull one of a set of headlines at the same level over to the left. If you try, its vertical position will also change. It will always move down to a position below the rest of the set.

This last point may cause you some grief, so here's an example with an explanation. Suppose your outline looks like Figure 3.12.

```
+   This is a superordinate headline
    -   This is the first subordinate headline
    -   This is the second subordinate headline
    -   I wish this headline were equal in importance to the superordinate
    -   This is the fourth subordinate headline
```

Figure 3.12: An outline with a headline to be moved.

Let's say you want to change it to look like Figure 3.13.

So you put your cursor on the **I wish this** line, and press the cursor-left key. However, the resulting change appears in Figure 3.14.

Again, the fact that you cannot simply pull a headline to the left preserves the logical structure of your outline. What you want to do, in effect, is to promote the **I wish this** headline to a higher logical level. If you were to do so, you might distort the relationship of the other headlines at the same level of indentation to their superordinate headline. ThinkTank forces you first to make those headlines to which it will be superior subordinate to it. You must therefore move **This is the fourth subordinate headline** to the right, and **then** move the **I want this** headline to the left.

```
+   This is a superordinate headline
    -   This is the first subordinate headline
    -   This is the second subordinate headline
+   I wish this headline were equal in importance to the superordinate
    -   This is the fourth subordinate headline
```

Figure 3.13: The intended result of a MOVE.

```
+   This is a superordinate headline
    -   This is the first subordinate headline
    -   This is the second subordinate headline
    -   This is the fourth subordinate headline
-   I wish this headline were equal in importance to the superordinate
```

Figure 3.14: The result of moving one headline of a group at the same level.

There are a few other restrictions on the MOVE command, all designed to preserve the logical structure of your outline:

1. You cannot move the summit line.
2. You cannot move anything left as far as the summit line; all other headlines in an outline must be subordinate to the summit.
3. You cannot move anything to a position that is more than one degree of indentation to the right of the headline above it. ThinkTank will not allow you to skip a logical level.
4. If you move an outline to the right beneath a collapsed headline, that headline will expand, and the material you are moving will appear below the newly-expanded headlines. You can then move it up or down among those headlines.

Moving over long distances in your outline can be particularly tricky. The easiest solution is simply to use the DELETE and UNDO commands, saving the MOVE command for situations when you simply want to move a headline to the left or right one degree, and similar simple situations.

Here are a few hints to simplify long-distance moving:

- If there are any paragraphs in the portion you want to move, collapse them before you begin. Better yet, collapse the entire portion you are moving, so that you are apparently moving only a single headline. In MOVE mode, the bar cursor will always appear on the screen, and if the section you are moving is expanded, especially if it includes a paragraph, it may fill the entire screen, so you can't see anything but the part you are moving. As a result, you won't be able to see where you are moving *to*.
- Be sure to collapse any portions of your outline that are between the section you are moving from and the section you are moving to.
- Be sure that the destination to which you are moving is sufficiently expanded so that you can see your target. Although moving something to the right under a collapsed headline will cause anything under that headline to expand one degree for

each step you take to the right, it's much easier if you can actually see where you are going before you get there.

To leave MOVE mode, you can press either Esc or F1 again.

The Paragraph Editor

We've made a lot of references to paragraphs. That's because ThinkTank's word processor is called the Paragraph Editor. You can enter up to 900 lines or 20,000 characters of text under any headline (about 30 double-spaced pages).

If you use the Paragraph Editor before you are familiar with it be aware that a paragraph in ThinkTank is *all* the text nested immediately below a given headline. Any command referring to a paragraph has its effect on the ThinkTank paragraph, not on the English paragraphs that may be included in it.

Also, the text in a paragraph is considered to belong to its superordinate headline. If you delete the headline, you will delete the paragraph as well. You can split a ThinkTank paragraph into several parts attached to different headlines, (see Chapter 7), but it's tricky.

You can type continuously, without pressing ← until you want to create a new paragraph, as with most word processors. To enter the Paragraph Editor, press F5, or E P (EDIT PARAGRAPH).

The Paragraph Editor is a fairly sophisticated word processor, including most of what you expect from a word processor except for printing-format commands and block-move and -delete. Even these limitations can be overcome with a little ingenuity. In Chapter 7, you'll learn how to use all its powerful features and get around its limitations. For now, remember that you can enter it from the top level using either of the above commands, and leave it by pressing Esc E.

There is a third way to enter the Paragraph Editor that's a bit tricky. If you press F6, you are supposedly in NEW PARAGRAPH mode, and can enter a paragraph where there is none. If you press F6 when there is already a paragraph under the bar cursor, ThinkTank will ask you if you want to delete it. This command is most useful only when there is a paragraph under a headline which you want to replace. If you simply wish to add a new paragraph, use F5.

The KEYWORD Command

The KEYWORD command gives you the options of searching for a word or exchanging it for another word. It will search only through the material nested under the current bar cursor headline. The KEYWORD command is entered by pressing the K key at the top level. You are then given the option of SEARCH (S) or XCHANGE (X). This command will be demonstrated in Chapter 5.

The PORT Menu

You were introduced to the PORT command in Chapter 2, in the section on backing up files. The other options of the PORT command will be dealt with in Chapters 8 and 9.

THE SECONDARY COMMAND MENU

The Main Command Menu gives you access to an additional set of commands which we'll look at now. First press F10 to display the Main Command Menu.

Next, move the menu cursor to **extra** and press ← or F10. You will now see the Secondary Command Menu, which is illustrated in Figure 3.15. Take a few minutes to browse through this menu. The PROMOTE command, which you have already used, appears here. The COPY and MERGE commands are somewhat advanced, and we will not explore them until later. When you are through browsing press Esc twice, or press F10, to return to the top level, and we'll go over the remaining commands.

The ALPHA Command

The ALPHA command will alphabetize all first-level headlines under a bar cursor headline. That's why it's important to arrange lists with last names first. To alphabetize your phone list, move the bar cursor to **PHONE LIST**, and press F10 F10 A to enter the ALPHA command. When the action stops, your outline should look similar to Figure 3.16.

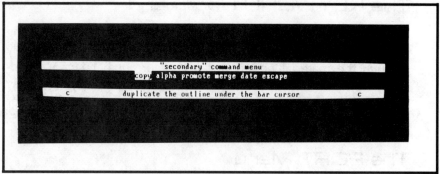

Figure 3.15: The Secondary Command Menu.

```
+   ThinkTank Book Exercises
    +   PHONE LIST
        +   Brown, Clarence G.          (504) 201-1642
        +   Carter, Bennett             (201) 767-2212
        +   Darnell, August             (212) 555-0326
        +   Denton, Arthur              (209) 901-6027
        +   Franklin, Howard K.         (415) 555-2651
        +   Hernandez, Andrew           (212) 112-9009
        +   Summers, Scott              (907) 936-1111
        +   Weinberg, Dr. Morton        (415) 211-9803
```

Figure 3.16: The phone list after using the ALPHA command.

Be aware that, if your headlines have numbers in them, numbers will appear before letters in the sorting sequence, and will be treated as a series of characters. Thus, 1000 will be placed before 20, and 111 will appear before 12.

Resetting the Date

If you forgot to reset the date when you fired up ThinkTank one morning, or if for some reason you want to arbitrarily change the date while you are working, the Secondary Command Menu includes a DATE command. Pressing F10 F10 D will return you to the first prompt that appears when you load ThinkTank. You still have the option of changing the date or not, as you do at the beginning.

A FINAL WORD

ThinkTank, like its outlines, is structured like an inverted tree. At the top level, you can enter any number of modes. You are said to be at the top level when you are not in any of the modes. In most cases, when you enter a mode, you are given a menu of options, and some of these options may present further choices. At any time, either a menu of choices is present on the status lines at the bottom of the screen, or one may be called up by a single keystroke.

This chapter explained the use of the INSERT, DELETE, MOVE, and Headline Editor modes. It also explained how to move the bar cursor, and a number of miscellaneous commands. You might regard this chapter as a reference guide to using the program, since all of its modes are explained briefly here. If you are a new user, I strongly suggest that you reread this chapter after you have had some experience using the program. Table 3.7 summarizes the top-level commands. COPY and MERGE, which are advanced commands, will be explained in later chapters.

TOP-LEVEL COMMANDS

+	EXPAND—reveals hidden text beneath current bar cursor.
–	COLLAPSE—hides all exposed text nested beneath current bar cursor.
Ins	Inserts new headlines.
Del	Deletes outlines, paragraphs; undoes deletions.
F1	Moves current bar cursor headline to a different location.
F2	Repositions the screen window.
F3	Enters the Headline Editor.
E H	Enters the Headline Editor.
F4	Erases the current bar cursor headline, enters the Paragraph Editor.
F5	Enters the Paragraph Editor.

Table 3.7: Top-Level Commands.

E P	Enters the Paragraph Editor.
F6	Enters a new paragraph; deletes an existing paragraph.
F7	Expands the paragraph under the bar cursor; collapses if expanded.
F8	Expands headlines without revealing paragraphs; collapses if expanded.
F9	Displays Function Key Menu.
F10	Displays Main Command Menu.
K	Searches or exchanges keyword.
P	Port Command Menu—sends and receives files.
F	Files Command Menu—opens and closes outlines on disk.
F10 F10	Extra—displays the Secondary Command Menu.

Secondary Menu Commands

F10 F10 P	Promotes all headlines below bar cursor one degree to the left (to delete superordinate headline).
F10 F10 A	Alphabetizes all first-level headlines below bar cursor headline.
F10 F10 D	Resets the date.
F10 F10 M	Merges the contents of one paragraph to a different headline.
F10 F10 C	Copies the entire outline nested under, and including, the current bar cursor headline.

Table 3.7: Top-Level Commands (continued).

4

FROM
A LIST
TO A
REUSABLE
CALENDAR

In this chapter we'll work our way through a few exercises which demonstrate effective ways of using ThinkTank. The MOVE and COPY commands are covered extensively, so you should have full mastery of them by the time we finish.

If you are like me, you often make lists: to-do lists, lists of phone calls to make, shopping lists, etc. Not only that, you tend to forget where you have put the list you need at the moment. ThinkTank is an essential aid for people like me. Even if you are not this sort of person, you may find that, by using ThinkTank in the manner I'm about to demonstrate, it will make several things that you are already doing easier.

A LIST OF THINGS TO DO

Let's start out by creating something that many people find helpful in getting organized—a simple list of things to do, and a vague schedule of when to do them. In the process, we'll see how ThinkTank facilitates both aspects of creative thought—the free-flow stage and the critical-judgment stage—and how it integrates the two.

If you don't already have ThinkTank up and running, reload it and reopen the **b:exercise** outline that you started in the last chapter. Move the bar cursor to **PHONE LIST,** collapse it (−), and press the Ins key. You should see a question mark directly below the plus sign in front of **PHONE LIST,** and a flashing cursor. You are now ready to insert a new headline at the same level of indentation as **PHONE LIST.** Since you will be adding new material that is not part of your phone list, *do not* indent this headline—it should be directly below **PHONE LIST.** We'll talk about why you should put it there later.

If you want to explore a bit first, expand your phone list, move your bar cursor to the last line of the last entry, and then press Ins. As you know, you can use the cursor-moving keys to move the question mark anywhere in your outline except more than one position to the right of the headline directly above it. You'll notice that you can move past hidden headlines; their contents won't become visible unless you position the flashing cursor to nest new information under the superordinate head.

When you are through exploring, move back to the bottom of the outline, and try to line up the question mark directly below the plus sign in front of **PHONE LIST.** If you have difficulty getting around in this mode, press Esc. This will allow you to get out of INSERT mode, go back to the top and collapse everything, expand it one level, and start over.

First we'll enter a general category **THINGS TO DO,** and then we'll brainstorm a little. Of course, your list of things to do will be quite a bit different from mine, but the principles will be the same. Figure 4.1 shows my first attempt at writing down a few items.

A quick glance reveals that it's fairly random. There are several ways to order it, and I'll demonstrate four of them. First, we'll look at two different techniques for classifying the items in the list. Next, we'll add a time dimension. Finally we'll subsume the entire list under a more powerful form of organization—a weekly calendar.

```
    +   THINGS TO DO
        -   Pick up xerox copies.
        +   Refinish the redwood table.
            -  Get new legs for it.
        -   Call Art.
        -   Set up data base for record collection.
        -   Home inventory.
        -   Find a more efficient method of accounting.
        -   Rebuild the picnic benches.
        -   Find music for Tom's party.
        -   Make a medical appointment.
```

Figure 4.1: A simple list.

To begin, there are several *types* of activities in my list, so I'll classify the activities under more general headlines: **Carpentry Projects, Computer Projects,** and **Other.**

A CLASSIFIED LIST

The first method I'll demonstrate is similar to the one in the *ThinkTank User's Manual.* This method will introduce the COPY command and the MOVE command, and involves extensive deleting. In essence, the method is to copy parts of the list, move the copies under the appropriate headlines, and then delete the items that are duplicated in the wrong place.

The first step is to make several copies of the list. Although it is not absolutely necessary, it will be easier to do if you collapse your headlines first by moving the bar cursor to **THINGS TO DO** and pressing − .

To use the COPY command, place the bar cursor on the first headline of the outline to be copied. In this example, the headline is **THINGS TO DO,** and if you followed my previous directions, the bar cursor should already be there. Next, press F10 to bring up the Main Command Menu and then press F10 again to display the Secondary Command Menu. The menu cursor will be on **COPY,** so you could just press ↵ , but press C instead, to get in the habit of entering commands by their keystroke. ThinkTank will copy the entire outline, and leave the bar cursor on the top headline of the second copy.

Since we have three categories in the list, repeat the procedure. Press F10 F10 C and you will have a third copy of the same thing. (You should also make an extra copy, so we can have a fresh one ready when we start over.) Your screen should look like Figure 4.2.

Now press E H to enter the Headline Editor. It doesn't matter where the bar cursor is when you enter, because you can move it with the cursor keys. Change one **THINGS TO DO** headline to **Carpentry Projects,** another to **Computer Projects** and the third to **Other.**

Next we're going to use the DELETE command to eliminate the unwanted duplicate entries. First expand the **Carpentry Projects** outline. Your screen should now look like Figure 4.3.

```
        +   ThinkTank Book Exercises
        +   PHONE LIST
        +   THINGS TO DO
        +   THINGS TO DO
        +   THINGS TO DO
        +   THINGS TO DO
```

Figure 4.2: The original outline with four copies of one category.

```
      +   ThinkTank Book Exercises
        +   PHONE LIST
        +   THINGS TO DO
        +   Carpentry Projects
            -   Pick up xerox copies.
            +   Refinish the redwood table.
            -   Call Art.
            -   Set up data base for record collection.
            -   Home inventory.
            -   Find a more efficient method of accounting.
            -   Rebuild the picnic benches.
            -   Find music for Tom's party.
            -   Make a medical appointment.
        +   Computer Projects
        +   Other
```

Figure 4.3: The same outline with the major headlines edited.

If you are using your own list, of course you should have used appropriate categories, but the principles will be the same. On my list, it's obvious that some of the items now under **Carpentry Projects** have nothing to do with carpentry. So I'll use the DELETE command to delete all the irrelevant ones.

First, move the bar cursor to the first item under the heading. Press Del for the DELETE command, which gives you the option of deleting the outline or undoing a deletion. Press O for the OUTLINE command. When you delete an outline, everything attached to the headline under the bar cursor will be deleted as well. In this instance, of course, there is nothing attached to it, so only the single headline will be deleted. **Pick up xerox copies** will disappear, leaving the bar cursor on **Refinish the redwood table,** which is a carpentry project. We want to keep this item under **Carpentry Projects,** so move the bar cursor down one more line to **Call Art,** and press Del O again. The bar cursor will move to **Refinish the redwood table** again. Move the bar cursor down and keep repeating Del O until nothing is left in this category except **Refinish the redwood table** and **Rebuild the picnic benches.**

Then move down to the next two categories, **Computer Projects** and **Other,** repeating the procedure until the outline looks like Figure 4.4. *Note:* This outline will not all fit on the screen at once.

Simulating a DEMOTE Command

There's just one more step to this procedure. Move the bar cursor to **PHONE LIST.** Press Ins. Create another headline that says **THINGS TO DO.** Now you need to nest the subcategories under your main head. In effect, you need to "demote" them— you want the effect opposite of the PROMOTE command we encountered in the previous chapter. Unfortunately ThinkTank has no DEMOTE command, so we'll improvise.

```
    +   ThinkTank Book Exercises
        +   PHONE LIST
        +   Carpentry Projects
            +   Refinish the redwood table.
            -   Rebuild the picnic benches.
    +   Computer Projects
            -   Set up data base for record collection.
            -   Home inventory.
            -   Find a more efficient method of accounting.
    +   Other
            -   Find music for Tom's party.
            -   Call Art.
            -   Pick up xerox copies.
            -   Make a medical appointment.
```

Figure 4.4: A classified list.

For this you need the MOVE command. First collapse each of the subcategories. Next, move the bar cursor to **Carpentry Projects.** Place one finger on F1 and a finger of the other hand on the cursor-right key. Press F1 to enter MOVE mode. Press the cursor-right key once. The headline will move one notch to the right. Press F1 again to get out of MOVE mode. Press the cursor-right key to move the bar cursor down. Press F1 to enter MOVE mode, cursor-right to move the headline, F1 to leave MOVE mode, and repeat the procedure one more time.

Most of the time it's just as easy to press Esc to return to the top level from MOVE mode, but when you want to simulate a DEMOTE command, this two-finger approach is very speedy.

When you're all finished, the list should look like Figure 4.5.

A SIMPLER METHOD

The method we just used to classify the items in the list took quite a few steps, but it gave you practice using the MOVE and COPY commands. Now we'll do the same thing by a simpler method, one which will again use our demoting process.

```
   +   ThinkTank Book Exercises
      +   PHONE LIST
      +   THINGS TO DO
         +   Carpentry Projects
            +   Refinish the redwood table.
               -   Get new legs for it.
            -   Rebuild the picnic benches.
         +   Computer Projects
            -   Set up data base for record collection.
            -   Home inventory.
            -   Find a more efficient method of accounting.
         +   Other
            -   Find music for Tom's party.
            -   Call Art.
            -   Pick up xerox copies.
            -   Make a medical appointment.
```

Figure 4.5: The list in its final form.

If you made an extra copy of the original **THINGS TO DO** list, expand both of your remaining versions (to make sure you are using the unclassified one), and delete the one we just classified, to keep your outline from getting cluttered up. If you didn't do the previous exercise, we'll work with the original **THINGS TO DO** list that you set up. In any case, make a copy of the list, because we're going to reclassify it once more.

First enter MOVE mode and rearrange the headlines under THINGS TO DO so that they are in logical order. As before, simply move the bar cursor to the headline you want to move and press F1. This time we'll use the cursor-up and cursor-down keys to move the headlines so that they are grouped logically, and press F1 after each entry is in its proper place. As before, you can toggle between MOVE mode and the top level, keeping one finger on F1 and using two fingers on the cursor keys. When finished, the list should look like Figure 4.6.

Next I'll enter INSERT mode, by pressing the Ins key. When in INSERT mode, remember, you can insert headlines anywhere in an outline, not just below the present position of the bar cursor. Just use the cursor-movement keys to move the flashing cursor and question mark wherever you want them. If you press ↵ after completing a headline, you will still be in INSERT mode. You don't get back to the top level until you press Esc, so once you are in the INSERT mode you can enter as many headlines as you like, anywhere you want them.

```
+   THINGS TO DO
    +  Refinish the redwood table.
    -  Rebuild the picnic benches.
    -  Set up data base for record collection.
    -  Home inventory.
    -  Find a more efficient method of accounting.
    -  Find music for Tom's party.
    -  Call Art.
    -  Pick up xerox copies.
    -  Make a medical appointment.
```

Figure 4.6: Classifying without copying by using the MOVE mode.

This time, enter the same subheads as before: **Carpentry Projects, Computer Projects,** and **Other.** When it's finished, you will have a classified list, but all the items will be at the same level, rather than properly nested, as shown in Figure 4.7.

ADDING SOME HIERARCHY

The next step is to repeat our simulated DEMOTE. Start with the bar cursor on **Refinish the redwood table.** Press F1 cursor-right F1 cursor-right F1 cursor-right F1. Now both carpentry projects should be nested under the subhead, which should have a plus sign in front of it. Skip over **Computer projects** to the next line (press the cursor-right key twice) and repeat the procedure. When you reach **Other,** skip over that and continue to the end. The final result should once again look like Figure 4.5.

By now, you should be quite good at simulated demotes and moves. But we're barely warming up!

Adding a Temporal Dimension

Now that you have added some order, the new organization begins to suggest other possibilities. Maybe the categories should

```
    +   THINGS TO DO
        -   Carpentry Projects
        +   Refinish the redwood table.
        -   Rebuild the picnic benches.
        -   Computer Projects
        -   Set up data base for record collection.
        -   Home inventory.
        -   Find a more efficient method of accounting.
        -   Other
        -   Find music for Tom's party.
        -   Call Art.
        -   Pick up xerox copies.
        -   Make a medical appointment.
```

Figure 4.7: A categorized list without hierarchy.

be given different priorities. Perhaps, now that you have a classified list, other types of activities come to mind and you want to add new subheads and entries to your outline. Or you might want to add a time dimension to the outline because all the items on your list are probably not equally urgent. To do this, we must generate some new headlines, at the highest level of this outline.

Before starting make a copy of your **THINGS TO DO** list, (F10 F10 C) because we're going to use it one more time. You may want to add something like **extra** to one of the copies using the headline editor, or label one **THINGS TO DO 1** and the other **THINGS TO DO 2,** so you can find the extra one later. (Remember to press ↵ when you are finished.)

To one of the two copies of your list, we'll add headings for **Today, This Week, This Month,** and **Eventually,** all under the **THINGS TO DO** headline. Your outline will now look like Figure 4.8.

```
 +   THINGS TO DO
   -   Today
   -   This Week
   -   This Month
   -   Eventually
   +   Computer projects
       -   Set up data base for record collection.
       -   Home inventory.
       -   Find a more efficient method of accounting.
   +   Carpentry projects
       -   Rebuild the picnic benches.
       +   Refinish the redwood table.
           -   Get new legs for it.
   +   Other
       -   Find music for Tom's party.
       -   Call Art.
       -   Pick up xerox copies.
       -   Make a medical appointment.
```

Figure 4.8: The first stage in adding a time dimension.

Reorganizing the Tasks by Time

The next step is to classify the tasks, so that they are all in the proper categories. You can do this either by moving things around with the MOVE command or by entering the various tasks a second time under the relevant time category. ThinkTank doesn't care which method you use. If you want a master list, keep the original and copy each entry before you move it. Then, when you refer to the master list you can add something like **done 4/28** after each entry, or delete the entry.

If you don't want a master list, you can maintain your list so that each entry appears only once. Simply move the individual tasks out and up to their appropriate time category, and then indent them (F1 cursor-left, cursor-up as many times as necessary, cursor-right, F1).

I chose to have a single list, and my final version looks like Figure 4.9.

```
    +   THINGS TO DO
        +   Today
            -   Pick up xerox copies.
            -   Call Art.
            -   Make a medical appointment.
        +   This Week
            -   Find music for Tom's party.
        -   This Month
        +   Eventually
            +   Computer Projects.
                -   Set up data base for record collection.
                -   Find a more efficient method of accounting.
                -   Home inventory.
            +   Carpentry Projects.
                +   Refinish the redwood table.
                    -   Get new legs for it.
                    -   Rent a heavy-duty sander.
                +   Rebuild the picnic benches.
            -   Other.
```

Figure 4.9: Giving priorities to the tasks.

How It was Done

In this example, I chose to retain each entry only once. Almost all of the **Other** category comprised things to do today, so I placed the bar cursor on **Other** and used the cursor-up key, in MOVE mode, and pressed the cursor-right key to move the entire **Other** list under **Today**. **Find music** was somewhat lower priority than the others, so I moved it left (to get around the **This Week** headline), and then inserted it under **This Week**. Since all the rest have no time limit on them, I simply moved the headlines one degree to the right under **Eventually.** *Note:* Any time you move a headline, everything subordinate to it moves with it.

Next, I used the PROMOTE command (F10, F10, P) to move all the items under **Other** one degree to the left, so I could delete the word **Other** from the **Today** section, because it was no longer relevant. To be complete, I inserted the word **Other** back in the **Eventually** category, so it would be available when I needed it. At the same time, I remembered that I needed some special equipment for one of the carpentry projects, so I inserted **Rent a heavy-duty sander** under **Refinish the redwood table.** This shows one of the prime virtues of ThinkTank—its flexibility. You can insert anything wherever you need to, whenever you think of it, and it will be in the appropriate place in the hierarchical organization.

Let's pause for a while now, while you reorganize your own list of things to do, and then we'll put the principles you have just learned to work, as well as introduce some new ones.

DEALING WITH INCREASING COMPLEXITY

Let's take another approach to our little outline. Suppose you require a greater degree of organization than we have established here. This time, instead of reorganizing a single outline, we're going to take advantage of one of the useful aspects of redundancy. If you made a copy (F10 F10 C) of your **THINGS TO DO** list prior to reorganizing it, use the MOVE command to place it *after* your reorganized list (F1 cursor-down Esc). If you haven't, first make a copy of your **THINGS TO DO** list. Next, we'll set up a new outline at the same level of indentation as the **THINGS TO DO** outline. This outline appears in Figure 4.10. Type in this new section exactly as it appears in the book.

You have just created a calendar for a week. If you anticipate the need for organization of larger amounts of information, you can add it right now.

If each day you want to keep track of appointments, phone calls to make, and miscellaneous other things separately, you can do so with the following procedure. Delete the outline under (and including) **Week of.** Place the bar cursor on **Week of,** and press Del O. Under **CALENDAR,** insert **Week of** once again. Press ←⏎ , then Indent one degree and type in **day.** Press ←⏎ , indent one more position and type **Appointments** ←⏎ . Directly below that, type **Phone calls** ←⏎ , and below that, **Miscellaneous,** or whatever categories you prefer. When you have finished entering your categories, press Esc to return to the top level. Now this portion of your outline should look something like Figure 4.11.

Next, move the bar cursor to **day** and copy that portion of the outline five times. When you have finished, move your bar cursor to **Week of,** collapse it, and expand it again. Below **Week of,** you should see the word **day** six times. Go into the Headline Editor (E H or F3). Then move the flashing cursor to the first line that says **day.** Press Home, and the flashing cursor should be on the **d.**

```
      +   THINGS TO DO (extra)
      +   CALENDAR
          +  Week of
             -   Monday
             -   Tuesday
             -   Wednesday
             -   Thursday
             -   Friday
             -   Weekend
          -  Future
```

Figure 4.10: Adding a calendar.

```
        +   CALENDAR
            +   Week of
                +   day
                    -   Appointments
                    -   Phone calls
                    -   Miscellaneous
            -   Future
```

Figure 4.11: Beginning a classified calendar.

Enter **Mon,** move down to the next line, press Home and enter **Tues,** and so on (you will have to delete the last **day** to enter **Weekend**). Press ← when you are finished. Now your calendar form for the week is complete, and you didn't have to add your three new categories more than once!

Now copy the calendar. In fact, you may want to make several copies. Move your bar cursor to the first **Week of** entry, and go back into the Headline Editor (E H, or F3). Your flashing cursor should appear after the word **of.** Enter Monday's date (or Sunday's date, if you prefer). If you've made more than one copy, you might want move down to the next **Week of** entry, and enter the following Monday's date. Press ← when you are through, or Esc if you've made errors. It's a good idea not to enter the date on the last copy you have, however, since you may want to use it to generate calendars for the following weeks (we'll deal with this technique more extensively in Chapter 5, "Creating Templates." Figure 4.12 shows the final result.

Using Command Prefixes

Now you are in a position to expand your list of things to do, expand your calendar, and start moving the various items from your list to the days you want to do them. In the process, we'll take a second look at two other features of ThinkTank: command prefixes and flexibility. Obviously, it would save time if you could expand your whole week's calendar and your complete to-do list in a minimum of strokes. As you may remember, a command prefix allows you to extend a command several levels deep into

```
+   CALENDAR
    +  Week of 5/12
       +  Monday
          -  Appointments
          -  Phone calls
          -  Miscellaneous
       +  Tuesday
          -  Appointments
          -  Phone calls
          -  Miscellaneous
       +  Wednesday
          -  Appointments
          -  Phone calls
          -  Miscellaneous
       +  Thursday
          -  Appointments
          -  Phone calls
          -  Miscellaneous
      +  Friday
          -  Appointments
          -  Phone calls
          -  Miscellaneous
       +  Weekend
          -  Appointments
          -  Phone calls
          -  Miscellaneous
    +  Week of 5/19
       +  Monday
          -  Appointments
          -  Phone calls
          -  Miscellaneous
       +  Tuesday
       +  Wednesday
       +  Thursday
       +  Friday
       +  Weekend
    +  Week of
```

Figure 4.12: Complete form for a weekly calendar.

an outline. Simply preface the command with a number. To expand your entire week's calendar, instead of moving the bar cursor to the name of each day and hitting the + key, you can just put the bar cursor on **Week of,** hit 3, and then hit +. That tells ThinkTank you want to expand your outline three levels deep from the current bar cursor position. If you're not sure how many levels are under a bar cursor and you want to see them all, prefix your EXPAND command with the # (⇧ -3) key and you will have a fully expanded outline. Once you have moved your various items of business to their appropriate places in your calendar, a portion of it will look similar to Figure 4.13.

```
+   PHONE LIST
+   CALENDAR
    +   Week of 5/12
        +   Monday
            +   Appointments
                -   Dept. meeting, 10 AM
                -   Clarence for lunch
            +   Phone calls
                -   Make a medical appointment
                -   Call Art re conference next week
                -   Call Clarence to confirm lunch
            +   Miscellaneous
                -   Make a dinner reservation for anniversary
                -   Order flowers
        +   Tuesday
            -   Appointments
            -   Phone calls
            +   Miscellaneous
                -   Pick up xerox copies
        +   Wednesday
            +   Appointments
                -   Current data to HQ by 3 PM today
            -   Phone calls
            +   Miscellaneous
                -   Pick up birthday gift for Aunt Martha
        +   Thursday
        +   Friday
        +   Weekend
```

Figure 4.13: A filled-in weekly calendar form.

Now is your chance to see why you added this new material to your existing outline with the phone list on it. Here it is Monday, and you need to call Clarence, Art, and your doctor. Their phone numbers are just a few keystrokes away! If you want to take the trouble, you can use the COPY command to duplicate the phone numbers, and then move them to today's schedule, beneath the names of the people you need to call. This is convenient if you have many calls to make and you expect to delete each week's outline at the end of the week (otherwise, your outline will get awfully cluttered, and you will crowd your disk and your computer's memory). However, if you have only a few, it's a simple matter to look them up.

Press Ctrl-Home to get the bar cursor to the top of the outline. Press − to close it up. Press + to see the major headings. (As you get comfortable with the program, you'll find yourself repeating this sequence of strokes frequently.) Move the bar cursor to **PHONE LIST** and press + once. All the phone numbers you might need are immediately visible. Having made your call, you can now press − to close up the phone list, move the bar cursor down to **CALENDAR**, expand it, and note your appointment with your doctor in the appropriate place. If your other calls generate new activities to be completed, it's a simple matter to add that information to the outline, if not under a particular day, then under **FUTURE**.

If there's a great deal of new information that results from your call, you can simply move to the end of your outline (press Ctrl-End), and insert a whole new outline.

WHAT YOU HAVE JUST DONE

This brief demonstration shows you several important things about ThinkTank. First, it demonstrates the program's flexibility. Second, it shows how ThinkTank can be used either to generate new material at random or to organize that material into progressively more complex forms, and how the more complex forms may themselves aid in generating further ideas. From this, you can see how ThinkTank can function as a spur to your creativity, and thus can make you more productive. Let's look at each of these things in turn.

As you have seen, headlines can be inserted anywhere in an outline, at any time. You need never think of any outline as finished. Once inserted, headlines can also be moved anywhere in the outline. This means you never have to worry about putting an item in the wrong place.

You can move freely from one part of an outline to another with the help of command prefixes. You can collapse or expand your outline to see any given level of organization or complexity, to find out if what you have done makes sense on that level. And you can safely ignore any part of your outline that you don't currently need. This is why it's often useful to include unrelated material in a single outline—you can keep everything you are currently working on at hand, so you don't have to swap disks repeatedly.

Moreover, with ThinkTank you can record fleeting but useful thoughts. If, for example, you are working on the marketing plan for your new product, and you remember that it's your anniversary this weekend, you can quickly close up your marketing plan outline, insert a note to buy a gift for your spouse and make reservations at your favorite restaurant in today's (or tomorrow's—I don't want to rush you) schedule, and return to your marketing plan, in about six keystrokes.

Another comforting ThinkTank feature is its tolerance for redundancy. Unlike a data base management program, ThinkTank doesn't care if you use the same headlines more than once for different things, so you can maintain several methods of organization of the same material for different purposes.

You have seen how useful this can be in combining the to-do list with a calendar. You might want to carry this principle even further, and use ThinkTank to reorganize the same material to generate shopping lists, errand lists, lists of calls to make, etc. Adding such new categories may jog your memory, so that you can add additional items to your lists. And it does no harm to retain duplicate information. If you open an outline and find a note reminding you to do something you've completed weeks ago, you can always delete it when you see it.

ThinkTank is equally useful at any stage in a project's development. If you already know what you want to organize (whether stages in a production process, days of the week, or ideas in a writing project), you can generate outlines to guide your work. This is what we did when we created our calendar.

On the other hand, if you're just getting started with something, you can begin with the simplest units, and just lay them out as they occur to you, as we did in establishing our to-do list. They'll stay where you put them until you decide what to do with them. Then, as you think about what you've done and patterns and relationships become clear, you can begin to group your items or ideas sensibly. As you build higher and higher levels of structure from your original thoughts, the makings of a course outline, a book, an invention, a product plan, or a new way of doing business may be taking shape. It is this free movement between top-down and bottom-up thinking, which you have now tried out for yourself, that makes ThinkTank such a useful aid to creative thought.

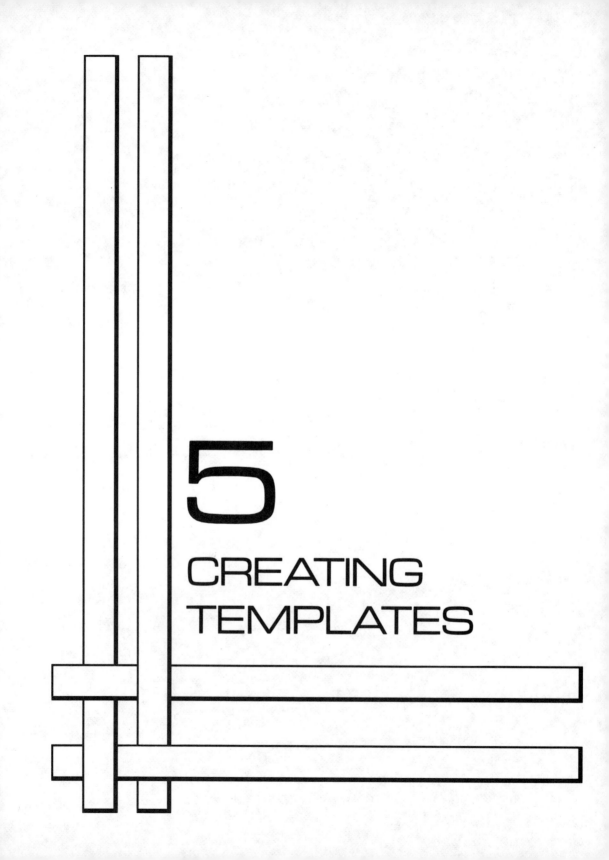

5
CREATING TEMPLATES

This chapter introduces a technique called *templating*—in essence, the creation of blank forms. You may already be familiar with creating forms in data base management programs. You will find ThinkTank considerably more flexible in the way you can create and use forms in it than most data base management programs. ThinkTank's two different EDIT modes, one for headlines and one for paragraphs, allow for entries of almost any length. And if you need a special field in just one of your records, you can add it without having to reformat your entire file.

Along the way, you'll learn the DELETE-UNDO command and the MERGE command, as well as a number of useful techniques you can use in a variety of situations.

LOGGING SALES CALLS

Richard Wells is a sales representative for an office supplies and equipment distributor. He has become one of the top sales reps in his territory by paying careful attention to the growth and progress of his customers, so that he can almost anticipate their needs. Another secret of his success is that he personalizes every call he makes. He uses ThinkTank to keep track of this constantly changing information. Let's take a look at how he does it. As we watch, we'll see one of the ways in which ThinkTank can be used as a data base manager.

The key unit in Richard's ThinkTank outline is a sales-call log which contains call records for all his customers. He has set up a template, which he uses to record all the information he needs to make a successful call. Figure 5.1 shows his sales call template before he has filled it in.

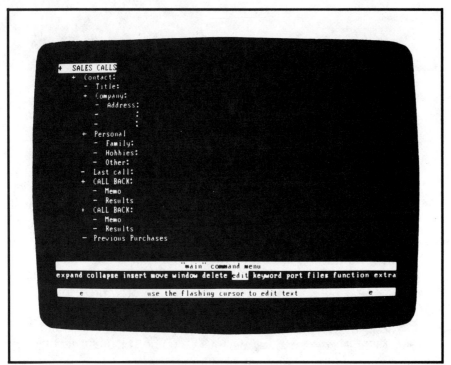

Figure 5.1: A template for sales calls.

Creating the Template

Richard's sales-call form includes both the information he needs while making a call and space for recording new information. For example, if a customer requires a certain type of catalog, or wants an order followed up, or wants to place a new order, Richard will record those facts under the **Memo** heading. Later, he can transfer the information to another part of his outline, so that all the orders he has taken for the day are consolidated in a single list for further action.

There are a few useful extras on the template form in Figure 5.1. First, note the two colons on their own lines, below **Address:**. These allow him to print out just the address information, in mailing-label form, if necessary. He placed them there by spacing over to just below the colon after **Address:** with the space bar. Second, although you can't see them on the screen, Richard has placed a space after each colon, so that the cursor will be properly positioned when he enters the Headline Editor to fill out his log.

ThinkTank does have a feature that will let you see the spaces. If you press Alt-F2, the background character will change from a blank space to a period, so you can see where the spaces are. Figure 5.2 shows the same screen as Figure 5.1, but with the background characters changed from spaces to periods.

You might want to take a few minutes now to create this template or one that might be more useful to you. Remember, to enter a group of headlines such as this template, all you need to do is press the Ins key and then press ←─ after each entry. If you find that you've left out a headline, you can insert it anywhere by using the cursor-movement keys to move the flashing cursor and question mark to the appropriate location. If you find that some are in the wrong place, you can move them after you're done by pressing F1. If you've made any mistakes, you can change them afterward using the Headline Editor (F3 or E H).

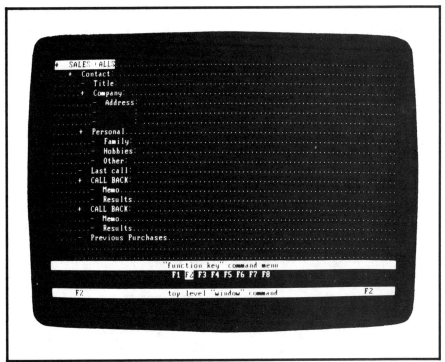

Figure 5.2: Sales call template showing periods in the background.

Building a File from the Template

To build a file from a template, begin by making several copies of the template. Be sure to make at least one more than you need, so that you will always have a blank one from which to generate more after you have filled the others in. Move the bar cursor to **Contact:** and press F10 F10 C to activate the COPY command. Repeat the procedure to make more copies. Now let's fill one in.

With the bar cursor on **Contact:,** enter the Headline Editor (F3 or E H). Notice that the flashing cursor appears after the space after the colon, ready for you to append information to the headline. You can type in the information, and then press the cursor-down key, and you will be at the end of the next line, ready to fill in the next blank. You can continue through the form, entering information and pressing the cursor-down key. If you follow the example below, however, you'll find that, as you skip some entries (the ones without the colons), the cursor moves directly below the previous entry. To get the cursor to the end of the line, press the End key on the numeric keypad. If you didn't expand the outline fully before you started, you can expand any portion while in the Headline Editor simply by pressing the + key on the numeric keypad. This way, you can even fill in lines that are hidden when you start.

A Filled-in Template

Now let's look at Richard's first call record (or your own). Move the bar cursor to **SALES CALLS,** collapse it (− on the numeric keypad) and expand it (+). The only headlines showing are the **Contact:** lines, which include both the customers' names and telephone numbers, as Figure 5.3 shows. This first expansion will allow Richard to see the names of all his customers at a glance.

When he is ready to make a sales call, he moves the bar cursor to the customer's **Contact:** line, and expands the entry. He sees the customer's title and company, and the dates of previous calls. If **CALL BACK** has today's date, he'll expand the **CALL BACK,** to see what he wants to discuss with his client. Figure 5.4 shows one completed record, before the current day's call.

```
        +   NEW ORDERS
        +   THINGS TO DO
        +   SALES CALLS
            +   Contact: Arthur Denton        (209) 901-6027
            +   Contact: George R. Forbes     (415) 911-2233
            +   Contact: Marie Lavereux       (415) 555-0602
            +   Contact: Molto Pozzo          (408) 311-6200
            +   Contact: Marcia Reeves        (916) 767-2222
            +   Contact: Chester Burnett      (415) 936-2211
```

Figure 5.3: First-level expansion of sales call log.

```
+   SALES CALLS
    +   Contact: Arthur Denton         (209) 901-6027
        -   Title: VP, Engineering
        +   Company: Sky High Technologies, Inc.
            -   Address: 11200 Dakota Avenue W., Suite 2112
            -            : Fresno, CA 93711
            -            :
        +   Personal
            -   Family:  Wife-Nancy, Son-Joe, 12, Daughter-Anita, 9
            -   Hobbies: Fishing, Golf, Tinkers w. tv sets
            -   Other: Bad back
        -   Last call: 4/22
        -   Last call: 5/12
        +   CALL BACK: 5/18
            +   Memo
                -   Says something big may be happening soon
                -   Ask about health, golf score
                -   How are Nancy, Joe & Anita?
            -   Results
        +   CALL BACK:
        -   Memo
        -   Results
        +   Previous Purchases:
            -   Megahype PC-compatible
            -   Super Spreadsheet
            -   Word Wizard
            -   Graphics Maker software for engineering
            -   ThinkTank
            -   3 file cabinets, letter size, 4-drawer, lockable
            -   5 blueprint cabinets, lockable
```

Figure 5.4: A completed sales call record.

If Richard doesn't know his customer very well, he may look under the **Personal** headline to remind himself of topics of conversation to put the customer in a favorable frame of mind. Seeing Arthur Denton's **Personal** information, for example, he'll be sure to ask about Nancy, Joe, and Anita, and to inquire about Arthur's golf game and his health, or to mention a problem he's having with his tv set.

When Richard makes the phone call, he expands his outline so that that his screen looks like Figure 5.5. Thus the information he needs is immediately visible. **CALL BACK** is expanded, and he is in INSERT mode, with the flashing cursor just below **Results,** ready even as he talks to record any vital new information.

Completing the Call

After completing his call, Richard makes several changes to his log. He will copy the empty **CALL BACK:** headline, so another

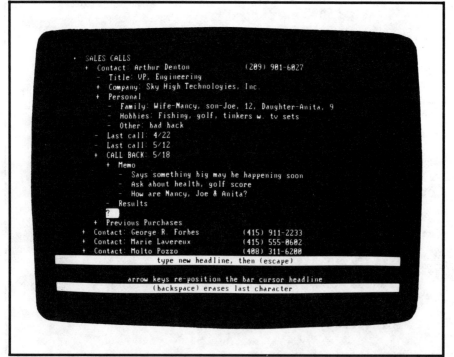

Figure 5.5: Sales call record ready to accept new information.

will be in reserve. Next, he will enter the date for his next call on the original empty **CALL BACK** line with the Headline Editor, and revise **CALL BACK: 5/18** to read **Last call: 5/18.** He will press Del O to delete the **Memo** from the day's call, and he may also delete the first of the **Last call** lines if he no longer needs it. Finally, he will copy the **Results** section, change the word **Results** to the name of his contact, and move it to his list of new orders. Figure 5.6 shows Richard's completed call record.

Keyword Search and Exchange

ThinkTank has one more feature to make Richard Wells's job easier: it will search for a *keyword* (any combination of up to 80 letters, numbers, punctuation marks, and spaces). When he starts the day's work, Richard wants to know who he promised to call

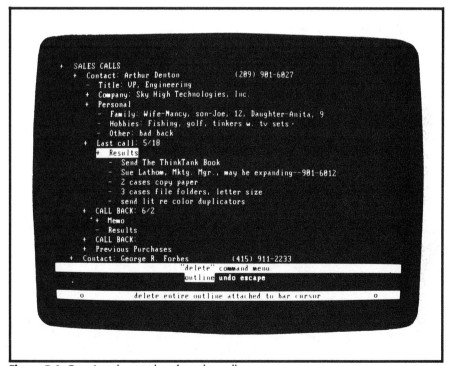

Figure 5.6: Entering the results of a sales call.

on a given day. All he has to do is search his records for the current date, 5/18.

Here's how to use this search feature:

1. Move the bar cursor to the outline to be searched (**SALES CALLS,** in this instance).

2. Enter SEARCH mode (K S, for KEYWORD SEARCH).

3. Enter **CALL BACK: 5/18** (or current date) when the prompt **pattern to search for?** appears.

As ThinkTank searches the outline under the bar cursor, it will automatically expand any portion that contains the keyword. When it finds the pattern, ThinkTank gives you the option of either continuing the search or stopping. The disadvantage of stopping is that when you want to continue the search, you must start again from the top. Richard habitually changes **CALL BACK** to **Last call** when he completes a call because the completed calls will say **Last call** instead of **CALL BACK.** When he searches for calls to make, ThinkTank will skip over the day's completed calls.

The KEYWORD command also has an exchange option, similar to the global find and replace option found in many word-processing programs. To select this option, press K X. ThinkTank will ask you to enter both a keyword to search for, and a keyword to replace it with. If Richard did not habitually change each **CALL BACK** to **Last call** as he completed each call, he could change **CALL BACK: 5/18** to **Last call: 5/18** for all his calls at once. The procedure is essentially the same as a search.

1. Enter XCHANGE mode (K X, for KEYWORD XCHANGE).

2. Enter **CALL BACK: 5/18** when prompted for a **pattern to search for.**

3. Enter **Last call: 5/18** when prompted for a **pattern to replace with?**

The computer will do all the work.

There's just one trick in exchanging keywords: a short word that you want to replace may appear as part of another word. For example, if you want to replace "for" with "to," then "former" would become "tomer" and "foreman" would become "toeman." You can avoid this problem by including a space before and after the keyword you want replaced, but then ThinkTank won't replace the word if there is a punctuation mark following it.

There is one important difference between searching and exchanging. When ThinkTank searches, it stops at every instance of the pattern that you specified, whether the letters it includes are uppercase or lowercase. When you exchange, however, only words with the same pattern of capital and lowercase letters as you entered will be replaced.

MAINTAINING A RESUME

Templates have many uses. Anything requiring a series of records of recurring types of information can be handled efficiently through ThinkTank templates. Moreover, templates can be used in situations that require a standard structure for different types of information. Let's look at one example of this type: a resume.

Howard Franklin is a market researcher, specializing in survey research. Since he works in advertising, a field where people change jobs often, he likes to keep his resume up-to-date. Lately, however, he's been thinking about a career change, so he has had to rethink the kinds of information he wants to present about himself. After using ThinkTank to brainstorm a description of his ideal job and working situation, he came up with the following system for creating a customized resume for each position about which he inquires.

This example introduces several new techniques: using headlines to format the appearance of the output, using the Paragraph Editor, and using the MERGE command. If you follow along and recreate the example, you will also gain practice in using the techniques you have just learned.

First, he has set up a blank resume template, which we see in Figure 5.7.

Formatting with Headlines

You'll notice that Howard has inserted apparently blank headlines between his major headings. Actually, you can't insert a

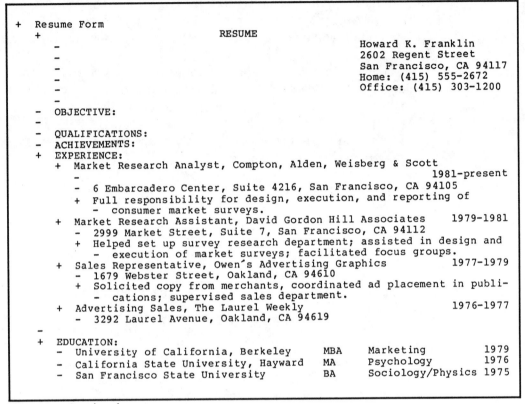

```
+  Resume Form
   +                           RESUME
      -                                              Howard K. Franklin
      -                                              2602 Regent Street
      -                                              San Francisco, CA 94117
      -                                              Home: (415) 555-2672
      -                                              Office: (415) 303-1200
      -
   -  OBJECTIVE:
   -
   -  QUALIFICATIONS:
   -  ACHIEVEMENTS:
   +  EXPERIENCE:
      +  Market Research Analyst, Compton, Alden, Weisberg & Scott
         -                                                   1981-present
         -  6 Embarcadero Center, Suite 4216, San Francisco, CA 94105
         +  Full responsibility for design, execution, and reporting of
            -  consumer market surveys.
      +  Market Research Assistant, David Gordon Hill Associates   1979-1981
         -  2999 Market Street, Suite 7, San Francisco, CA 94112
         +  Helped set up survey research department; assisted in design and
            -  execution of market surveys; facilitated focus groups.
      +  Sales Representative, Owen's Advertising Graphics        1977-1979
         -  1679 Webster Street, Oakland, CA 94610
         +  Solicited copy from merchants, coordinated ad placement in publi-
            -  cations; supervised sales department.
      +  Advertising Sales, The Laurel Weekly                     1976-1977
         -  3292 Laurel Avenue, Oakland, CA 94619

   +  EDUCATION:
      -  University of California, Berkeley      MBA   Marketing         1979
      -  California State University, Hayward    MA    Psychology        1976
      -  San Francisco State University          BA    Sociology/Physics 1975
```

Figure 5.7: Template for a resume.

blank headline, but if you want to create a line space, you can insert a headline consisting of one blank space.

Howard has included his major work experience in his template, as he doesn't expect to change that portion of his resume for each interview. One of the unfortunate limitations of ThinkTank is that, although it will let you create headlines up to 76 characters on screen, it will not print them on two lines; a long headline that is nested several levels deep will almost undoubtedly be truncated. Therefore, to keep his lines from getting too long, Howard has simply broken some of the headlines into separate headlines when describing his experience, nesting the following line under the first.

On the other hand, he has left the sections labeled **OBJECTIVE, QUALIFICATIONS,** and **ACHIEVEMENTS** empty, including only the major heads, as he will want to vary these sections to match the prospective job specifications.

Next, he maintains a file of statements of achievements, set up as a series of short paragraphs, each with an identifying headline. Since they are all available in his outline, it's a simple matter to move any combination of them into place to create a custom resume.

Introducing the Paragraph Editor

Howard uses the Paragraph Editor to create this part of his outline, because it has a few important features not available in the Headline Editor that are very useful for printed output. Let's glance at them before we go on.

Unlike headlines, which will be truncated if they are too long to fit on a printed page, lines created in the Paragraph Editor will *wrap*—that is, words at the end of a printed line will not be cut or separated if they are too long to fit, but will be moved to the following line. Also, in the Paragraph Editor, a *hard carriage return* is displayed on the screen as a small triangle when the ← key is pressed. You can see, for example, if you have used hard carriage returns for line spacing. Both of these features will be useful to Howard in creating his Achievements outline. *Note:* If you *don't* want to see the hard carriage returns, you can turn them off by pressing Alt-F3.

We won't examine the Paragraph Editor in detail until Chapters 7 and 8, but if you follow Howard through this exercise, you should know enough to get started. The first step is to place the bar cursor on the headline under which you want the paragraph, and press F5 or E P. A pair of dotted lines will appear, with a flashing cursor at the left edge of the screen, beneath the top line. You can type up to 20,000 characters, 900 lines, or a point at which you want a new paragraph.

In the Paragraph Editor, the delete keys and cursor-movement keys work the same as in the Headline Editor, with a few additions which we'll look at in Chapter 7. The Paragraph Editor, like the Headline Editor, is normally in INSERT mode, so if you want to add text somewhere in an existing paragraph, simply move the flashing cursor to the point at which you want to enter text, and begin typing. Any text following the point of insertion will move to the right. When you finish entering text, and are satisfied with it, press Esc E to return to the top level.

Setting up the Achievements Outline

Howard begins setting up his outline of achievements by delineating the areas in which his most significant achievements have occurred. Since he's brainstorming at this point, he will let achievements come to mind at random, and insert them in the appropriate places.

In contrast to the Headline Editor, which lets you edit a headline anywhere in your outline, the Paragraph Editor restricts you to the paragraph under a single headline. Then you must return to the top level to edit the next paragraph. Therefore, it's simpler to enter a headline and then add text than it would be to set up a series of headlines and enter text under each one later. Figure 5.8 shows Howard's initial outline.

Adding Text to the Outline

As Howard remembers each of his achievements, he will enter a headline nested one level deeper below the headlines shown in Figure 5.8. After he presses Esc to return to the top level, his bar cursor will be on the new headline. He will enter the Paragraph Editor, write a short description of his achievement, and then return to the top level to go on to his next achievement. Figure 5.9 shows his outline after he has entered one achievement and Figures 5.10a and 5.10b show portions of the completed outline.

```
        +   Achievements
            -   Organizational
            -   Research
            -   Advertising
            -   Sales
```

Figure 5.8: An outline for brainstorming on personal achievements.

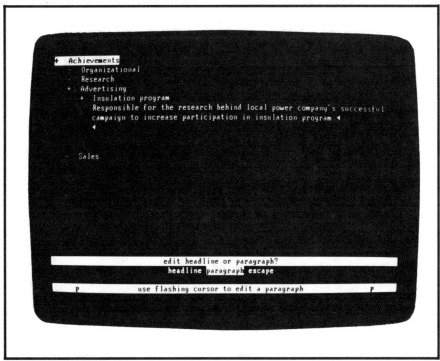

Figure 5.9: The Achievements outline with one paragraph added.

ThinkTank automatically places a carriage return at the end of a paragraph, so it is not necessary to enter a carriage return when you exit. As Figure 5.10b shows, however, Howard has ended each of his achievement paragraphs with a carriage return, and then added a second carriage return to create a line space.

Combining Text with Template: The DELETE-UNDO and MERGE Commands

Now that Howard has set up a file of achievements, he can produce a final, customized resume in only a few keystrokes. We'll walk through the process with him, and in the process gain some practice with the DELETE-UNDO and MERGE commands.

Howard will create a single paragraph under the headline **ACHIEVEMENTS:** delineating several accomplishments he

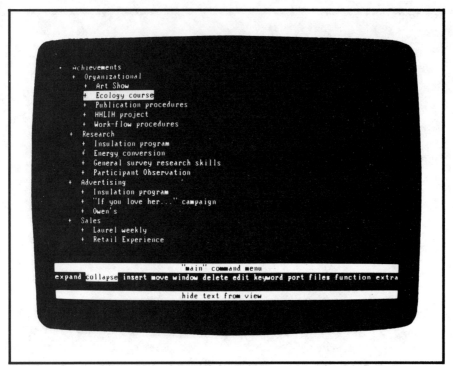

Figure 5.10: Two different expansions of the Achievements outline.

feels will be especially relevant to the job in which he is interested. For example, if he were seeking a senior research position,
he might stress his achievements in research. If he were seeking a
managerial position, he would emphasize his organizational
achievements as a team leader; if he were interested in moving to
a small company with significant growth opportunities, he might
point up those achievments showing initiative and skill in setting
up new procedures.

At present, Howard will create a resume for the latter type of
position. Since he knows that the company president is con-
cerned with ecological issues, he will also mention his achievements in this area.

Figure 5.11 shows Howard's resume form and Achievements
outline as he gets ready to begin. He has already made a copy of
the blank resume form, so that he will have a blank form to use
later. He has used MOVE mode to place the new copy below his

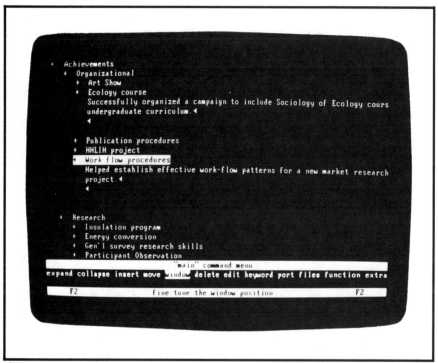

Figure 5.10: Two different expansions of the Achievements outline (continued).

Achievements outline. The bar cursor is on **Work-flow proce-dures.** He will copy that portion (F10 F10 C), so that it will still be available to use in other resumes after he has used it in his current one.

Next, he must move the copy into position for a merge. In order to merge any paragraph to another, the headline of the paragraph to be merged from must be below the headline to be merged to, and at the same level of indentation. As I mentioned earlier, you can move a headline, and its subordinate material anywhere in an outline using MOVE mode. However, as you probably noticed, MOVE mode is tricky to use when moving items over long distances. The more efficient, and less confusing, way to move text a long way is to use the DELETE-UNDO commands. These commands allow you to delete text at one point in your outline and then insert it in another.

When the copy process is completed, the bar cursor will be on the new copy of the **Work-flow procedures** headline. Next,

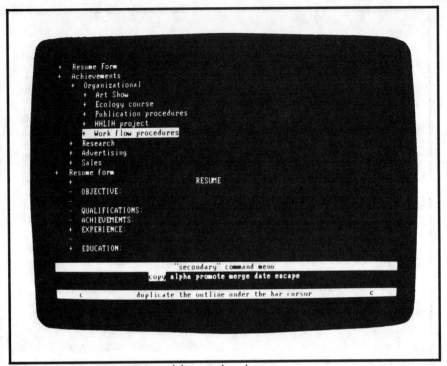

Figure 5.11: Preparing to copy, delete, and undo.

Howard will delete it. First he enters DELETE mode, by pressing Del. The DELETE menu offers three choices:

Use O (OUTLINE) to delete an outline;

Use P (PARAGRAPH) to delete the paragraph attached to the bar cursor headline;

Use U (UNDO) to undo the previous deletion.

Although he only wants to move a paragraph, any paragraph once deleted cannot be restored, so he chooses the OUTLINE command by pressing O, deleting the headline along with the paragraph. Next, he moves his bar cursor to **ACHIEVEMENTS:**.He presses Del, and U (UNDO), and the deleted **Work-flow procedures** reappears, with a plus sign indicating that the paragraph is still present, as shown in Figure 5.12.

There is one very important thing to keep in mind when you want to move something with the DELETE-UNDO commands.

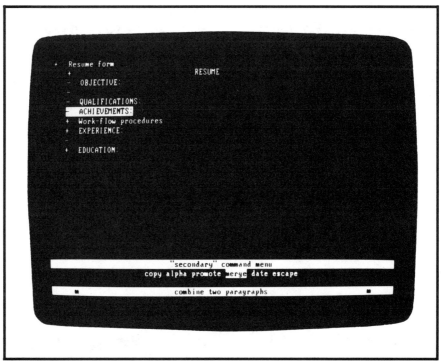

Figure 5.12: Setting up a merge.

You must never delete anything else before you perform the undo, or the first item you deleted will be lost forever!

Next, Howard will perform a merge. The MERGE command moves a paragraph from one headline to another. If a paragraph is already present, the new text will be appended to the old. In this instance, the headline that text will be merged *to* is empty—it has no paragraph attached to it. In order to perform a merge, three conditions must be met:

1. The two headlines between which the merge will take place must be at the same level of indentation.

2. The merge-from headline must be below the merge-to headline.
   Note: If either of these conditions is not met, you must move one headline. It's easier to get them in the right place if you collapse them both first.

3. The bar cursor must be on the merge-to headline.

Since the first three conditions are met, Howard moves his bar cursor to **ACHIEVEMENTS:** and enters the MERGE command (F10 F10 M). The menu will offer the options of deleting the paragraph from under the old headline (D), or copying it, so that both headlines will have the material from the merge-from headline under them. Since he copied the **Work-flow procedures** headline and paragraph from his achievements outline, Howard will have no further need of these copies, so he chooses to delete (D). After the merge, his resume looks like Figure 5.13.

Howard will then repeat the procedure of merging several additional paragraphs under the **ACHIEVEMENTS:** headline, until this portion of his resume appears as in Figure 5.14.

You'll notice that Howard has not yet deleted any of the empty headlines from which he merged the text. He could have deleted each one in succession, and his screen would have been less cluttered, but it doesn't matter when he performs the delete as long

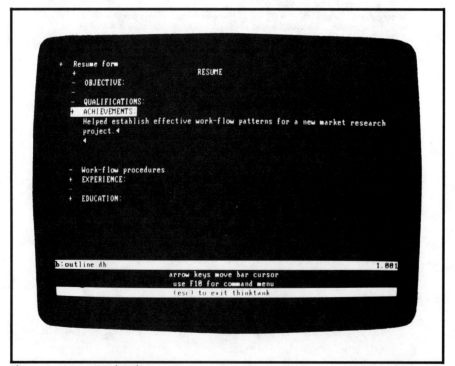

Figure 5.13: A completed merge.

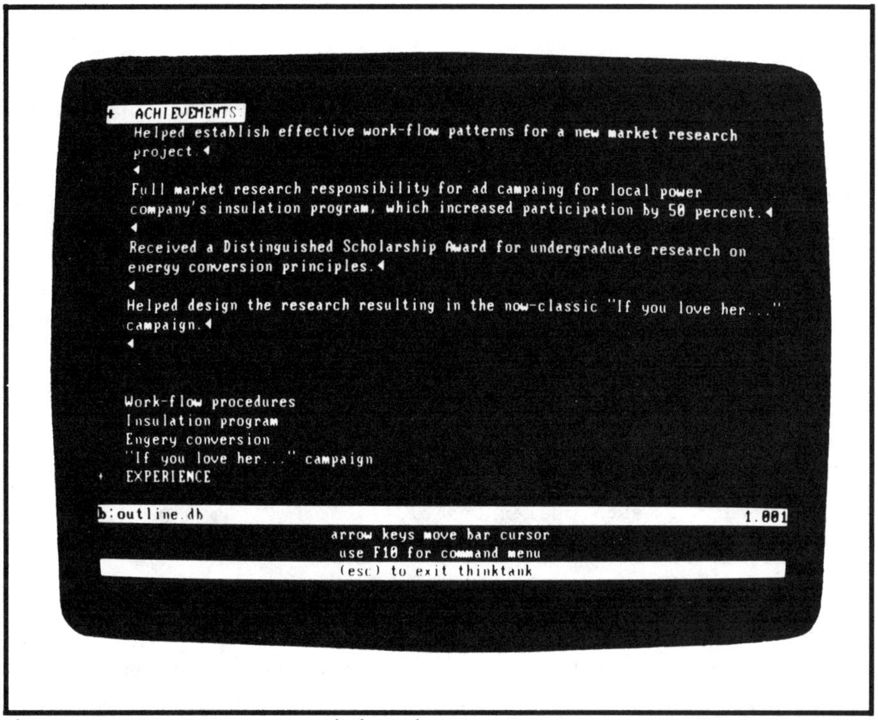

Figure 5.14: Creating a paragraph from four merges.

as the undo is executed while the bar cursor is on **ACHIEVE-MENTS:,** to assure the correct placement of the merge-from headlines.

After deleting the empty headlines, he will use the Headline Editor to fill in his objective, and the Paragraph Editor to summarize his qualifications for the job in question. When he is all finished, he will print out the resume as it appears in Figure 5.15.

OTHER USES FOR TEMPLATES

We have already seen how templates can be used to maintain a daily calendar/schedule/to-do list. Templates can also be set up for such varied uses as:

- personnel records
- inventory lists

```
                        RESUME
                                        Howard K. Franklin
                                        2602 Regent Street
                                        San Francisco, CA 94117
                                        Home: (415) 555-2672
                                        Office: (415) 303-1200
OBJECTIVE: A senior market research position in a growing company
   dedicated to soft-path energy development.

QUALIFICATIONS:
   Eight years of progressively responsible experience in advertising,
   sales, and market research; design, administrative, and supervisory
   experience; skills in all phases of market research; commitment to soft
   energy development; and an entrepreneurial imagination.


ACHIEVEMENTS:
   Helped establish effective work-flow patterns for a new market research
   project.

   Full market research responsibility for ad campaign for local power
   company's insulation program, which increased participation by 50
   percent.

   Received a Distinguished Scholarship Award for undergraduate research
   on energy conversion principles.

   Helped design the research resulting in the now-classic "If you love
   her..." campaign.



EXPERIENCE:
   Market Research Analyst, Compton, Alden, Weisberg & Scott
                                                1981-present
      6 Embarcadero Center, Suite 4216, San Francisco, CA 94611
      Full responsibility for design, execution and reporting of
         consumer market surveys.
   Market Research Assistant, David Gordon Hill Associates    1979-1981
      2999 Market Street, Suite 7, San Francisco, CA 94112
      Helped set up survey research department; assisted in design and
         execution of market surveys; facilitated focus groups.
   Sales Representative, Owen's Advertising Graphics          1977-1979
      1679 Webster Street, Oakland, CA 94610
      Solicited copy from merchants, coordinated ad placement in publi-
         cations; supervised sales department.
   Advertising Sales, The Laurel Weekly                       1976-1977
      3292 Laurel Avenue, Oakland, CA 94619

EDUCATION:
   University of California, Berkeley   MBA  Marketing          1979
   California State University, Hayward MA   Psychology         1976
   San Francisco State University       BA   Sociology/Physics  1975
```

Figure 5.15: The completed resume.

- catalogue entries
- medical records
- minutes of formal meetings
- bibliographic references.

The important points to remember in templating are:

1. Duplicate your original template before adding any information to it.
2. Set up the entry spaces in your headlines so that you can use the headline editor to fill out a complete form.
3. Duplicate any *parts* of your template that you will need to reuse—like the **Call back:** line in our sales calls example—prior to filling them in.
4. If you expect entries to be longer than a headline, simply add a headline to remind you of the contents, and fill in either by using the Paragraph Editor or by inserting short, nested headlines. We have seen both of these techniques in the resume example.

ThinkTank does have some limitations as a data base manager in the areas of searching and sorting: searching is a rather slow process; and, while it can sort alphabetically, it will sort only the first-level headlines beneath the bar cursor. So, if you need complex, nested sorts, or extemely fast record retrieval, you are probably better off with a dedicated data base program.

On the other hand, if you don't want to spend the time learning to use a data base program, or don't need the specialized capacities of a dedicated package, ThinkTank is a reasonably powerful record-keeping tool; and the ease with which information can be moved and copied is one of its great virtues.

6

FROM AN IDEA TO A MASTER PLAN

In this chapter we'll depart from the guided series of exercises in other chapters. As we follow the adventures of the staff of Sky High Technologies, we'll see how a ThinkTank outline can be used as a framework for the development of a complex body of information. We'll also see how ThinkTank can *transform* such information into numerous different forms for different purposes.

In the course of the chapter, you'll see demonstrations of brainstorming, organizing the resultant material, project planning, scheduling, maintaining a modular file, and sharing of files with other users. These illustrations should help you to form a conception of the numerous ways ThinkTank can be employed, some of which you may be able to adapt to your own work.

A NEW VENTURE

One fine morning in May, Bernie Richman, president of Sky High Technologies, called in his managerial team for a conference. Bernie had an announcement to make that would change the company forever. Sky High had until now done a steady, respectable business as a manufacturer of passive solar water heating systems, based on solar collectors of the company's own design and manufacture. But on this day, Art Denton, the head of Sky High's Engineering Division, had announced that his research and development group had successfully tested a revolutionary new product.

The group had developed a new energy-conversion and -storage system that could increase the efficiency of the company's solar collectors. As part of a properly designed system, Sky High's collectors could now be used not only for passive heating, but for generation of electricity as well, even in climates with a limited number of days of sunlight.

Up to now, Sky High had marketed complete systems. While the energy converter could be marketed to third parties for use in complete systems, Bernie was quite unhappy with this idea. He preferred to continue marketing complete systems, but the systems would have to be considerably larger than those the company had previously produced. He had to be sure that the system was one that had a good chance to compete in the marketplace. He also wanted assurance that his company was capable of marketing the system.

Since this venture would take Sky High into a new area, there were some risks involved. Loans would have to be floated to cover the costs of expanding the plant to handle construction of the new units. The expense of producing and marketing several systems at once appeared to be prohibitive. So Bernie wanted to enter the market with a system that had a strong promise of a quick return on investment. To convince the bank that the company was capable of handling the job, Bernie had to present the loan officer with the single most marketable version of the system.

Bernie asked Sue Lathom, his marketing director, to take charge of gathering the necessary information to help them select the design with which to enter the market, and to develop a marketing strategy based on that design. He also asked all the other department and division heads to give Sue their full cooperation. Sue was to report in six weeks, during which time Bernie would confer with George Yamamoto, his production manager, and Art, on alternative product designs. They would draw no conclusions, however, until the results of Sue's research were in. Art supplied Sue with all the available technical data about the system, and she set to work.

STEPS TOWARD A MARKETING PLAN

She went directly to her computer, on which she always has ThinkTank up and running, except when she needs a spreadsheet. Let's take a peek at how she organizes her work. Her outline appears in Figure 6.1.

```
+  Good Morning Sue. This will be one terrific day!!!
   +  Rolodex
   +  To do this week
      +  Monday
      +  Tuesday
         +  9am - conference room - IMPORTANT!!!
            -  New product announcement
      +  Wednesday
         +  10am - meeting with Freddie Perez from engineering
            -  Get some kwh-per-hour figures
            -  Any other hard figures re $ savings
         -  Department lunch at Sweet Lorraine's - 12:30
         +  3:30 - sales meeting
      -  Thursday
      +  Friday
   +  FORMS
      +  To do this week
      +  Rolodex entry
      +  Memo
      +  General Marketing Plan Outline
      +  Expenses
   +  DRAFT: Letter to Homebuilders' Society of America
   +  DISTRIBUTOR CONFERENCE NOTES
   +  Random notes
```

Figure 6.1: Sue's working outline.

At the summit of her outline is an encouraging message. It gives Sue a little lift to have the computer say something nice to her as she browses through her outline files, and this line will show up between the menu bars. Next is her address and telephone list, which she has called **Rolodex** (she no longer has a Rolodex on her desk). Following that is a weekly calendar. Tuesday's meeting appears along with an entry for the next day, showing an appointment Sue set up to get more information on the new product. Next is a section labeled **FORMS,** in which she keeps an assortment of templates. Following that are two projects in progress, and a section for notes.

Among Sue's templates is a **General Marketing Plan Outline.** This is a dummy form, with all the categories she needs for creating a marketing plan. Her general marketing plan outline is shown in Figure 6.2.

```
+  General Marketing Plan Outline
   +  Global Strategy Statement
      -  One-year goals
      -  Five-year goals
   -  Pertinent product characteristics
   +  Customer characteristics
      +  Able to use
         -  Geographic distribution
         -  Demographic characteristics
      +  Want to use
         -  Geographic distribution
         -  Demographic characteristics
      -  Price sensitivity factors
   +  Nature of the competition
      +  Supplier:
         -  Nature of product line
         -  Geographic distribution
         -  Market shares
   +  Promotional strategy
      +  Advertising
         +  method:
            +  frequency:
               -  dates:
         -  cost
      +  Direct promotions to dealers
         +  method:
            +  frequency:
               -  dates:
         -  cost
      +  Other PR
         +  method
            +  frequency:
               -  dates:
         -  cost
```

Figure 6.2: Sue's general marketing plan outline.

To begin the project, Sue made a copy of this outline. She changed the name (temporarily) to "Marketing Plan for Art's New Baby," filled in as much of the product description as she could from Art's tech sheets, and added a few new categories. For example, she would need information on weather conditions and prices for heating fuels and electricity in various parts of the country, so she added a headline to hold it when it arrived.

Since this was a new type of product for the company, she did not know who the customers were likely to be. So she called in her new market research manager, Howard Franklin, and asked him to do a market survey to find out. She ported part of her marketing plan outline to a structured text file, and gave it to Howard, who, as we know, was also a ThinkTank user. Howard incorporated the marketing plan into his own ThinkTank outline, and used it as the basis for developing several survey questionnaires for homeowners, distributors, and builders, any of whom might be interested in the system.

Sue would not need the **Promotional strategy** section of her outline until later. Once she had all her information, she would rough out a strategy in that section, which could then serve as the basis for discussions with the advertising and sales managers. From those discussions, Sue would later flesh out a full-fledged marketing plan, complete with a detailed schedule and allocation of responsibilities.

Sue also gave a copy of her structured text file to Julia Lee, her administrative assistant, who would research energy rates and weather conditions. Sue would research the competition herself, while waiting for the results from Howard and Julia.

DESIGNING AND MAINTAINING THE SURVEY QUESTIONNAIRE

Let's now look at how Howard handled the project. He worked up a research design and a series of questionnaires to gather the information that Sue needed. To begin, he ported Sue's text file into his general working outline.

In Figure 6.3, we can see how Howard uses ThinkTank. Like Sue, he has edited the summit line (with a quote from San Francisco's favorite columnist, to remind himself of home), to identify his general working outline. Since he has been with the company only a short time, he has very little in the outline, so Sue's text file appears as the second first-level headline, after his calendar.

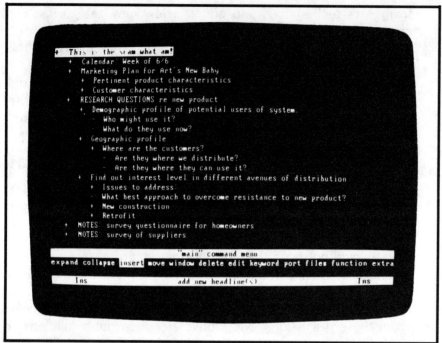

```
+ This is the scam what am?
  + Calendar: Week of 6/6
  + Marketing Plan for Art's New Baby
    + Pertinent product characteristics
    + Customer characteristics
+ RESEARCH QUESTIONS re new product
  +  Demographic profile of potential users of system.
    - Who might use it?
    - What do they use now?
  + Geographic profile
    + Where are the customers?
      - Are they where we distribute?
      - Are they where they can use it?
    + Find out interest level in different avenues of distribution
      + Issues to address:
      - What best approach to overcome resistance to new product?
      + New construction
      + Retrofit
  + NOTES: survey questionnaire for homeowners
  + NOTES: survey of suppliers

                        "main" command menu
expand collapse  insert  move window delete edit keyword port files function extra

    Ins                  add new headline(s)                 Ins
```

Figure 6.3: Howard's working outline.

Beneath that, Howard has started a brainstorming section in which to plan his work. Notice how he has inserted a series of blank headlines, each indented one level under the previous one. This will give him room to move when he starts to add structure to his outline. (As we know, it's a bit easier to move headlines to the left than to the right.) Figure 6.4 shows the **NOTES** portion of his outline expanded, so we can get a glimpse of his brainstorming process.

In a separate file on another disk, Howard has over the years built up a file of useful survey research questions. Each time he works on a new project, he extracts any questions from the survey that might be useful in other surveys, and adds them to his outline file, classified by topic. When he has progressed from the brainstorming phase to the survey design phase, Howard loads up his question file. He begins by creating a special first-level head at the end of his file, where he will store copies of the questions he wants to use. Next, he looks through the file to locate any questions that he might be able to use in the present survey,

```
+   NOTES: survey questionnaire for homeowners
    +
      +
        +
          +  Special areas needed to develop:
             +  reactions to specific aspects of product
                -  ease/difficulty of installation
                -  initial cost vs. long-term savings
             +  desirability of various options
                -  what the heck are the options?
                -  Does Sue know, or should I see Freddie?
             +  favorable predispositions-
                -  correlated w. what?
          -  Sample design should take care of geographics
          +  Suggest broad-based sample for initial pass
             -  follow w. focused sample of most interested cats.
          -  TELL SUE WE SHOULD HAVE FOCUS GROUPS!!!
+   NOTES: survey of suppliers
    +
      +
        +
          -  Get a list from Homebuilders' Assn.
          +  Phone survey, followed w. mail
             -  Start w. unstructured, to find out issues
          -  Wholesalers?
```

Figure 6.4: Howard's brainstorming outline.

whether in their current form or with some rewriting. This saves Howard a lot of time in the long run, because he doesn't have to start each survey from scratch.

As Howard finds useful questions, he copies them, deletes the copies, and undoes the deletions under the special head. When he has copied all the usable questions from the file into his new section, he will place his bar cursor on the special head, port to a structured text file, and port that file into his working outline.

Then he will be in a position to create his questionnaires within his working outline, with the notes he has received from Sue constantly available. He might go through this process more than once, as he thinks through the details, and uncovers subtleties that his first design may not have tapped. Figure 6.5 shows Howard's file of questionnaire items, as he has begun to extract the questions he will actually use.

BRINGING IT ALL TOGETHER

When they were at the end of the allotted research period, Howard and Julia showed Sue their conclusions. Howard's analysis of the market for the system among homeowners revealed that:

- Geographically, there was the most interest in California, Colorado, New England, and the upper Midwest.
- Politically, those expressing the most interest seemed to be either strongly liberal or strongly conservative.
- Interest among those with a college degree or higher was more than doubled that of the next lowest educational category.
- Income had no effect on interest in the product, but it had a strong effect on price sensitivity.
- There was about equal division between those who wanted to be able to do the installation themselves and those who preferred to have the product installed by a qualified contractor.
- Other demographic factors had very little effect.
- The vast majority of those who expressed even a moderate interest in the product would look favorably upon a future home in which the system had already been installed.
- Nearly all those who thought energy conservation issues were somewhat or very important were favorably disposed toward the product, although not all of them foresaw any immediate chance that they would install it in their present home.

Regarding builders, Howard drew the following conclusions:

- Geographically there was extremely strong interest by homebuilders in the middle Atlantic region.
- Many of the builders surveyed saw the system's potential for usefulness in multi-unit home and commerical buildings as even greater than in SDUs.
- Builders were generally favorable everywhere, except for those who specialized in existing forms of heating installation.
- Builders in general saw the greatest problems with the system as maintainability (especially if parts were not available), and problems with local building codes and zoning ordinances. Many feared that they would not be knowledgeable enough to install the system, as it was outside their experience.

```
+  Questionnaire Item File, version 7.43, updated 5/12/84
   +  Demographics
      +  Home Ownership
      +  Mobility
      +  Marital Status
      +  Household composition
      +  Education
      +  Occupation
      +  Chief Wage Earner
      +  Union Membership
      +  Group Membership
      +  Ethnic Background
      +  Political Affiliation
      +  Religion
      +  Income
      +  Sex
      +  Age
      +  Name, Address, Phone #
   +  Opinions - political
   +  Opinions - energy issues
      +  Nuclear
      +  Solar
      +  Conservation
      +  Gasoline consumption
      +  Price sensitivity issues
   +  Energy Consumption Questions
      +  Insulation items
      +  Power sources used
      +  Types of appliances
      +  Transportation
      +  Conservation measures
   +  Product reaction questions
   +  ART'S NEW BABY
      +  Do you own your own home, or do you rent?
         -  own__
         -  rent__
         +  IF OWN: How much is your monthly payment?
            -  under $200    __
            -  $201-$350     __
            -  $351-$500     __
            -  $501-$800     __
            -  $801-$1200    __
            -  over $1200    __
      +  There has been a great deal of discussion these days about

         -  energy conservation. Do you feel that energy conservation is
         +  very important, somewhat important, or not important at all?
            -  very  important    __
            -  somewhat important __
            -  not important      __
            -  other              __
            -  DK/NA              __
```

Figure 6.5: Howard's ThinkTank file of questionnaire items.

Sue took Julia's report on prevailing climate conditions, and, matching that data with the product description and technical specifications from the engineering department (and after extensive discussions with Art and Freddie), came to the following conclusions:

- The system as originally conceived would require no modifications in the southeast and southwest.

- Installations in the Pacific northwest would definitely require some sort of backup system, as there were barely enough sunny days to operate the system.

- Installations in the northern-tier states would require some kind of backup heating system, but would be able to generate adequate electricity, provided the electricity was not used as the principal source of heating fuel.

- Given the interest by both SDU developers and by those involved in multi-unit construction, high priority should be given to developing some sort of a central collection system. Such a system could be used not only in multi-unit structures, but (Sue surmised) by tract developers as well, to greatly reduce the cost of installation.

With this additional information, Sue returned to her outline to begin hammering out the specifics of a marketing plan.

As you can see in Figure 6.6, Sue simply plugged in the information under the appropriate headlines, and edited the headlines as needed to conform to her own style. At this point she has begun entering goals, which she will later revise using the Paragraph Editor, to create something suitable for formal presentation. In Chapter 7, we will watch as she uses the Paragraph Editor to create and revise her Global Strategy Statement.

Given the results of the survey, Sue has added a new category of customers—OEMs, builders of new housing, who appear to be the best market for the system. She has also created a brainstorming section under **Promotional strategy**, where she has simply entered a series of ideas. If you look at the details, you can see that, where her dummy included a space for a description of one promotional method, she has used the COPY command to duplicate it several times, so that she can fill in specifics for various methods. She has already begun doing so. You can see that ideas regarding ads with a reply coupon, a brochure for those who send in the coupon, a conference for home builders, and a brochure for a mass mailing to builders are already under development in the more structured portion of the **Promotional strategy** section. When all her ideas have either been worked into a usable form or discarded, she will delete the brainstorming section.

Later when the outline was fully filled in, she passed copies to Advertising Manager Ruth Brown, Public Relations Specialist Gail Altman, and Sales Manager Joe Donato, as structured text files. They would fill in the details of the proposal in their own areas of expertise and return the results to Sue as structured text files, so she could add them to her outline, replacing her own rough draft.

In the meantime, Sue planned follow-up research with Howard, and discussed details of development schedules with George and Art, so that she could plan a coordinated schedule for everyone.

SETTING UP A SCHEDULE

When preliminary discussions were completed, it was time to set up a timetable to coordinate the activities of everyone in the department, and to assure that the various projects dovetailed correctly. Sue began by adding a schedule template to her outline.

A portion of the template is shown in Figure 6.7. She has set up a blank headline, under which she has created a project-item form. She will duplicate the outline attached to the blank headline 12 times, once for each month, and enter the names of the months with the Headline Editor. As you can see, this process is partially completed. As information becomes available regarding a given project, she will duplicate the project-item form, complete the headlines with the Headline Editor, and enter a list of goals for the project for the month as a series of individual headlines.

Before Sue could fill in the details, however, she needed to know what they were. She asked her managers and assistants to prepare proposed schedules and budgets for the various projects she assigned to them. The proposals would come back to Sue in the form of structured text files, so that, after discussing and finalizing the details with her staff, she could fill in her template simply by moving and copying items, doing a little editing along the way.

```
+  Marketing Plan for SkyPower Home Heating/Generating System
   +  Global Strategy Statement
      +  One year goals
         +  Stress developing of presence & credibility
            -  Establish sales where distribution & demand coincide
            -  Seek success stories
         +  Use in heavy promotion to dealers in other regions
            -  STRESS availability of regionalized collector systems
            -  Market multi-unit system by end of first sales year
            -  Build name recognition in consumer market
      +  Five year goals
         -  Expect break-even by 2 1/2 years
         -  Full national coverage of builders by 2 years
         -  Homeowner retrofit for gas-fired available by 1 year
         -  Other homeowner retrofit by 3 years
         +  Owner-builder package by 2-3 years?
            -  Check w. engineering for details.
   +  Pertinent product characteristics
   +  Customer characteristics
      +  OEM Customers
         +  Geographic distribution
            -  Interest everywhere
            -  Most interest in Middle Atlantic region
         +  STRONG INTEREST IN MULTI-UNIT
      +  Able to use
         +  Geographic distribution
            -  Southeast, Southwest, West Coast
            -  Northern tier with some modifications
            -  Potential problems in Pacific Northwest, Maine
         +  Demographic characteristics
            -  homeowners
            -  avg. house price $78,000
            +  income factors - check
               -  Financial market for financing of installation?
      +  Want to use
         +  Geographic distribution
            -  California
            -  Colorado
            -  New England
            -  Upper Midwest
         +  Demographic characteristics
            -  strongly liberal or strongly conservative
            -  concerned re ecological issues/conservation
            -  college educated
            -  generally favorable attitude, needs cultivation
      +  Price sensitivity factors
   +  Promotional strategy
      +  POTENTIAL PROMOTIONAL STRATEGIES
         -  Heavy direct-mail campaign to developers
         -  Big product-intro conference for builders
         -  Press releases to trade journals
         -  press releases to general press
         +  Advertising in Mother Earth News, other ecology-oriented pubs
            -  coupon for more info
         +  Advertising in regional mags where most homeowner inst
```

Figure 6.6: Sue plugs the new information into her outline.

```
              -  e.g., Sunset
              -  Coupon
         -  Brochure for coupon responses - medium scale
         -  Full color slick for builders
         +  Set up a builders' hotline!
              +  Technical/installation info
                   -  Can engineering provide notes, info for mail response?
              +  Legal info
                   -  See if Legal can work up standard briefs, phone info
    +  Advertising
         +  method: Coupon ads in Ecology/Conservation Publications
              +  frequency: Monthly
                   -  dates:
              -  cost
         +  method: Coupon ads in regional homeowner mags
              +  frequency: Monthly
                   -  dates:
              -  cost
         +  method: Brochure for coupon responses
         +  method:
         +  method:
    +  Direct promotions to dealers
         +  method: Developers' Conference at major SF hotel
              +  frequency: once
                   -  dates: Aim for early November?
              -  cost: sky's not the limit, how about low clouds?
         +  method:
         +  method:
    +  Other PR
```

Figure 6.6: Sue plugs the new information into her outline (continued).

Figure 6.8 shows Ruth's schedule for completion of the color brochure for builders. Sue can add this information to her outline, along with all the other schedules.

In Figure 6.9, you can see the schedule beginning to take shape. Notice how the items from Ruth's outline have been moved to their proper places with a minimum of alteration.

Finally, Sue reorganized her master plan into a day-by-day schedule, which she used as a calendar to keep track of the entire project. First, she made a copy of each **Goals** line in the project-item forms for the month. Next, she used the Headline Editor to revise the various goal statements so she knew which item belonged to which project. Then she moved each of the **Goals** sections into a part of her outline headed **SKYPOWER MASTER SCHEDULE**. After each move, she performed a PROMOTE on the items under each **Goals** line, so she could delete the headlines that simply said **Goals**. Finally, she used the MOVE mode to put the goals in order by date.

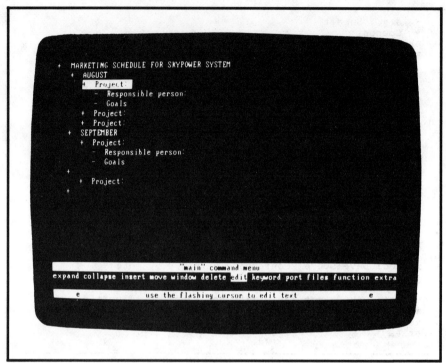

Figure 6.7: Sue creates a schedule template.

```
+   Builders' Brochure
    -   Determine contents by Aug. 12
    -   Copy completed by Aug. 17
    -   Contract w. Western Photo to be signed by Aug.5
    -   Photos to be completed by Aug. 20
    +   All materials to Leong Design Associates by Aug. 22
        -   Expect 2-3 week turnaround
    +   Pages to Tollber Color Labs for color sep - 2 weeks
        -   To us for approval by Sept. 24
    +   To K&M for printing by Sept. 25.
        -   K&M will deliver to Mary's Mail Service by 6/28
    -   Expect replies by Oct. 15
+   Mailing List
    -   Review of in-house lists by Aug 14
    -   Contact Modern Marketing for additional lists - when
    -   Hopefully, mailing lists should be ready by Mid-September
```

Figure 6.8: A portion of Ruth Brown's advertising schedule.

```
+   MARKETING SCHEDULE FOR SKYPOWER SYSTEM
    +  AUGUST
       +  Project: Builder Conference
          -  Responsible person: Gail
          +  Goals
             -  Aug 20: Begin researching SF hotels
             -  Aug 31: Deadline for finding someone to build the models
       +  Project: Builder Brochure
          -  Responsible person: Ruth
          +  Goals
             -  Aug. 6: Sign Contract w. Western Photo
             -  Aug. 6: Contact Modern Marketing re mailing lists
             -  Aug. 12: All contents of brochure to be determined
             -  Aug. 17: Copy completed
             -  Aug. 20: Photos to be completed
             -  Aug. 22: All materials to Leong Design Associates
       +  Project: Legal/Technical Hotline
          -  Responsible person: Julia
          -  Goals
                Get the Legal Dept. working on a set of briefs to be sent
                to builders on request, to assist in dealing with zoning
                variances, building code waivers, lobbying for building
                code changes, etc.

                Start machinery to get 800 line set up.

                Locate appropriate personnel in Engineering and Legal to
                handle phone inquiries.


       +  Project: Focus Groups
          -  Responsible person: Howard
          +  Goals
             -  Aug. 7: Deadline for agreeing on goals
             -  Aug. 21: Sample to be selected, site to be chosen
    +  SEPTEMBER
       +  Project: Builder Conference
          -  Responsible person: Gail
          +  Goals
             -  Sept. 10: Drawings for models to be submitted
             -  Sept. 12: Meet w. Leong's to discuss display designs
             -  Sept. 26: Display designs approved
       +  Project: Builder Brochure
          -  Responsible person: Ruth
          +  Goals
             -  Sept 10: Designs from Leong Design Associates
             -  Sept. 11: Pages to Tollber Color Labs
             -  Sept. 21: Mailing lists should be completed
             -  Sept. 24: Color seps returned for approval
             -  Sept. 25: Color seps to K&M Printing
             -  Sept. 28: Delivery to Mary's Mail Service
       +  Project: Focus Groups
       +  Project: Dummy for magazine ads
```

Figure 6.9: Sue creates a schedule from her template and outline.

```
            -  Responsible person: Ruth
            +  Goals
               -  Sept. 5: Contents to be determined
               -  Sept. 12: Copy to Leong's
               -  Sept. 26: Galleys for approval
    +  OCTOBER
       +  Project: Builders' Brochure
          -  Responsible person: Ruth
          +  Goals
             -  Oct. 15: BEGIN EXPECTING REPLIES
       +  Project: Research responses to brochure & conference mailing
          -  Responsible person: Howard
          +  Goals
             -  Oct. 28: Begin research
       +  Project: Builders' Conference
       +  Project: Focus Groups
       +  Project: Magazine ads
    +  NOVEMBER
    +  DECEMBER
    +  JANUARY
    +  FEBRUARY
```

Figure 6.9: Sue creates a schedule from her template and outline (continued).

Figure 6.10 shows her calendar for August. As you can see, all the items from her colleagues' individual schedules have been arranged into a single continuous list, put in order by date.

In this chapter, we have followed a group of coworkers as they developed a project. We have watched them use ThinkTank as an


```
    +  AUGUST
       -  Aug 1: Memo to Legal Dept. re hotline, standard briefs
       -  Aug. 3: Contact phone co. re additional 800 line
       -  Aug. 6: Sign Contract w. Western Photo (Brochure)
       -  Aug. 7: Deadline for agreeing on goals for focus groups
       -  Aug. 12: All contents of brochure to be determined
       -  Aug. 17: Copy completed for builders' brochure
       -  Aug. 20: Begin researching SF hotels (Conference)
       -  Aug. 20: Photos to be completed for builders' brochure
       -  Aug. 20: Legal & Engineering hotline people to be selected
       -  Aug. 21: Sample to be selected, site to be chosen
       -  Aug. 22: All materials for builders' brochure to Leong Design
Assoc.
       -  Aug. 31: Deadline for finding someone to build conference models
```

Figure 6.10: Sue creates a calendar from the master plan.

organizational tool for planning, as a filing system for modular information, as a brainstorming tool, and as a scheduling tool. These are but a handful of the myriad uses to which the creative person can put ThinkTank.

In this chapter, you see how ThinkTank can aid you in ordering information in different forms, and in providing an organizing framework within which ideas and plans can be developed creatively. In studying these examples, perhaps you have found new ways to create, organize, and communicate information that you use in your own work.

7

USING THE PARAGRAPH EDITOR

In this chapter you will learn all you need to know about ThinkTank's Paragraph Editor. By the time you are finished, you should be able to use it with ease and grace to complete a draft of a written document. You will find the Paragraph Editor a highly flexible, easy-to-use word processor with a few significant limitations, most of which concern formatting for printing, (see Chapter 8). Here I will show you how to get around the Paragraph Editor's other limitations.

We will watch Sue Lathom and Ruth Brown, whom we met in Chapter 6, use the Paragraph Editor to create a presentable prose version of the marketing plan and to develop copy for the brochures. By the end of this chapter, you should be comfortable with all of the Paragraph Editor's commands and options.

THE NATURE OF THINKTANK PARAGRAPHS

As we have noted before, in ThinkTank every paragraph must be nested under a headline. You can create a paragraph under a headline with no words in it (a blank headline such as we have encountered in Chapter 5); you can change the headline over a paragraph; you can combine the contents of several paragraphs under one headline (as Howard Franklin did when creating his resume in Chapter 5); you can even delete the paragraph from beneath a headline. But you cannot create a paragraph that has no headline.

This is one of the greatest strengths and the greatest weaknesses of the Paragraph Editor. It is a strength because it allows you to move a large block of text any place within an outline easily (or, through the PORT command, into another outline). Moving a block of text from two pages after the beginning to two pages before the end is a quick and simple business because you can collapse the parts of the outline that you aren't currently using, and can perform a DELETE-UNDO. There's no need to scroll through pages of text.

On the other hand, it is a weakness because ThinkTank regards a paragraph nested under a single headline as a single unit, it's rather complicated to move a small block of text *within* a paragraph. In this chapter you'll learn how to do it.

This brings up another important characteristic of ThinkTank paragraphs: each paragraph is regarded by ThinkTank as a single unit. No matter how many grammatical paragraphs may exist in a block of text below a single headline, to ThinkTank, the entire block is a single paragraph and is treated as such.

ThinkTank is ideal for developing a large written document, such as a research report, a novel, a presentation text, or a computer book, expecially if you organize your work logically. (Using ThinkTank will almost force you to develop logical habits of thought.)

You may find the limitations regarding ThinkTank paragraphs cumbersome if you do not develop detailed outlines prior to writing the text. Either that, or you will become skilled enough at using the tricks presented here that you no longer notice the limitations.

ThinkTank paragraphs can be quite long—up to 20,000 characters and 900 lines, or about 3,400 words. That's about 30 pages of normal double-spaced typescript. This gives you ample room to develop an idea. (In the course of writing this book, I've reached this limitation only once.) But you will find your text easier to work with if you keep your paragraphs relatively short, and use many subheads.

AN OUTLINE FOR WRITING

As you develop a document, you may find that some ideas come to you more readily than others. If you already have a partially developed outline of your end product, you can insert paragraphs as they come to you. You might want to keep your paragraphs hidden while you work, expanding with the F8 key and command prefixes. This will allow you to maintain a clear overview of your project.

Clearly, the more comfortable you are working from outlines, the easier it will be for you to use the Paragraph Editor for serious writing, as opposed to note-taking. But if you find that the details of an outline don't fall into place until much of the work is done, ThinkTank can still enhance your ability to complete a writing project.

First, you can take advantage of the fact that a ThinkTank outline does not have to be a single, unified whole. As so many of our examples have demonstrated, you can begin by simply taking random notes. If you are afraid you won't leave yourself enough flexibility for organizing the notes, you can create some indented, blank headlines at the top of you notes outline, as we saw Howard Franklin do in Figure 6.4.

Second, you can organize your notes into the outline of a document using ThinkTank. As various ideas find their place, they can be moved out of the random notes section into the appropriate portion of your document outline.

Third, at the same time, you can use ThinkTank to keep track of your progress, as we saw Sue Lathom do in the previous chapter. If parts of your project require additional information before they can be completed, and you have an idea when that information will arrive, you can include those facts in your outline and schedule your work accordingly. Or, you can include a memo section, with notes to yourself regarding steps you must finish prior to completing a given phase of the project. This way, you won't lose track of the things you need to do. Figure 7.1 shows a sample outline with all of these elements.

USING THE PARAGRAPH EDITOR

To enter the Paragraph Editor, place the bar cursor on the headline under which you want to insert text and press E P or F5. Once you have entered this mode, you cannot move to another paragraph without first exiting to the top level and relocating the bar cursor. Two lines of dashes will appear beneath the headline to remind you that you are in the Paragraph Editor. No matter how long your paragraph gets, these two lines will remain on the screen. The Paragraph Editor cursor will appear at the left edge of the screen, directly below the upper line of dashes.

The Paragraph Editor cursor, like the Headline Editor cursor, is a small, flashing rectangle. You can move it anywhere in a paragraph by using the the four arrow keys on the numeric keypad

```
+  A Sample Outline for Writing
   +  Manuscript Outline
   +  Notes
   +  Project schedule
      -  Product info expected January 23
      -  Price info expected February 1
      -  Sales info expected February 4
      +  DEADLINES:
         -  Price report due Feb. 15
         -  Complete report due Feb 24
   +  Remember to:
      -  Get demographic data from U.S. Census
      +  Check last summer's sales figures for accuracy
         -  Call sales department for update
```

Figure 7.1: A sample outline for a writing project.

and then start typing. If you want your text to be indented, you must use the space bar or the cursor-right key, as there is no tab function.

Once you have entered text, there are two keys you can use to make changes. The Del key deletes the letter under the flashing cursor and then to the right, while the Backspace key deletes to the left, exactly as in the Headline Editor. There is no need to press the ← key unless you want the succeeding text to begin on a new line. Text will wrap to the next line, as in most word processors, so that if the last word on the end of a line is too long to fit on the screen, it will not be broken. Instead, it will be moved to the following line. (When you are printing a document, paragraph lines will wrap in the same manner, even if the paragraph is under a headline that is deeply indented in an outline.)

The ← key is like the carriage return on a typewriter: it moves the cursor to the beginning of the next line. Whenever you press the ← key in the Paragraph Editor, a small isosceles triangle, pointed to the left, will appear on the screen where the cursor was located. Use the ← key to start a new grammatical paragraph. If you want to insert a line space, press the ← key twice. You can also control the appearance of the printed output somewhat by inserting carriage returns, a technique we will look at later in this chapter.

Let's look over Sue Lathom's shoulder as she begins to fill out her marketing plan with text. The last time we saw the marketing plan, it was in the form of notes. Sue will begin by entering a paragraph under the headline **Global Strategy Statement,** which is shown in Figure 7.2. Notice that this "paragraph" is in the form of minimal sentences containing a series of thoughts without regard to proper sentence structure. None of these words are divided at the right-hand edge of the screen. However, unlike some word processors, ThinkTank's Paragraph Editor does not justify the right margin. Later, we'll watch Sue edit and revise this paragraph.

To leave the Paragraph Editor, press Esc. This will display the menu shown in Figure 7.3.

The EXIT Command Menu

Let's look at the options available in the EXIT Command Menu. As with other ThinkTank menus, you can enter its commands either by moving the menu cursor to the command and pressing ← or by pressing the letter key that activates the command. You can also use the menu as an aid to learning the commands,

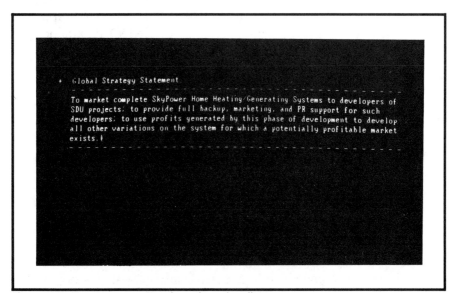

Figure 7.2: Creating a paragraph under a headline.

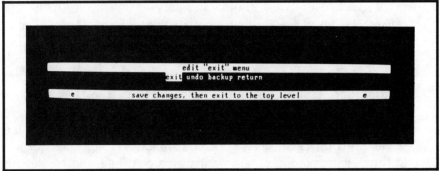

Figure 7.3: The Paragraph Editor EXIT Menu.

using the menu cursor to highlight the command you want, and then pressing the letter indicated on the lower bar of the menu.

The EXIT Menu has four options. You can exit to the top level, saving everything in your paragraph as it currently stands, by pressing E. You can back up, or save the paragraph in its present condition and then return to the Paragraph Editor by pressing B (in case of a power failure). You can undo any changes you have made to a paragraph by pressing U. This will restore the paragraph to its form when you entered the Paragraph Editor, or if you have used the BACKUP command, to the appearance it had when you last did a BACKUP. If you began a new paragraph when you entered the Paragraph Editor, the UNDO command will delete it. Finally, if you pressed Esc by mistake, or if you notice a change you want to make while the EXIT menu is on display, you can simply return to the Paragraph Editor by pressing either R or Esc again. If you choose any option other than EXIT, the Paragraph Editor cursor will be exactly where it was before you entered the command, and will again respond to the keyboard. Table 7.1 summarizes the EXIT commands.

Moving the Paragraph Editor Cursor

The Paragraph Editor cursor is like the Headline Editor cursor. Its movements in response to the arrow keys are identical to those of the Headline Editor cursor. But you should know about its other features as well.

First, it will move anywhere in a given ThinkTank paragraph, but will not move beyond the limits of a paragraph. If you want to edit

EXIT COMMANDS FROM
THE PARAGRAPH EDITOR

E   Exit to top level, saving paragraph in its current form.

B   Save current form of paragraph, then return to Paragraph Editor.

U   Undo changes made to paragraph, restoring it to condition at time of entering Paragraph Editor.

R   Cancel the EXIT command given by pressing Esc.

Esc   Cancel the EXIT command given by pressing Esc.

Table 7.1: Paragraph Editor EXIT Commands

text in a paragraph under a different headline, you must exit to the top level, move the bar cursor to the headline over the paragraph you wish to edit, and then reenter the Paragraph Editor.

Second, *all* of the cursor-movement keys work in the Paragraph Editor. Home takes you to the beginning of a line, End to the end of a line, PgUp takes you 21 lines up (or to the top line, if your paragraph is shorter than 21 lines), but leaves the cursor in the same left-to-right position as it started in. PgDn, similarly, will move the cursor 21 lines down or to the end of the paragraph if the paragraph is shorter than 21 lines, and will not move it left or right.

Third, the Ctrl key can be used in conjunction with the cursor-movement keys to speed up your movement through a paragraph. Ctrl-Home moves the cursor to the first character of a ThinkTank paragraph (even if that character is a space), Ctrl-End to the last (including a hard carriage return). Ctrl-cursor-left moves the cursor to the last letter of the previous word, and Ctrl-cursor-right to the first letter of the next word. The Ctrl key has no effect on the cursor-up and -down keys, however. Table 7.2 summarizes the Paragraph Editor cursor movements.

Inserting New Text in a Paragraph

It's easy to insert new text in a paragraph. Just move the cursor to where you want to start inserting, and type. Let's look over Sue Lathom's shoulder again. She wants to add additional text at the end of the existing paragraph, but she wants it to be separate from the present paragraph. Before she starts, the Strategy Statement looks like Figure 7.2. First she presses Ctrl-End, which places the cursor just after the period on the last line. She hits the ↩ key twice, to create a line space, and simply types in the second sentence, finishing with a carriage return. When she is done, she presses Esc-E to return to the top level. The result is shown in Figure 7.4.

PARAGRAPH EDITOR CURSOR COMMANDS

Moving Left

cursor-left	Moves cursor left one character.
Ctrl-cursor-left	Moves cursor to end of previous word.
Home	Moves cursor to beginning of current line.

Moving Right

cursor-right	Moves cursor right one character.
Ctrl-cursor-right	Moves cursor to beginning of next word.
End	Moves cursor to end of current line.

Moving Up

cursor-up	Moves cursor to character directly above present position.
Ctrl-Home	Moves cursor to first character of ThinkTank paragraph.
PgUp	Moves cursor up 21 lines, without moving left or right. If less than 21 lines of text, moves cursor to first line, without moving left or right.

Moving Down

cursor-down	Moves cursor to character directly below present position.

Table 7.2: Paragraph Editor Cursor Movement

Ctrl-end	Moves cursor to position just after last character of ThinkTank paragraph. (This is irregular; sometimes it will move cursor to last character, rather than to the position after last character.)
PgDn	Moves cursor down 21 lines, without moving left or right. If less than 21 lines of text, moves cursor to last line, without moving left or right.

Table 7.2: Paragraph Editor Cursor Movement (continued).

When a ThinkTank paragraph ends with a carriage return, one of two things may happen when you try to add new material at the end. Sometimes pressing Ctrl-End places the cursor at the beginning of the line below the final carriage return, and sometimes it places the cursor directly on the carriage return, and you can't move the cursor forward or down. In the former instance there is no problem, but if you get stuck, simply press the ← key to insert an extra carriage return. The cursor will stay on the

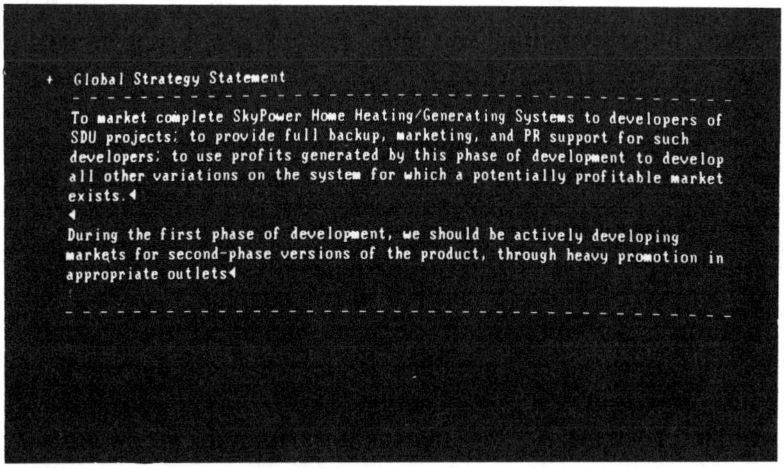

Figure 7.4: Adding text to an existing paragraph.

carriage-return marker, but you can insert text in front of the cursor as usual. If the marker bothers you, press the Del key after
you have inserted at least one character, and then you will be
able to add text to your heart's content or 900 lines, whichever
comes first.

Now Sue wants to rewrite the first paragraph as a series of sentences, rather than shorthand phrases. She enters the Paragraph
Editor (E P), and the cursor appears in the top left corner, on the
T in **To.** She begins by typing **Our primary goal is.** The first
line will now read:

> **Our primary goal is To market complete SkyPower Home
> Heating/Generating**

The remainder of the first line has been wrapped to the second
line. Sue now wants to change the capital T to lowercase, so she
moves the cursor right one more space, presses Del, and then
presses T. She wants to change part of the name of the product
from **Home** to **Structural,** since her market survey revealed
strong interest in the product for multiple-unit structures. So she
holds down Ctrl, presses the cursor-right key four times, and
presses Del four times. (She could have simply held the keys
down, rather than pressing them four times, and the cursor
would have continued moving. *Note:* This would be helpful over
long distances, but hard to control over short ones.) Now the first
line reads:

> **Our primary goal is to market complete SkyPower
> Heating/Generating**

and the cursor is in the second space before the H. Notice that
Systems did not move back to the first line. It will move only
when Sue moves the cursor to the end of that line, or to another
line, or enters a new character. Next she simply types the word
Structural. Everything following the inserted word moves to the
right. The first line now reads:

> **Our primary goal is to market complete SkyPower
> Structural**

The slash mark between Heating and Generating indicated to
ThinkTank that it is one word, which is too long to fit on the

remainder of the line. She can solve this by moving the cursor to the slash mark and pressing the space bar once. Then the first line would read:

Our primary goal is to market complete SkyPower Structural Heating/

The normal setting for the Paragraph Editor is Insert mode. Sue can therefore continue making modifications to her paragraph by moving the cursor to the point at which she wants to make a change, deleting the old information, and inserting new words. She could just as easily insert before deleting—it makes no difference in which order these steps are performed. When she is finished, her first paragraph looks like Figure 7.5.

The SELECT Menu

Now let's suppose that Sue wants to make further changes to this paragraph. She decides that the separate sentence at the end

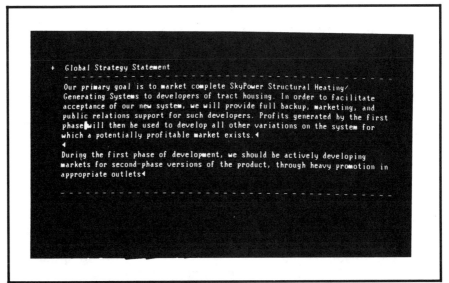

Figure 7.5: The same paragraph after editing.

should come before the preceding sentence, so that the paragraph reads:

> Our primary goal is to market complete SkyPower Structural Heating/ Generating systems to developers of tract housing. In order to facilitate acceptance of our new system, we will provide full backup, marketing, and public relations support for such developers. During the first phase of development, we should be actively developing markets for second-phase versions of the product, through heavy promotion in appropriate outlets. Profits generated by the first phase will then be used to develop all other variations on the system for which a potentially profitable market exists.

Unfortunately, the Paragraph Editor does not permit you to move something by deleting and undoing the deletion elsewhere. Sue could simply insert the new material a second time, and then delete it from the end.

But there is an easier way. ThinkTank's Paragraph Editor has a SELECT mode, which lets you deal with blocks of text all at once. You can enter SELECT mode by pressing Alt-S, but we're going to look at all of the options first. To display the SELECT mode options, you must first press F10 to display the EDIT Command Menu (which you can see at the bottom of various figures throughout this chapter), and then either press Alt-S or move the menu cursor to **select** and press ↩ . The only selections displayed at first are START and ESCAPE. START means to start selecting a block of text with which to work, and since this must be done first, you can't see the other options until you have done so.

What Sue will do is to SELECT the block of text beginning with **Profits generated by** and ending with **appropriate outlets,** copy the entire block, and then delete the redundant parts. We'll walk through the process with her.

First she moves the cursor to the end by pressing Ctrl-End. This leaves the cursor directly below the extra carriage return at the end. She could have moved down four lines with the cursor-down key and then right four words using Ctrl-cursor-right, and started from the beginning of the text she wants to work with, but since the selection she wants to work with goes all the way to the end of the ThinkTank paragraph, it's quicker to start from the end, because she can get there in one keystroke. She presses Alt-S to start her selection, and then presses the cursor-up key. Each time she presses the cursor-up key, a line of text is highlighted in reverse video. Since she started with the cursor at the extreme left, every time she moves to a new line, the entire line is highlighted. If she had started with the period after **appropriate outlets,** the highlighted section would end directly above the point at which the cursor appeared on the line below.

If you are following along on your computer, you might want to try selecting both ways. Press Esc to cancel the selection, and the highlighting disappears. You can then move the cursor to another point and start over. Remember, the selection always starts where the flashing cursor is located before you enter SELECT mode.

Since all the cursor keys work the same way in SELECT mode as they do in the Paragraph Editor's normal mode, you can stretch the selection to the beginning of the line by pressing Home if your starting point was at the middle of a line. If you are moving down rather than up, you'll find that the right-hand end of the line is not highlighted, but you can stretch the highlight to the end of the line with the End key.

Since Sue's cursor is already at the extreme left, she will just press the cursor-up key six times. The highlighted portion will then run from the words **public relations** to the end, as Figure 7.6 shows. Then Sue will press Ctrl-cursor-right six times to move the beginning of the selected area to the word **Profits.** The flashing cursor indicating the current cursor position is now on the space before the P in **Profits.**

Moving Text Within a Paragraph   *Note:* When you are selecting text from top to bottom, the cursor keys will behave in the opposite manner. That is, moving the cursor right along a partially highlighted line will stretch the highlight to the right, rather than shrink it, and moving the cursor left will shrink the highlight.

Now we are in a position to look at the SELECT Command Menu, which appears at the bottom of the screen in Figure 7.7. When in SELECT mode, press F10 to display the EDIT Command Menu, and then either press Alt-S again, or move the menu cur-

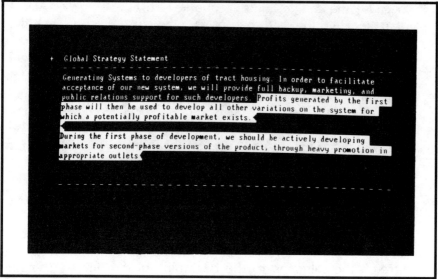

Figure 7.6: Using the SELECT command highlights a section to copy or delete.

sor to SELECT and press ⏎ . You will see the options DELETE, COPY, FINISH, and ESCAPE. Sue will choose to copy, which she enters by pressing Alt-C. When she presses this key, the entire highlighted portion will be copied, so that her paragraph now looks like Figure 7.7.

When she is finished, the part to be copied and the new copy of that part are both highlighted, and ThinkTank remains in SELECT mode. To leave SELECT mode, press Esc (the ESCAPE command), and the highlight will disappear and normal cursor movement will return. Pressing Alt-S (the FINISH command) will also return you to the normal paragraph-editing mode, but leave the highlight in place until you press a key.

The steps in moving text within a ThinkTank paragraph are summarized below. If your paragraph has gotten long enough to fill several screens, however, you may find this method unduly cumbersome. Indeed, if you are near the limit on paragraph length, and you want to move something from the end of your ThinkTank paragraph to the beginning (or vice versa), you may find it easier to copy the paragraph, and then delete the unwanted sections.

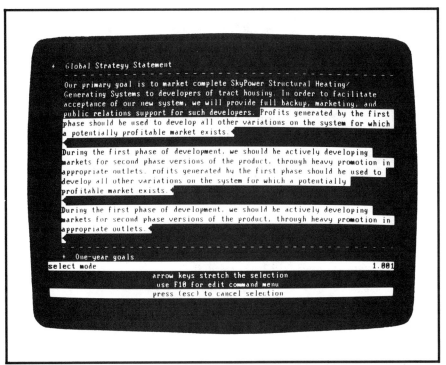

Figure 7.7: The SELECT Command Menu and the effect of the COPY command.

Here is the procedure for dividing paragraphs:

MOVING TEXT WITHIN A PARAGRAPH

KEYSTROKES	COMMANDS, ACTIONS, EFFECTS
cursor keys	1. Place your cursor at the point where you want the new material to appear.
Alt-S Ctrl-End Alt-C	2. Copy everything from the point of insertion to the end of the ThinkTank paragraph. (If you want to move something that's not at the end, use the cursor keys to mark the part to be copied, from the point where you want it to appear to the end of the part you want moved.)

cursor keys Alt-S	3. Place your cursor at the point of insertion, and use the cursor keys to mark everything up to the beginning of the text to be inserted.
Del Y	4. Delete the marked block. Now the material to be inserted should appear where you want it, as well as further down, below the copied section.
cursor keys	5. Move the cursor to to the beginning of the **second** appearance of the passage you have just inserted in its proper place.
Alt-S cursor keys	6. Enter SELECT mode. Use the cursor keys to stretch the highlight to the end of this passage.
Del Y	7. Delete the passage.
Esc	8. Leave SELECT mode and return to the Paragraph Editor.

Deleting Large Blocks of Text Within a Paragraph   Next Sue will use the DELETE command, also from the SELECT Menu. As before, she will have to select the portion she wants to work with. She moves the cursor to the **P** in **Profits,** presses Alt-S to activate SELECT mode, presses End to highlight the line, and then presses the cursor-down key three times to mark the section to be deleted, ending at the second carriage return (on the line by itself). Next she presses the Del key. On the top line of the menu ThinkTank will ask, **really delete the selection?,** as a sort of safety valve. She presses Y, and the result looks like Figure 7.8.

Note again that the Paragraph Editor's DELETE command does not have an UNDO command, but if you delete something in error, you can restore the entire paragraph to its condition before editing by pressing Esc U.

Next, Sue repeats the procedure. She presses Ctrl-End to get to the end of the selection, presses Alt-S to return to SELECT mode (ThinkTank automatically returns to the Paragraph Editor after a deletion), presses the cursor-up key five times, and presses Del,

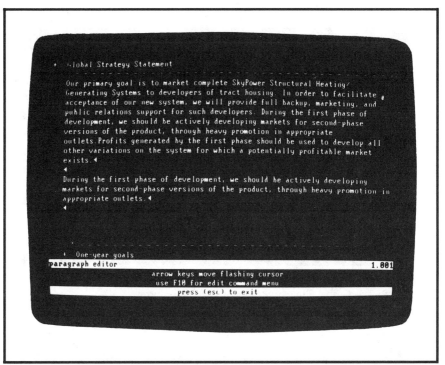

Figure 7.8: Continuing a block-move by deleting intervening material.

followed by Y. Then all she has to do is delete the two internal carriage returns using the delete keys Del or the Backspace key, change a few words, and finally achieves her goal—the paragraph shown in Figure 7.9.

The EDIT Command Menu

As you probably remember, we went through an EDIT Command Menu to get to SELECT mode. The EDIT Command Menu is shown in Figure 7.10. It includes three commands with which you are already familiar—DELETE and BACKSPACE, which are the character-by-character delete modes activated by the Del and Backspace keys, respectively—and the SELECT command. But there are three new commands on this menu which we will now examine.

The TYPEOVER Command The TYPEOVER command simply takes the Paragraph Editor out of INSERT mode, so that anything

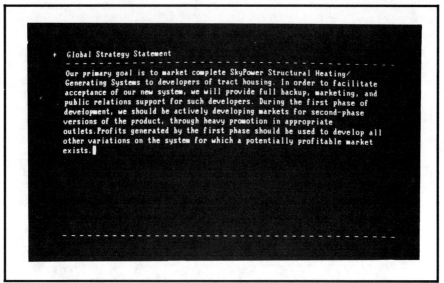

Figure 7.9: The Global Strategy Statement in its final form.

Figure 7.10: The EDIT Command Menu.

you type will replace what's already on the screen, instead of pushing it to the right. This is especially useful when you want to make certain types of changes. For example, if you want to replace a word with another of the same length, change capitals to lowercase or vice versa, or replace some text toward the end of a paragraph with something longer, you can use TYPEOVER and skip the extra step of deleting the text to be replaced.

Suppose, for example, that Sue wanted to change the product name, **SkyPower Structural Heating/Generating Systems** to all capital letters. She could turn on TYPEOVER mode by pressing Alt-T, move the cursor to **SkyPower,** press the Caps Lock key, and type the same words. The capital letters would replace the letters now in her paragraph, and when she was done, **SKYPO-WER STRUCTURAL HEATING/ GENERATING SYS-TEMS** would replace the original copy, with no deleting needed.

ThinkTank will not type over carriage returns in TYPEOVER mode. If you are typing in TYPEOVER mode and come to a carriage return, the carriage return will move to the right under the flashing cursor, just as it does in INSERT mode under the same circumstances.

As usual, you can exit TYPEOVER mode by pressing Esc.

The FIND Command   The FIND command is activated by pressing Alt-F. It functions essentially the same as KEYWORD SEARCH, except that its scope is limited to the single ThinkTank paragraph you are editing. It has one other notable difference from KEYWORD SEARCH. You don't have to be at any particular position in the paragraph to search for something.

When you enter the FIND command, you will be asked for a group of characters to search for. Type them in and press ↵ . You will then have the option of searching forward from the current cursor position, which you select by pressing the cursor-right key, or backward, which you select with the cursor-left key. The flashing cursor will move to the first letter of the selected pattern in the direction chosen, and give you the option of searching in either direction again, or ending the search by pressing the Esc key. If ThinkTank has searched as far as it can in the chosen direction and has not found the characters you are searching for, it will give you the message **pattern not found!** on the lower bar of the menu. You can then either press Esc, or continue the search in the opposite direction. Below is a summary of the steps in using the FIND command.

USING THE FIND COMMAND

KEYSTROKES	COMMANDS, ACTIONS, EFFECTS
Alt-F	1. Enter the FIND Command.
[pattern to search for]	

↵	2. Enter the pattern of characters you want to find.
cursor left or right	3. Search forward or backward.
Esc	4. End the search.

The XCHANGE Command   The XCHANGE command is also similar to the top-level KEYWORD XCHANGE command but will work only in a given ThinkTank paragraph. There are two forms of XCHANGE. You can either replace all instances of a given pattern automatically, exactly as in the top-level XCHANGE command, or you can replace selectively. The global XCHANGE command will search only forward, and will replace all instances of a given pattern of characters with the pattern of your choice. You will be returned to the Paragraph Editor with the cursor at the beginning of the last replacement. The steps in using this command are summarized below.

GLOBAL XCHANGE WITHIN A PARAGRAPH

KEYSTROKES	COMMANDS, ACTIONS, EFFECTS
Ctrl-Home	1. Move the cursor to the beginning of the ThinkTank paragraph.
Alt-A [pattern to search for]	2. Enter the XCHANGE ALL command.
↵	3. Enter the group of characters that you want to replace.
[pattern to replace with] ↵	4. Enter the pattern you want to substitute for the existing pattern.

   The selective XCHANGE, activated by Alt-X, is a combination of the FIND command and the XCHANGE ALL command. You can choose to replace a given instance of the pattern being searched for by pressing ↵ , or you can continue the search with the cursor-left and cursor-right keys, or end the search by pressing Esc. The steps in using the two XCHANGE commands are summarized below.

SELECTIVE REPLACEMENT OF CHARACTERS

KEYSTROKES	COMMANDS, ACTIONS, EFFECTS
Alt-X	1. Enter the selective XCHANGE command.
[pattern to search for] ↵	2. Enter the group of characters you want to replace.
[pattern to replace with] ↵	3. Enter the group of characters you want to substitute for the existing pattern.
cursor left or right	4. Search forward or backward from the current cursor position.
↵	5. (A) Replace an instance of the old pattern with the new pattern, *or*
cursor left or right	(B) continue the search, *or*
Esc	(C) end the search.

We have now examined all the commands available within the Paragraph Editor itself. Table 7.3 summarizes these commands. Next we will look at ways of manipulating text from the top level.

PARAGRAPH EDITOR COMMANDS

Del	Delete character under flashing cursor, and subsequent characters to the right.
←	Delete character to left of flashing cursor, and subsequent characters to the left.
Alt-T	Put Paragraph Editor in TYPEOVER mode. Press Esc to return to INSERT mode.
	SELECT Mode Commands
Alt-S	Enter SELECT mode, to select a passage to copy or delete.

Table 7.3: Paragraph Editor Commands

Alt-C	Copy passage highlighted through SELECT mode.
Del Y	Delete the passage highlighted through SELECT mode.
Alt-S	Leave SELECT mode with highlight in place.
Esc	Leave SELECT mode with highlight eliminated.

Search and Replace Commands

Alt-F	Find a given pattern in the paragraph.
cursor-right	Search toward the end.
cursor-left	Search toward the beginning.
Alt-A	Replace all instances of a given pattern after the current cursor position with a new pattern.
Alt-X	Search for a given pattern to be replaced in the paragraph.
cursor-right	Search toward the end.
cursor-left	Search toward the beginning.
	Replace the old pattern with the new pattern.
Esc	Return to Paragraph Editor from FIND or selective XCHANGE.

EXIT Commands

Esc E	Save current version of paragraph and return to top level.
Esc B	Save current version of paragraph and return to Paragraph Editor, with cursor at current position.
Esc R	Cancel EXIT command, return to Paragraph Editor, with cursor at current position.

Table 7.3: Paragraph Editor Commands (continued).

Esc Esc	Same as Esc R.
Esc U	Undo any changes made to paragraph and return to top level.

Table 7.3: Paragraph Editor Commands (continued).

TOP-LEVEL COMMANDS FOR HANDLING PARAGRAPHS

There are many top-level commands that act on paragraphs as well as outlines, or on paragraphs exclusively. Let's look now at the ways you can use them to make effective use of ThinkTank's word-processing capabilities.

Moving Paragraphs Within an Outline

As you have just learned, you can move grammatical paragraphs (or any other size unit) *within* a ThinkTank paragraph by using the COPY and DELETE commands from the SELECT menu. Granted, it's clumsy, but it does work, and with practice, it becomes quite easy.

When you want to move an entire ThinkTank paragraph from one part of an outline to another, however, the process is much simpler. Since every ThinkTank paragraph belongs to a single headline, you can move a paragraph the same way you move a headline. This is done from the top level, rather than from within the Paragraph Editor. First, place the bar cursor on the headline of the paragraph you want to move. Then either use the MOVE command (F1), which is suitable for short moves, or the DELETE OUTLINE (Del O) and DELETE UNDO (Del U) commands for long moves.

As we saw with the Headline Editor, the MOVE command moves headlines (and the paragraphs attached to them) in accordance with your outline's presumed logical structure, not linearly up and down. Consequently, using MOVE for anything but minor adjustments can be rather frustrating. Here are a few hints to make moving paragraphs easier:

1. Always collapse your paragraphs before moving them with the MOVE command. Paragraphs take up so much space on the screen that you will have trouble orienting yourself in the outline.

2. When moving text over a long distance, by either method, collapse any parts of your outline not involved in the move before you start. Press Ctrl-Home − + to get your outline opened only to the first level of indentation, and then expand the portion that contains the paragraph to be moved and the portion that includes the place you want to move it to. If your outline contains a book with chapters, for example, and you want to move a paragraph from Chapter 6 to Chapter 1, you'll find the move simplified considerably if Chapters 2 through 5 are completely collapsed, with only their titles showing.

3. When moving toward the top of your outline, a DELETE and UNDO may be simpler than a MOVE. The bar cursor tends to place itself at the top of the screen while you are moving, and you sometimes can't tell whether you've gotten where you want to go until you have passed the point, as each headline that was above the one you are moving appears below it when you press the cursor-up key.

4. When you undo a delete, the headline that you bring back will always be at the same level of indentation as the one directly above it. You may have to use the MOVE command to reposition your paragraph with regard to indentation.

Experiment with these MOVE and DELETE-UNDO combinations, perhaps on an outline that you no longer need, until you feel comfortable with them.

Merging Paragraphs

You have already been introduced to the top-level MERGE command. Howard Franklin used it when setting up the **Achievements** portion of his resume. But it has additional uses that you might need. Here is a quick review of the necessary steps:

MERGING TWO PARAGRAPHS

KEYSTROKES	COMMANDS, ACTIONS, EFFECTS
F1 cursor keys Esc	1. Move the merge-from paragraph to a position below the merge-to paragraph, at the same degree of indentation. There should be no intervening headlines at the same degree of indentation.
cursor-up –	2. Collapse any intervening headlines.
F10 F10 M	3. Enter the MERGE command.
C	4. (A) Copy the merge-from paragraph to the end of the merge-to paragraph and retain the original, *or*
D	(B) copy the merge-from paragraph to the end of the merge-to paragraph and delete the original.

Now for some of the whys and wherefores. When you merge, the new material will appear at the end of the material in the old paragraph. So if you want to merge several paragraphs into one long one, it pays to line them all up in order before you start, so you don't have to do a bunch of copying and deleting after the merge is completed. You can merge text to a headline that has no paragraph under it. Then the text you merge will be the first text under that headline.

Merging with the COPY command can be useful if you are putting something together out of parts. If, for example, you have a series of standard paragraphs that you use in a number of contexts, you will want to copy rather than delete them. This way, you can use the paragraphs over again (as Howard did with the achievement items for his resume in Chapter 5). When you have completed the document that you are creating out of standard paragraphs, you can can port it to a text file and delete it from your outline. The materials from which it was created will remain in your outline for future use. If the original paragraphs were logically placed in an outline before you started, however, you would be better off following this procedure:

CREATING A LONG PARAGRAPH BY MERGING WHILE RETAINING THE SOURCE PARAGRAPHS IN THEIR ORIGINAL POSITIONS

KEYSTROKES	COMMANDS, ACTIONS, EFFECTS
cursor keys	1. Place the bar cursor on the headline of the paragraph whose contents you want to merge.
F10 F10 C	2. Copy the paragraph.
Del O	3. Delete the copy.
cursor keys Del U	4. Move the bar cursor to the merge-to headline, and undo the delete.
cursor-up	5. The bar cursor will jump to the headline that has reappeared. Move it back to the merge-to headline.
F10 F10 M D	6. Merge and delete.
cursor-down	7. Move the bar cursor back to the merge-from headline and delete it.

If you follow these steps, your paragraph will appear both in its new position and in its original place in the outline. This is much easier than moving a paragraph, merging with copy, and then moving the original back to its original location.

On the other hand, your shorter paragraphs may be elements of a work in progress, held in reserve under their own headlines until you come to the point where they fit. In that case, you may want to delete them during the merge.

After you have performed a merge, you will probably want to do something with the old headline. If you keep an outline of the structure of your work, you may want to move the headline back where it came from (in which case, it would have been easier to copy the headline and its paragraph before merging). Otherwise, just delete it. This will help you keep your outline in order.

Moving Parts of Paragraphs

Sometimes you find that you want to move *part* of a paragraph from one headline to another. You can't do this directly, but you can do it using a combination of the steps you just learned. The procedure below shows you how.

MOVING PART OF A PARAGRAPH
TO ANOTHER HEADLINE

KEYSTROKES	COMMANDS, ACTIONS, EFFECTS
F1 cursor keys Esc	1. Move the headline of the paragraph containing the text you want to move to a position below that of the paragraph you want to move it into, at the same degree of indentation.
cursor-up	2. Place the bar cursor on the merge-to headline.
F10 F10 M C	3. Perform a merge with COPY.
cursor-up	4. Move the bar cursor to the headline of the merge-from paragraph.
E P or F5	5. Enter the Paragraph Editor.
Alt-S cursor keys	6. Enter SELECT mode and mark the part of the text that you no longer want in the move-from paragraph.
Del Y	7. Delete the marked section.

Next, you will want to edit the paragraph that has had the new material added to it. The steps you will follow are the same as those Sue used when editing her Global Strategy Statement. The first thing you will want to do is delete the part of the new material that you left in the old paragraph. The procedure is as described above. If you need to rearrange the material—if the new text belongs somewhere in the middle of your paragraph, for example—the procedure is quite similar to that described earlier for moving text within a paragraph.

MOVING THE NEW MATERIAL TO
ITS PROPER PLACE IN THE PARAGRAPH

KEYSTROKES	COMMANDS, ACTIONS, EFFECTS
cursor keys	1. Move the bar cursor to the headline over the paragraph with the new material added.
E P or F5	2. Enter the Paragraph Editor.
cursor keys	3. Start with your cursor at the point where you want the new material to appear.
Alt-S Ctrl-End Alt-C	4. Select and copy both the new material and the text that should appear after it.
cursor keys	5. Place your cursor at the point of insertion,
Alt-S cursor keys	6. Use the cursor keys to select everything up to the beginning of the new material.
Del Y	7. Delete any material between the point where you want the merged material to appear and the beginning of the merged section. The new text should now be in its proper place.
cursor keys	8. Move the cursor to the beginning of the new text at the end of the paragraph.
Alt-S Ctrl-End Del Y	9. Delete the merged material from its orginal position at the end of the paragraph. Everything should now be as you want it.

If you want to intersperse parts of the new text throughout the original paragraph, you can follow the same procedures, but you will mark your blocks using the various cursor-moving keys, instead of Ctrl-End.

Deleting Paragraphs

There are three ways to delete a paragraph from an outline. First, you can use the top-level DELETE OUTLINE command (Del O), which will delete the paragraph's headline along with the paragraph. Second, the DELETE menu also includes a DELETE PARA-GRAPH option (Del P). This deletes the paragraph under the bar cursor headline *without* deleting the headline, which is useful if you want to keep the headline. However, if you delete the paragraph without deleting its headline, you can't undo the deletion— the paragraph is gone forever. If there's a chance of making a mistake, it's safer to delete the outline and then insert a new headline with the same text as the old. Then you can still undo the deletion any time up to the next time you use the delete function. You can always delete the extra headline later.

If you want to be extra careful, first copy the headline and its paragraph, then delete the paragraph from under one headline and delete the other outline. If you choose this or any other procedure for copying a paragraph or deleting an outline to get rid of a paragraph, be sure that no additional headlines are nested under the one you are working with. Otherwise you will be copying and deleting them along with the one you want to work with.

The third way to delete a paragraph is to enter the Paragraph Editor by pressing F6 instead of F5 or E P. This is useful if you know you want to enter a totally different paragraph under a headline. When you press F6 and a paragraph is present, ThinkTank will ask you whether you want to remove it. If you press Y, it will be gone forever. If you want to, you can use the F6 key as a delete key by pressing F6 Y Esc E. You are then, in effect, entering a new paragraph with nothing in it, and leaving the Paragraph Editor. The result is identical to Del P.

Dividing Paragraphs

Sometimes you may create a single, long paragraph, and decide that parts of it belong under two or more different headlines. For example, you may want to insert a numbered figure between the first part of a ThinkTank paragraph and the last part. Or you may be merrily typing away at a paragraph when the error message **too many lines!** or **not enough room for the last keystroke!,** with its attendant alarm, appears on one of the menu bars. In either of these circumstances, it is time to divide your paragraph and parcel it out among two or more headlines. It is easy to accomplish this.

DIVIDING A PARAGRAPH AMONG TWO OR MORE HEADLINES

KEYSTROKES	COMMANDS, ACTIONS, EFFECTS
F10 F10 C	1. Copy the paragraph you want to divide.
E P or F5	2. The bar cursor will move to the copy. Enter the Paragraph Editor.
Alt-S cursor keys	3. Enter SELECT mode and stretch the highlight to the end of the part you want in the first paragraph with the cursor keys.
Del Y	4. Delete the highlighted part.
Esc E	5. Exit the Paragraph Editor.
F4	6. Before you go any further, you may want to edit the headline of the second paragraph, where your bar cursor now rests. This is one of those times when F4, which erases the headline, is useful.
	7. When you finish, press ↵ to enter the change into the outline.
cursor-up	8. Move the bar cursor to the first copy of the copied paragraph.
E P or F5	9. Enter the Headline Editor.
Ctrl-End	10. Move the cursor to the end of the paragraph.
Alt-S cursor keys	11. Enter SELECT mode and stretch the highlight to the beginning of what is now the second paragraph.

Del Y   12. Delete the second paragraph.

Esc E   13. Exit the Paragraph Editor.

If you are inserting a figure between the two parts of the paragraph, and your figures are numbered, you can use a short-cut to renumber your figures. You can renumber the figure captions (which presumably are headlines) all at once using the Headline Editor. Place the bar cursor on the paragraph before any given figure, and do a KEYWORD XCHANGE (K X), replacing the old figure number with the new figure number. Repeat this procedure for each paragraph preceding a figure. This is faster than entering the Paragraph Editor to find and change each figure number.

TEMPLATING IN THE PARAGRAPH EDITOR

In Chapters 4 and 5 you learned various ways to use the Headline Editor to set up templates. There are times when templating is useful in the Paragraph Editor as well. Let's look at a couple of examples.

Setting a Limit on Text Size

At the end of the previous chapter, Sue had given Ruth Brown, her advertising manager, the task of developing a four-color, $8\frac{1}{2}$ × 11-inch brochure to send to developers, describing the SkyPower system and its advantages. Each page was to be illustrated, with text to accompany the illustrations.

For the sake of clarity, Ruth wanted to set up the text in small blocks, so that the text on each page would be relevant to the picture. Ideally, the text accompanying a given illustration should not run onto the next page. So Ruth needed a means of marking off a block that would fit in the available text space on each page. To make sure her text would be of the right length, she created the template shown in Figure 7.11.

This template consists of nothing more than a line of dashes, a series of carriage returns, and another line of dashes. When Ruth

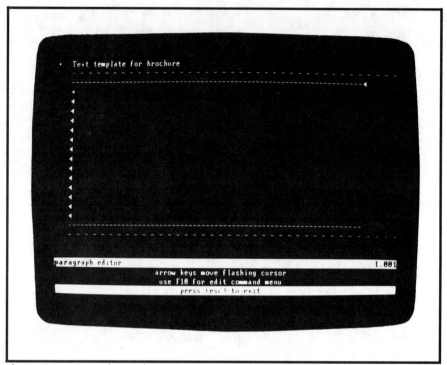

Figure 7.11: A template to limit text size.

wants to insert text, she will copy the template, enter the Paragraph Editor, move her cursor to the first carriage return below the line of dashes, and start entering text. The carriage return will move forward under the flashing cursor. When it is almost up to the carriage return at the end of the line of dashes, Ruth knows that she should move her cursor to the carriage return at the beginning of the next line (by pressing cursor-down home) before entering any further text. Figure 7.12 shows how she uses the template to set up a paragraph for the brochure.

If you prefer to work in TYPEOVER mode (Alt-T), you can set up your text space block with the carriage returns at the *ends* of the lines, rather than at the beginning. It takes longer to set up this way, but it's easier to see what you are doing. Figure 7.13 shows a text space template set up in this manner.

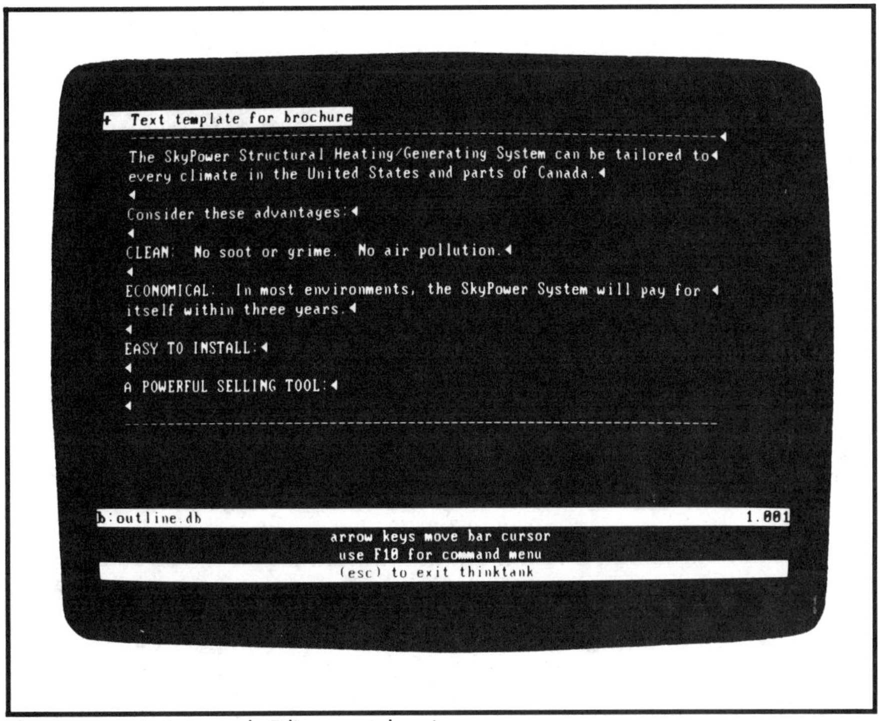

Figure 7.12: A Paragraph Editor template in use.

Setting up a Table

Ruth will also want to include tables in her brochure, to give comparisons of running and installation costs of the Sky Power System with other types of energy. She has created a table template for the purpose, shown in Figure 7.14.

Ruth created this empty table with spaces, underline characters, and vertical bars (shifted backslashes made with the key next to the letter Z on the keyboard). When she had set up the first two lines, she simply used the COPY command (Alt-S Ctrl-End Alt-C) to make a second copy for an additional line. If this table is not long enough for her data, she can add additional lines when she needs them using the same process. Of course, she will have to enter the information into the table in TYPEOVER mode (Alt-T), or the vertical divisions will move one space to the right with each letter entered.

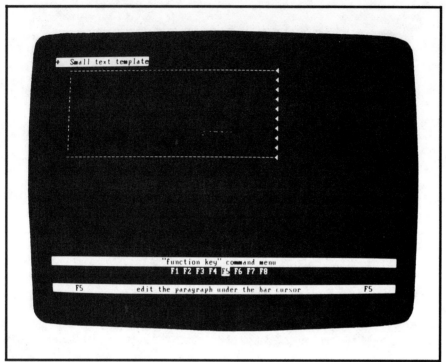

Figure 7.13: Another method of setting up a template.

A FINAL WORD

In this chapter we have reviewed all the features of ThinkTank's Paragraph Editor. You have learned how to move around in ThinkTank paragraphs and the peculiar limitations of these paragraphs. If you followed through with all the examples, you should have learned to use all of the commands for creating and editing text. We have also explored ways to use top-level commands for manipulating text, and have glanced at ways to gain control of your output through templating in the Paragraph Editor. In the next chapter we will explore the various ways to format a document for printing, and their effects.

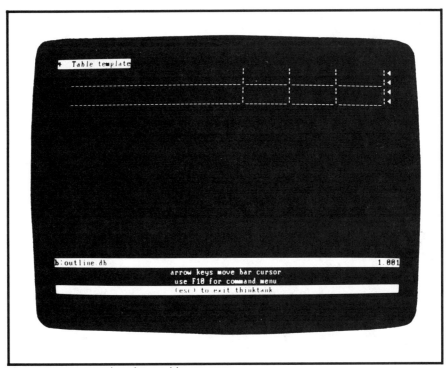

Figure 7.14: A template for a table.

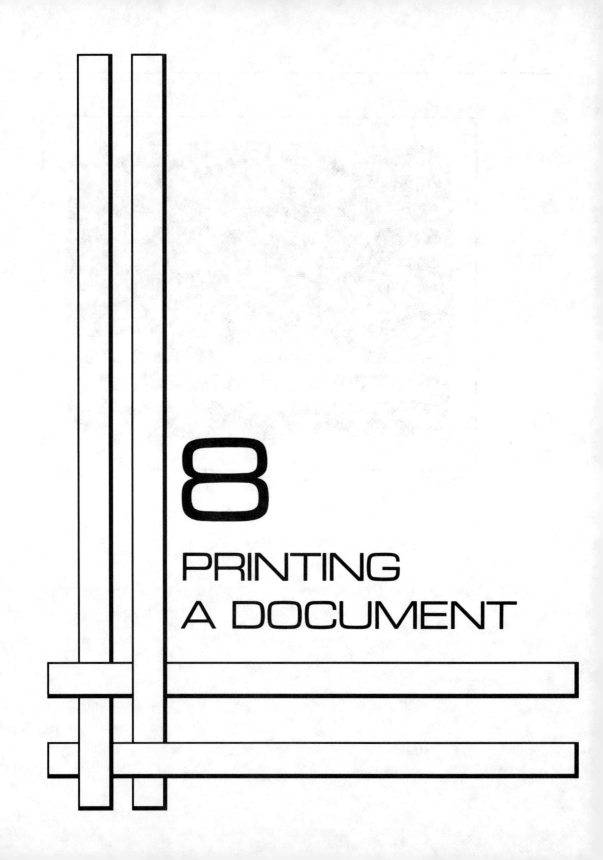

8

PRINTING
A DOCUMENT

Now that you have full control over the Paragraph Editor and are able to create long and complex outlines, you are ready to see the results on paper. With ThinkTank, you can have myriad varieties of printed output. About the only style you can't get from within ThinkTank is right-justified paragraphs.

Granted, if you want to print a great variety of type styles—underlining, doublestrike, boldface, superscripts, etc.—it *might* be easier to go through a word-processing program like WordStar as an intermediary between ThinkTank and your printer. But don't bet on it. We'll look at all the possibilities available, and you may be pleasantly surprised.

FORMATTING OUTPUT BEFORE PRINTING

Before we look at the ThinkTank formatting options, let's examine some formatting possibilities within the Headline and Paragraph Editors. You have already been introduced to one valuable technique for formatting printed output—templating. In Chapter 5, you saw Howard Franklin produce a resume using a template. His resume was created from a template set up in the Headline Editor, and contained only one paragraph generated by the Paragraph Editor. It took some experimentation to organize everything so that it appeared on paper just the way he wanted it, but once he had the template laid out properly, he could create any number of variations on his resume with no further experimenting.

Formatting Techniques
in the Headline Editor

Among the most important formatting techniques available in the Headline Editor is the use of blank headlines. Remember, if you enter nothing in a headline, the headline will disappear when you return to the top level. But if you enter a single space, you will create a headline that displays as a + or − on the screen and prints as a line space on paper. You can insert several of these blank headlines to create a wide space, just as though you had pressed the carriage return several times in succession in a word-processing program. If you want to indent some text to a greater degree than it would normally be in your outline, you can create several blank headlines, each indented one degree more than the previous one, and each ensuing line will be indented three additional spaces, as Figure 8.1 shows.

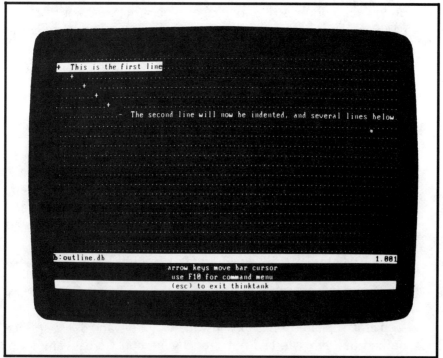

Figure 8.1: Indenting with blank headlines.

Formatting Techniques in the Paragraph Editor

In the Paragraph Editor, as in the Headline Editor, templating will give you a great deal of control over the appearance of your printed output. In Chapter 7, you saw Ruth Brown create a box just big enough to hold the amount of text that she wanted on a single page. You can create boxes to limit your output to any given size.

Although ThinkTank has no automatic centering function, you can create a *rule* and use it as a basis for centering. A rule for centering might look like this:

```
----------------------------------------- | -------------------------------------------
```

Since there is also no tabulating function, you can set up a rule consisting of these two headlines:

```
      1     2     3     4     5     6     7
 ----|----|----|----|----|----|----|----|----|----|----|----|----|----|
```

If you set up the tab rule as a pair of headlines, you can copy them, and move them to the place where you want to insert text, and insert text under the ruler line. That way, the rule will always be at the top of the screen as you enter text. When you finish the paragraph, you can delete the headline with the numbers and change the ruler line to a meaningful headline with F4.

You should also be aware of the effect of carriage returns. If you insert a carriage return in the Paragraph Editor, you create a line space, but you must be careful about adding a carriage return at the end of a ThinkTank paragraph. If you end a paragraph with a carriage return, and you print it as part of an outline, there will be an extra line space at the end of the paragraph. If you end *without* a carriage return, the following headline will automatically be printed one space below the end of the paragraph.

Printer Codes

Any high-quality printer, whether dot-matrix or letter-quality, will allow you to print in a variety of styles—underlined, boldface, doublestrike, italic, double-width, condensed, etc. If you have taken the time to learn the codes that activate various type styles on your printer, you can use any of them in ThinkTank headlines or paragraphs to control the appearance of your output.

Printer codes are called *escape sequences,* because they are sequences of characters preceded by the character generated by the escape key. When the printer receives the escape character, it interprets the following character (or characters) as a signal to do something, rather than as a character to be printed. But the escape key is a *dedicated* key in ThinkTank—it has a specific function in virtually every mode, and doesn't print anything. For this problem, fortunately, there is an easy solution.

The character normally printed by the escape key is ^[(Ctrl-left-bracket). You can generate this character by pressing Ctrl-[. It will print on the screen as a ←, but the printer will recognize it as the escape code, and interpret succeeding characters accordingly.

Here are some examples of escape sequences for specific printers. If you want emphasized print on an Epson printer, you can press Ctrl-[⇧-E, which the printer will understand as Esc-E. If you want correspondence-quality type on an Okidata 92 with a Plug 'n' Play kit, you can type Ctrl-[⇧-X 1 and the printer will go into correspondence mode. You can use these techniques equally well in the Headline Editor and the Paragraph Editor.

The only difficulty with using escape sequences to control your printer (aside from learning all your printer's escape codes), is that they take up space on a line. If a line of your text includes an underlined word, then you must include two characters at the beginning of the word to turn on underlining, and two more at the end to turn it off. When ThinkTank determines the line length for printing, it will count the escape codes as part of the line to be printed. Therefore, on the printed copy, the line will be four characters shorter than it ought to be. I haven't found any way to get around this limitation yet.

Inserting WordStar Codes

Up to now, we've been looking at ways to format your printed output without interfacing ThinkTank to WordStar. But, if you have already decided that you will use WordStar for final formatting, here are some time-saving techniques. You can adapt these techniques to many other word-processing programs.

Like most word-processing programs, WordStar controls formatting through *control codes,* rather than escape sequences. Control codes are inserted by holding down the Ctrl key and pressing another key at the same time. The code for underlining in Word-Star, for example, is Ctrl-P Ctrl-S. If you want to transfer your ThinkTank files to a word processor, you can insert your word processor's control codes into your text while you are writing in ThinkTank. This will save you the trouble of later searching through your text to the places you want to insert codes.

WordStar's other commands will have no effect in ThinkTank, but all the Ctrl-P codes can be inserted in the usual manner, while you are entering text. However, because Ctrl-P in WordStar is merely a signal to the program that you want to insert a print-formatting code, you don't have to type Ctrl-P at all. You can simply type Ctrl-S for underlining, Ctrl-B for boldfacing, and so on. When you enter Ctrl-P Ctrl-S in WordStar, you see ^S on the screen. In ThinkTank, these codes are represented by graphics characters from the computer's alternate character set, and they are a little strange. Figure 8.2 shows a ThinkTank paragraph with some WordStar control codes inserted, along with explanations for them. These characters will not show up at all if you send text to the printer directly from ThinkTank. However, when you port to WordStar, the characters will appear on the screen as they usually do in WordStar, and will have the usual effects when printing.

One word of caution: if you use WordStar's print-formatting toggles at the ends of headlines, be sure to add a space after the last control character. Otherwise the final control character will be stripped off when you port the outline to a word-processor file.

SENDING TEXT TO THE PRINTER

When you want to transfer anything from a ThinkTank outline to a different outline, another type of file, or a printer, you have to go through the PORT menu. You have already learned how to use the PORT command to back up your outlines with structured text files. In this chapter we'll use the PORT menu for sending text to the printer and for interfacing with WordStar. In Chapter 9 you'll learn a few other interesting uses for PORT command.

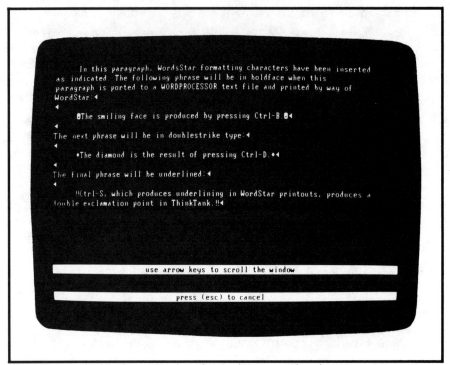

In this paragraph, WordsStar formatting characters have been inserted as indicated. The following phrase will be in boldface when this paragraph is ported to a WORDPROCESSOR text file and printed by way of WordStar:◄
    ◄
        ⊘The smiling face is produced by pressing Ctrl-B.⊘◄
    ◄
The next phrase will be in doublestrike type:◄
    ◄
        ◆The diamond is the result of pressing Ctrl-D.◆◄
    ◄
The final phrase will be underlined:◄
    ◄
        !!Ctrl-S, which produces underlining in WordStar printouts, produces a double exclamation point in ThinkTank.!!◄

use arrow keys to scroll the window

press (esc) to cancel

Figure 8.2: A ThinkTank paragraph with WordStar control codes.

What Gets Printed

Let's examine what gets printed when you send text to the printer. In ThinkTank, a command has its effect *only on that part of the outline nested under the bar cursor headline.* You *must* position the bar cursor on the headline superordinate to the material you want to print. ThinkTank will then send to the printer everything from that headline up to, but not including, the next headline at the same level.

If you want to print several parts of an outline at once that are not all subordinate to a given headline, you may have to do some rearranging before you send the text to the printer. Suppose, for example, you want to print the contents of the first three of seven first-level headlines, but not the remainder. You can begin by moving your bar cursor to the summit and inserting a dummy headline. Then perform a simulated DEMOTE on the three sections you want to print. When you finish printing, the bar cursor will still be on your dummy headline, and you can simply do a PROMOTE (F10 F10 P) and delete the dummy.

There is an alternative, but it has a drawback. When ThinkTank is porting, the material being ported scrolls across the screen, in the form in which it will reach its destination. You could place the bar cursor at the summit, and then watch the screen until the end of the part you want printed appears, and press the Esc key. That will end the printing operation, but your timing may be a bit off, and you could print a few extra lines, if they are already in the printer buffer.

Except for placement of the bar cursor, what you see on the screen has no effect on what is printed. The same text will be sent to the printer whether the outline is collapsed or expanded. The format options and not the screen display determine the degree of detail printed. The plus and minus signs will not be printed.

If you want to print an outline in a form that shows some parts more expanded than others, you can do a *screen dump,* a direct printout of the screen display. With your printer on line, hold down the ⇧ key and press PrtSc. Everything on the screen, including the menu, and the dotted lines at the top and bottom of a paragraph, if they are present, will be sent to the printer. However, most printers will not print visual representations of the hard carriage returns, the cursor, or any of the reverse video highlights.

As you know, ThinkTank will allow you to write headlines as long as 76 characters. If a long headline is nested several levels deep, the right end of the headline extends beyond the right margin of the screen when the bar cursor is on a superordinate headline. Headlines do not wrap on the screen and they don't wrap on the printed page, either. If your line is too long to fit the page, the rightmost portion of it will simply be lopped off.

There are several ways to get around this limitation. You can either choose the printing option that lets you print everything flush with the left margin (in which case you will lose the visual representation of your outline structure), or keep your headlines relatively short. If you want a long headline and it won't fit, you can simply press ↵ when you have reached the maximum length that will fit, and continue the headline as a new headline, indented below its beginning. It may take several trial print runs with your chosen format before you know what will work.

There is a third alternative, which works if you are printing only headlines, and not paragraphs. You can set the right margin at 131, even if you have an 80-column printer. With this method, your headlines will wrap, but they may break in the middle of a word. *Note:* This works on an Epson and IBM printer. You might have to experiment with other kinds to see what happens. See the section below on setting the right margin for further details.

Getting the TANKOPTS.DAT File to Work for You

If you send text to the printer often, the **TANKOPTS.DAT** file on the program disk can be extremely helpful. Once you have set up your formatting options, you can save them in the **TANKOPTS.DAT** file automatically, as I'll explain later.

As you know, if you have a two-drive system, you can work with data disks in both drives once you set the date. But if you want to print, ThinkTank will look for the **TANKOPTS.DAT** file in drive A, and if it isn't there, you will get the error message **can't read from "options"file!** and you will be stuck with the default format settings, which you will have to reset each time you print.

The easy solution for this problem is to use DOS to copy the **TANKOPTS.DAT** file onto all your data disks. (See Appendix B if you don't know how.) If you have several different groups of format settings that you use regularly, you can group all the files for which you use those settings on a single disk, and save the format options for them in a copy of the **TANKOPTS.DAT** file on the same disk. Then you won't have to look at and reset the options each time you want to print. This saves time. The only wrinkle is that the copy of **TANKOPTS.DAT** that you want to use *must* be in drive A. ThinkTank won't look for it in drive B.

Formatting Options

In order to send text to the printer, press P to display the first-level PORT menu. You will be given the option of sending text to a text file or to the printer. Press P (PRINTER).

You are then given the choice of three types of files—structured, formatted, and word-processor. Normally, files sent to the printer are always of the formatted type. You can print the other two types of files, but they are more useful for other purposes. As we've already seen, the structured file type is designed primarily for compact backup files. You can reconstruct the structure of your outline from a structured file with a lot of practice, but they aren't very pretty to look at or easy to understand. Word-processor files also have a number of drawbacks, which we'll discuss shortly, and you can create identical files to the word-processor type using the formatted type. So press F (FORMATTED).

The next choice you will be given is to look at the format options. *You always want to look at the format options! Press Y!* I have heard many users complain about the difficulty of getting printed output that is reasonably arranged on a page without going through WordStar. This is because they didn't understand the format options.

We will now consider each of the format options. Then we will look at ways to use specific groupings of options for various purposes. When we're finished, you should be comfortable with porting from ThinkTank to the printer. I'll also give you some tips to avoid the most annoying pitfalls.

Now we will look at how to access ThinkTank's 17 print formatting options, and consider their effects. When you answer Y to **look at the format options?** ThinkTank displays each one, one at a time. They cycle in either direction, and you can move to the next with the cursor-right key, or to the previous one with the cursor-left key. For example, if you know that you only want to change option #17 (the printer initialization message), you can start by pressing the cursor-left key.

There are basically two types of options. One type has a numerical value, such as settings for the left and right margins, and the other offers a choice between several alternatives, such as whether or not to print headers and footers. When you want to change a numercial option, you press ← , enter the numeric values you want to use, and then press ← again. If you select a number that is out of range in any of the formatting options, the computer will beep at you and wait for you to enter an acceptable number. Pressing Esc reenters the previous value for a numerical option.

The other type of option can be chosen either by a single letter or by using the menu cursor. As with numeric options, you must first press the ← key if you want to make a change. If you use the menu cursor, you must press the ← key to record your choice. Again, Esc returns the option to its previous setting. If you press one of the letters that signifies a value for a given option, it is recorded instantly. As always, it pays to learn the letter keystrokes that enter the commands.

Line Spacing   Option 1 lets you choose whether your copy is single, double, or triple spaced. Single spacing means that no lines are skipped (except, of course, for a blank headline, or an extra carriage return in the Paragraph Editor). Double spacing adds a single line space after each line of print, and triple spacing adds two. The default setting is double spacing. If you want single or triple, you can select it with the menu cursor, or by pressing S, D, or T. Simply pressing ← twice will give you single spacing, because the menu cursor starts at single if you choose to change this option. Selecting by letter enters the selection automatically.

Left Margin   The left margin may be set anywhere from column 0 to column 40. The default setting is 3. To change this setting, press ← , enter a number from 0 to 40 from the keyboard, and press ← . If you press Esc, the option is returned to its previous setting.
  There is a bug in the program regarding the left margin. The left margin option assumes that you will print page headers—lines at the top of each page containing the date, the superordinate headline, and the page number—and sets the left margin of the header. Unless you opt to print everything flush left, the next-level headlines after the superordinate headline will be printed *two* degrees of indentation from the left margin you set, *whether or not you actually print the headers.* So if you set your left margin at 0, for example, and indent your headlines three spaces, your first subordinate headline will be indented *six* spaces.

Right Margin   The right margin may be set anywhere from 39 to 131 spaces from the left edge of the page. It is set in the same manner as the left margin. Do not set the right margin at 39 if your left margin is 40.

If you have an 80-column printer, be aware that ThinkTank regards the columns as numbered from 0 to 79. If you set the right margin at 80, one letter of a truncated headline will appear at the left margin of the following line, on a line all by itself.

The default margin settings—3 on the left and 76 on the right—have a distinct advantage, in that you can see *all* your text on the screen as it scrolls by. If you set a longer right margin you will truncate the right-hand end of the line on the screen. However, up to 80 columns will print on an 80-column printer if the right margin is set to 79.

If you have a 132-column printer, you may not have a problem with truncated long headlines. With margins of 0 and 131, a 76-character headline will be printed in its entirety even if you indent each level three spaces and the headline is nested 15 levels deep.

Number of Lines   Option 4 sets the number of lines printed on a page. The default setting is 66, which neatly breaks your text into pages 11 inches long. You cannot cram more text onto an 11-inch page by changing this setting. All that will happen is that the visual page breaks will be progressively further toward the bottom of each succeeding page.

The range of acceptable settings is from 20—about 3 1/2 inches at six lines per inch—to 32,767 lines per page. Normally, you would change this setting only for different lengths of paper, but if you want continuous printing on fan-fold or roll paper, *without* skipping over the perforation, choose 32,767 lines per page.

Indented or Flush-Left Copy   Option 5 gives you the choice of printing everything either flush with the left margin, or indented, as it appears on the screen. Despite what the manual says, the default setting is flush left (called *flat* on the menu). You can select with the menu cursor, or by pressing F (flat), or I (indented), which is faster. Specific uses for these settings are discussed below.

Degree of Indentation   ThinkTank will show a setting for the degree of indentation even if you choose to print flush left. As with all the options, you can opt not to change this one (option 6) by pressing the cursor keys to go on to the next.

The default setting is three spaces, which is the same degree of indentation as that on the screen. If you have set up a template on the screen, choose the default setting to have your printed copy match the screen.

You may choose any degree of indentation between 0 (which is the same as choosing flush left instead of indented) to 15. Enter the setting the same way as the other numerical settings.

Be aware that if you choose indented printing, *both* headlines and paragraphs will be indented. Paragraphs will be indented one degree more than the headlines they belong to. Even if you choose the flat printing in option 5, ThinkTank will indent paragraphs under their headlines the number of spaces to which option 6 has been set. If you want the paragraphs as well as the headlines to be flush left, you must set this option at 0.

Depth of Headlines   Option 7 lets you control to what degree of detail you will print your outline. If you set headline depth at 1, only first-level headlines subordinate to the bar cursor will be printed. If you set it at 10,000 (the default) every headline subordinate to the bar cursor will be printed. Using this option in conjunction with option 8 gives you a great deal of control over what portions of your outline will be printed. For example, in the course of writing this book, I included numerous outlines as illustrations, interspersed among my paragraphs. When I wanted to print just the text as you see it now, I chose to print a chapter at a time, with headlines only to depth 2, and all my paragraphs. That printed the major subheads, minor subheads, and figure captions, but skipped all of the illustrative outlines, which were nested one level deeper than the figure captions.

Depth of Paragraphs   You can also print paragraphs from any depth from 0 (none, usually) to 10,000 (all). Contrary to what the *User's Manual* suggests, you don't have to merge all your text into one long paragraph to print a report. All you have to do is choose 0 (or 1) for option 7 (headlines) and 10,000 for option 8 (paragraphs).

If you choose to print headlines only (paragraphs to depth 0), and there is a paragraph attached to the bar cursor headline, it *will* be printed, because the bar cursor headline is considered level 0. One way around this is to create a dummy headline above the one you want to start with, as described above, and demote everything that you actually want to print.

Section Numbers   Option 9 allows you to print your outline with engineering/military-style numbers. Section numbers seem to give ThinkTank users more trouble than any of the other printing options, so lets look at them in some detail.

Each degree of indentation is given a separate decimal place, and each succeeding headline at the same level of indentation is given a higher number. For example, if you print flush left, with section numbers to depth 3, your outline will look like Figure 8.3 when it is printed. But if you print *five* levels of headlines and print section numbers only to depth 3, your outline will look like Figure 8.4.

If you print section numbers with indented format, an indentation of one or two spaces will be overridden by the section numbers, because each degree of indentation requires two more places for its section number. If you indent each level three or

```
        1: This is a first-level headline.
        1.1: This is a second-level headline.
        1.1.1: This is a third-level headline.
        2: This is the second first-level headline.
        2.1: This is a second-level headline.
        2.2: This is another second-level headline.
```

Figure 8.3: Printing flush left with three levels of section numbers.

```
        1: This is a first-level headline.
        1.1: This is a second-level headline.
        1.2: This is another second-level headline.
        1.2.1: This is a third-level headline.
        This is a fourth-level headline.
        This is a fifth-level headline.
        2: This is another first-level headline.
```

Figure 8.4: Printing flush left with five levels of heads and three levels of section numbers.

more spaces, the indentation will follow its normal pattern, no matter to what depth you print section numbers.

Section numbers are always printed flush left, whether or not the outline is indented. Paragraphs do not receive section numbers separate from the headline to which they belong.

Figure 8.5 shows an outline printed in indented format, with an indentation of 5, and section numbers printed to depth 3.

Table of Contents   Options 10 and 11 control the printing of a table of contents. A table of contents can be quite useful in a long document with many headings and subheadings. The table of contents will be printed at the end of the document, with pagination beginning at i. It consists of all the headlines in the portion of the outline you have printed, to a level of nesting of your choice. The pattern of indentation will be the same as that for the rest of your document. Each entry in the table of contents is followed by a line of alternating periods and spaces, followed by the page number on which the headline appears.

Option 10 determines whether a table of contents is printed. After pressing ↵ , then press Y (or ↵ again) if you want a table of contents, N if you don't.

Option 11 determines how detailed the table of contents will be, by letting you choose the number of levels of headlines to be printed. You may choose to print the table of contents to a greater depth than you have printed headlines, and ThinkTank will gladly print a table of contents with headlines to a greater depth than you have printed in your outline. *But the table of contents will only be as long as the number of headlines printed.* Suppose your outline has twelve first-level headlines, and the first section has four second- and five third-level headlines. Suppose, further, that you print your outline only to a depth of one, and your table of contents to a depth of three. Your table of contents will then include the first first-level headline, all the second- and third-level headlines from the first section, the second first-level headline, and the first second-level headline beneath it. Figure 8.6 illustrates the problem. Figure 8.6 shows the entire contents of this book at an early stage of development, printed with headlines to depth 1 and paragraphs to depth 0. Figure 8.7 shows the table

```
1:    This is a first-level headline.
1.1:        This is a second-level headline.
1.1.1:          This is a boring outline.
2:    This is another first-level headline.
2.1:        You know what this is.
2.1.1:          You know what this is, too.
                    This is a fourth-level headline.
                        This is a fifth-level headline.
3:    This is a riddle with two answers.
3.1:        Why did the chicken cross the road?
3.1.1:          To get to the other side.
3.1.2:          For fowl purposes.
3.2:        What did you expect?
3.2.1:          You expected an original joke?
                    You should live so long!
```

Figure 8.5: Printing with a five-space indentation and three levels of section numbers.

of contents, printed to depth 3. Notice that it ends at the beginning of Chapter 2.

The default settings for options 10 and 11 print a table of contents to a depth of 3 levels of nesting.

Headers Option 12 determines whether your output will have a header at the top of each page. The default is yes. To eliminate headers, press ◄─┘ , then press N. If you choose to print headers,

```
+   Introduction
+   Chapter 1.  What Is ThinkTank?
+   Chapter 2.  Setting Up Housekeeping
+   Chapter 3.  The Grand Tour
+   Chapter 4.  Learning by Doing--A Personal Application
+   Chapter 5.  Templating
-   Chapter 6.  ThinkTank in Action
+   Chapter 7.  Using the Paragraph Editor
+   Chapter 8.  Printing Your Files
+   Chapter 9.  Advanced File Management, Working around Bugs, and Miscel
-   Chapter 10. Thinking About Thinking
+   Appendix A.
-   Appendix B.
+   Appendix C.
```

Figure 8.6: An early outline of the ThinkTank Book, with headlines to depth 1.

Figure 8.7: Table of Contents of the same outline, to depth 3.

ThinkTank will place the system date flush left, the bar cursor headline centered, and the word "page," followed by the page number, at the right margin at the top of each page. If you choose not to print headers, ThinkTank will still leave space for them, and begin printing four lines down from the top of the page, indenting (if you have chosen indented printing) the first-level headlines twice the number of spaces chosen for indentation.

Footers   Option 13 controls the printing of footers. ThinkTank's footers are identical to its headers, except that the last first-level headline on the page appears at their center, in place of the bar cursor headline. Again, ThinkTank allows space for them whether or not they are printed.

Continuous Printing   Option 14 controls whether the printer will stop at the end of each page or print continuously, to allow you the choice of using single sheets or fan-fold paper. When you set this option, ThinkTank's menu will display the question, **pause at the end of each page?** Choose by pressing Y or N. The default value is continuous printing.

If you wish to print one page at a time, press Y and ThinkTank will pause at the end of each page. When you insert the next sheet, press the space bar to continue. If you wish to switch from single-page to continuous printing during a printing operation, press Esc instead of the space bar.

Number of Copies   Option 15 sets the number of copies to printed. You may choose any number from 1 to 10,000. If you want more than three copies, however, it's probably cheaper and faster to make photocopies, rather than to print the document several times.

If you choose to print more than one copy, ThinkTank will send the entire document to the printer once, and then begin again at page one for each additional copy. This saves you the trouble of collating your copies.

Line Feed   Option 16 is designed to ensure that ThinkTank interfaces properly with your printer. Some printers proceed to the next line only if they receive an escape sequence generated by the computer telling them to do so; others proceed automatically at the end of each line. Your printer will probably wait for this escape sequence, so the default setting of Y is correct. Pressing Y will send line feed characters to the printer from the program. If your printer automatically inserts line feeds, your copy will have too many line spaces, and you should change the setting to N. If all your text overprints on a single line, change the setting to Y.

Printer Initialization Message   Some printers require a special initialization message in order to begin printing. If your printer is this type, consult your printer manual to find out the correct message. The default setting for option 17 is no initialization message. To enter an initialization message, press ↵ , type in the message, and press ↵ again. If the message includes Esc or CHR$(27), type Ctrl-[to substitute for these values.

If your printer has special printing modes, such as emphasized, enhanced, or correspondence-quality printing, and you want your document to be printed in this mode throughout, you can enter this code in the printer initialization message. For example, if you have an Epson or IBM Graphics Printer, to print a document in emphasized type, enter the message Ctrl-[⇧ -E. If you have an Okidata 92 or 93 with Plug 'n' Play, type Ctrl-[⇧ -X 1 to print in correspondence-quality type. You must use the ⇧ key with these codes because the escape code is represented by the capital letter. The lowercase letter will generate a different code, which will not have the same effect as the code generated by the uppercase letter.

Starting and Stopping the Printing Operation

When you have set all the format settings, you are ready to start printing. First, press Esc to get out of the OPTIONS mode. You will then be asked whether you wish to save the settings. Press S to save the settings (ThinkTank will record them in the **TANKOPTS.DAT** file on the disk in drive A, if the file is present, or give you an error message if it isn't), N if you don't want to, or R or Esc if you decide to review the options further.

As a general rule, it's a good idea to save your settings. Things can go wrong—paper may be misaligned, the printer may be set for a different computer, you may have made a mistake in your settings, etc.—and you may find yourself starting over several times. It's a lot easier to figure out what went wrong if you can take another look at the settings you have been using, and if the settings are not the problem, then at least you don't have to go through the labor of resetting the options each time you start over. The only time you should *not* save your settings is when you have already recorded a format that you use frequently, and just this once you want to do something different.

Having exited the OPTIONS mode, you can now start printing. ThinkTank will display the messages, **press (spacebar) to start printing** and **press (esc) to cancel** in the menu area. *Do not press the space bar until you have made sure that your printer is turned on, connected, and on-line!* If you try to print and your printer is not ready, ThinkTank will crash, and will probably make a mess of your data base in the process (see Chapter 9 for instructions on how to recover a crashed data base).

When you start printing, a box appears on the screen, and the text being sent to the printer will scroll by on the screen (the right margin may be cut off on the screen if your right margin for printing is greater than 76). If you see on the screen or the printer, that your copy is not coming out correctly, press Esc. In a few seconds, the computer will beep, and you will receive the message **press (spacebar) to continue.** Pressing the space bar will not continue the printing operation, but will return you to the top level, so you have a chance to make the necessary changes before you start printing again.

If you have a serial printer, or some other type of printer to which the computer does not automatically send text, you may need to make some special arrangements before you start printing. For example, many serial printers require a DOS redirect command. If you have this type of printer, issue the DOS commands *before loading ThinkTank;* otherwise the program will crash. If you're lucky, the Esc key will return you to the top level. If you're not, see Chapter 9 on recovering a crashed data base.

If you find yourself at the **press (spacebar) to start printing** message, and you haven't entered your redirect commands, only one course of action is open to you:

AVOIDING A REDIRECT CRASH

KEYSTROKES	COMMANDS, ACTIONS, EFFECTS
Esc	1. Cancel the printing operation.
Esc Y	2. Close the file and return to the operating system.
	3. Perform the necessary DOS operations.
tank ↵	4. Reload ThinkTank.
	5. Be glad you saved the formatting options.

Summary of Formatting Options

Table 8.1 summarizes the formatting options for printing available in ThinkTank, along with their default values.

PRINT FORMATTING OPTIONS

OPTION	SETTINGS		DEFAULT
Line Spacing	S	Single spaced	Double spaced
	D	Double spaced	
	T	Triple spaced	
Left Margin	Column 0 to 40		3
Right Margin	Column 39 to 131		76

Lines per Page	20 to 32767 lines	66
Indentation	F Flush left (flat)	flat
	I Indented	
Degree of Indenting	0 to 15 spaces	3

Note: No effect unless previous setting is I.

Depth of Headlines	0 to 10,000 levels	10,000
Depth of Paragraphs	0 to 10,000 levels	10,000

Note: If set at 0, will print paragraph attached to bar cursor headline, if one is present.

Depth of Section Numbers	0 to 10,000 levels	3
Print Table of Contents	Y Yes	Yes
	N No	
Table of Contents	Depth 0 to 10,000	3

Note: No effect unless previous setting is Y. Do not set higher than setting for depth of headlines.

Page Headers	Y Print page headers	Yes
	N Do not print headers	
Page Footers	Y Print page footers	Yes
	N Do not print footers	
Print with or **without Pausing**	Y Pause after each page	Continuous
	N Continuous printing	
Number of Copies	1 to 10,000 copies	1

Line Feed	Y	Sends line feeds to printer	Yes
	N	No line feeds sent	
Initialization message		enter message	no message

Table 8.1: ThinkTank's print formatting options

USING THE OPTIONS TO CONTROL PRINTED OUTPUT

Now that you know all the different ways ThinkTank can format your text as it is printed, you might want to think about the most useful formats for various purposes. Some of these formats have already been suggested in the previous section. This section shows some of the ways to use the format options to deal with the relationship between headlines and text in a given outline. This will help you to control the structure and appearance of your printed text.

Printing Text without Headlines

If you want to create a narrative report, you will find ThinkTank useful for setting up the structure of your report prior to writing. If you want the printed form of your report to be a continuous narrative, uninterrupted by subheads, then you will probably want to use the following settings:

- Output not indented
- Headlines to depth 0
- Paragraphs to depth 10,000 (or possibly 4, depending on the depth to which your outline is constructed)
- Page headers printed
- Page footers not printed
- Table of contents not printed.

These settings will give you a continuous report with a heading and page number at the top of each page. You can set the margins where you wish, and the text will conform to them, but it will not be right justified. There will be an extra line space at the end of each ThinkTank paragraph. If you have several grammatical paragraphs within each ThinkTank paragraph, you may want to use the carriage return to add line spaces between them for consistency. On the other hand, if your ThinkTank paragraphs are each devoted to a separate topic, you may wish to leave out the extra line spaces, so that the extra space between ThinkTank paragraphs will provide a visual break between sections.

Since you have not printed headlines, there will be no entries for the table of contents. Section numbers will not be printed because headlines have not been printed.

Printing Text with a Few Levels of Headlines

If you are printing a long and complex narrative report, you may want to use a few levels of headlines to make the structure of your narrative clearer to your readers. There is no difficulty in doing so—simply set headlines to, say, depth 3 and paragraphs to whatever depth necessary to assure that they are all printed.

But introducing headlines among the paragraphs raises a few questions about formatting. If you use the indented format, each level of headline will be indented under the superordinate level, but the paragraphs will also be indented one degree more than their headlines. This may result in some strange-looking output.

For this situation I would suggest using the flush-left option, and either setting section numbers to the same depth as your headlines or using other means to distinguish between various levels of headlines. For example, you might type your first-level headlines in capital letters, use printer codes for boldfacing on your second-level headlines, and use printer codes for underlining on your third-level headlines.

It is with combined headlines and text that a printed table of contents becomes most useful, especially if the document is long. Page footers will put section titles at the foot of your pages, if you find that helpful. I would suggest using either page headers or page footers, if not both, as they are the only ways to get ThinkTank to print page numbers on your output.

Printing Outlines without Paragraphs

You can print outlines without including any paragraphs attached. This is extremely useful at various developmental stages in a project. If the outline you are working on is an especially long one, for example, the level of organization to which you may need to refer at a glance may result in an outline too large to fit on the screen. To print an outline without paragraphs, simply set the paragraph depth to 0 and the headline depth to whatever level will give you the degree of detail you want. The only catch is that a paragraph attached to the bar cursor headline will be printed regardless, as the bar cursor headline is theoretically depth 0.

You have many options in printing an outline without paragraphs. You probably won't want to print flush left, unless you include section numbers to the same depth as headlines. You can indent any number of spaces you choose, with or without section numbers. If you have long headlines, you can capture the right ends of them on an 80-column printer by setting the right margin as high as necessary up to 131. Then your headlines will wrap. This may be acceptable for a working draft, but is not suitable for presentation material.

An alternative way to get all of your long headlines on paper is to use the printer initialization message to set the printer so that it uses a smaller type style. Most quality printers have optional *print pitches* of 12 characters to the inch, and many also have 15, 16, 17.2 or 18, as well. If you are using an 80-column printer, remember that with one of these optional pitches, you must calculate the number of columns per page based on the number of characters in eight inches of type.

Special Cases

ThinkTank's flexibility makes it useful for a number of special cases as well. If you are developing teaching materials, you may want to print both a text for your students and an outline for yourself. You might print the entire outline, text and paragraphs, with section numbers, for your students, and then do a second print run for yourself, printing only indented headlines. Or you could print the text for your students with only one or two levels of heads, as described above, and print a full outline for yourself. Alternatively, you may want to print both a text and the outlines for your students, so that they can get a view of the overall structure as well as the details.

If you are preparing a report that includes condensed outlines interspersed with the text, and you want to be sure that your outline examples are not divided across pages, you can arrange that, too. Set up your examples under headings that indicate where the example belongs, e.g., **Figure 5** or **Table 3.2**. Set up the outline so that these captions are nested to the deepest level that you intend to print. Then print the text with a limited number of headlines. At any point where an example should appear, its caption will be present. Then go back and print the various examples, one at a time, with the bar cursor on the caption line, so that it can be used as a page header. The figures can then either be inserted at appropriate points in the text, or grouped together at the end.

If you want to present part of an outline, and the part you want to present requires greater depth at some points than at others, consider doing a screen dump. You can use the screen dumps illustratively in the manner described for inserting illustrations. Unfortunately, your screen dumps will all include whatever ThinkTank menu happens to be present on the screen.

Printing Parts of Outlines or Paragraphs

When printing from ThinkTank, you can print:

1. Part of an outline by placing the bar cursor on the highest level head under which you want to print everything.

2. Only headlines by using the FORMAT option to set **Paragraphs are printed to depth 0.**

3. Only paragraphs by using the FORMAT option to set **Headlines are printed to depth 0.**

You can*not* print part of a paragraph. You can select a part, which you can then copy or delete, but you can't move just the copied part. Also, you can't undo a paragraph deletion at another point in your outline. ThinkTank regards all text under a given headline as a single unit, and regards it as permanently attached to its first superordinate headline.

The best method is to copy the headline under which the ThinkTank paragraph appears, which will copy the paragraph as well; move it to a place where it's at the highest logical level, so nothing under it will be included, delete the parts of the paragraph you don't want to print, and then print it with headlines to depth 0. When you copy a headline to duplicate a paragraph, however, be sure there are no additional paragraphs nested further beneath the headline, as they will be copied as well. There is no way to cancel this operation once you start it.

CREATING WORDSTAR FILES

Even with all these myriad options, you may find that simply porting your text to a printer does not give you as much control over its appearance as you would like. You can't force a page break, for example, so a first-level headline may appear at the bottom of a page, rather than with its subordinate material. (A headline will never be separated from a paragraph belonging to it, however.) And you can't right-justify your paragraphs.

When you find yourself in this situation, you will probably want to port your file to a word-processing program such as WordStar before you format your final output for printing. To do so, you must go through the PORT menu, as described below.

1. Place the bar cursor on the highest-level headline of the portion of your outline you want to send to WordStar.
2. Press P to display the PORT options.
3. Press T (TEXTFILE).
4. Press S (SEND).
5. Press W (WORDPROCESSOR).

6. Enter the name you want the text file to have. Remember to prefix it with **b:** if you want it on the disk in drive B. If your file name has no extension, ThinkTank will give it the extension .**TXT.**

ThinkTank will do all the rest. Let's see what gets sent to the file.

You'll be able to see what is being sent to the file as it is being ported, because it will scroll by on the screen. You will find that there is no way to preserve the structure of your outline in a word-processor file. All headlines appear flush left, followed by carriage returns. Paragraphs are flush left too, but carriage returns will appear only where you have inserted them, or at the end of ThinkTank paragraphs.

This is fine if you just want to deal with text. If you have masses of headlines with no text embedded, you can simply delete them using WordStar's block-delete system. If you know you will be porting to WordStar, you can insert WordStar print-formatting codes as you enter the text in ThinkTank.

However, if you want to preserve the structure of your outline, things get a bit sticky. There are several half-measures that work tolerably well. Most of them involve some rather complex file-handling techniques, which will be discussed in the next chapter.

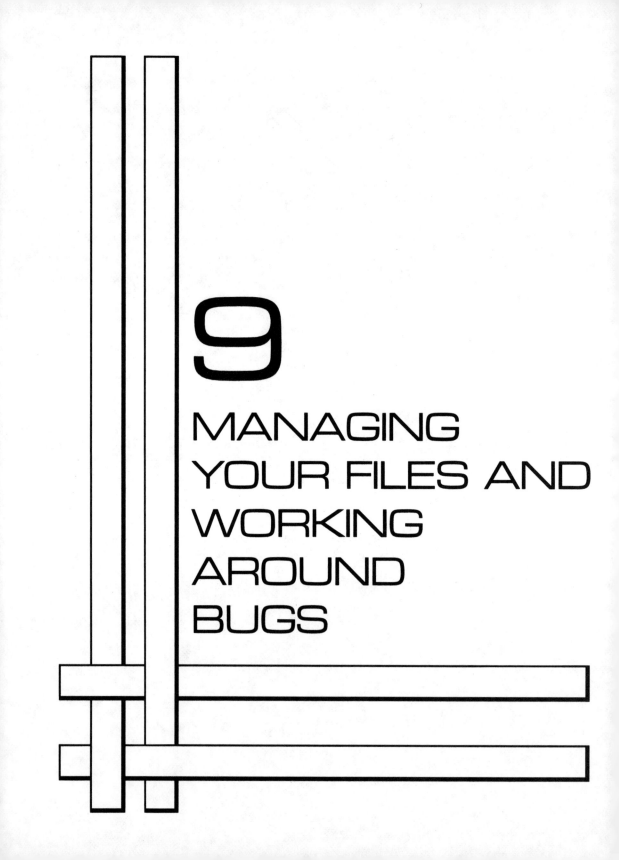

9

MANAGING YOUR FILES AND WORKING AROUND BUGS

In this chapter we'll deal with some loose ends that couldn't logically fit into the other chapters. First, we'll explore thoroughly the options available on the PORT menu, and look at some interesting ways you can use them to simplify other tasks and solve some sticky problems. You will also learn how to deal with some recurring problems, so that you can minimize panic and proceed peacefully.

STILL MORE ABOUT THE PORT MENU

As you have already learned, you can use the PORT menu to create compact backup files of your outlines, send text to a printer, and create files that can be read by WordStar. There are several other uses for the PORT command, some of which involve less-than-straightforward approaches that may not be obvious. Among them are copying and renaming files, creating files that will allow you to preserve the structure of your outlines in a WordStar file, decreasing the size of your file, and recovering from a crash that messes up your file.

To begin, let's review the PORT menu's options. When you press P to enter the PORT menu, you have two choices: port to a printer (P) or to a text file (T). We already reviewed the PRINTER commands in the previous chapter; let's now look at the text file options.

Receiving a Text File into Your Outline

When you choose text file (T), your next choice is between sending (S) and receiving (R). (You don't get this choice with the printer because you can't receive text from your printer.) So far, you have only used the SEND command, for creating word processor files and for creating structured backup files. You need to use the RECEIVE command when you want to port something from a text file back into an outline. If you are receiving a text file, be sure your bar cursor is at the headline after which you want the file to appear.

Incidentally, you can use this option to add files to your outline that were not created by ThinkTank. In fact, you can port any DOS text file into a ThinkTank outline. This makes ThinkTank compatible, to a degree, with any program that creates DOS text files.

When you press R, you will be asked whether the file is to be received in word-wrapped (W) or line-oriented (L) form. As a general rule, you will want word-wrapped, which inserts *hard*—i.e., fixed—carriage returns only at those points where they appear in the text file. This allows ThinkTank to reformat paragraphs to fit the screen or the printer in its usual manner. Line-oriented receiving inserts a hard carriage return at the end of each line of text as it is received. With ThinkTank's pattern of indentations, this can result in some strange screen and printer formatting, which you probably don't want. (In a little while, though, we'll look at some specialized uses for line-oriented receiving.)

ThinkTank will then ask you for the name of the file to be received. Type in the file name. If the extension is something other than .**TXT**, you must type it in as part of the file name. If you do not, ThinkTank will assign the extension .**TXT**. If the file is on a disk in drive B, be sure to include the **b:** prefix.

Unfortunately, you don't have an option to browse at this point, so you must remember the exact spelling of your file name. If you do not, you will receive the error message, **can't open text-file!**, along with ThinkTank's characteristic alarm. If you have many text files on disk, and you are not sure of their names, use the DOS **DIR** command to review your file names, and write them down or dump them to the printer (⇧ -PrtSc) before you load ThinkTank. If you are already in ThinkTank, your only recourse is to leave the program, (Esc Y), look at the directories, reload ThinkTank, and start the process over.

However, if the text file you want to receive is the last text file you created, you can use the RECALL command. Press F4, and the last file name you entered will be reentered.

The entire contents of your text file will then be transferred into your outline. It will scroll by in a box on the screen, so you can check to be sure it's the right file. If it's not, or if you don't want all of it in your outline, you can interrupt the transfer at any point by pressing Esc. If the text file was of the structured type, its entire contents will now be in your outline, collapsed under the headline on which the bar cursor was located when you created the file. The bar cursor will move to the new headline. If the text file was of another type, it will be collapsed under a headline reading **TEXT FROM FILE [FILENAME.EXT]**, which will be under the bar cursor. It will not be in outline form, however, but will be treated by ThinkTank as a single ThinkTank paragraph. This may create a problem if your text file exceeds 20,000 characters or 900 lines. If so, some of the file will not be transferred, as that is the maximum length of a ThinkTank paragraph.

If your text file comes from a source other than ThinkTank, and is too long to fit into a single ThinkTank paragraph, you should first use the program that created the file to break the file into smaller units, and port the shorter files in separately. If the text file is a formatted or word processor file created by ThinkTank, you can avoid this problem by creating the transitional formatted or word processor files from units of your outline that will be small enough to fit into a single ThinkTank paragraph. For reference, Table 9.1 summarizes the PORT menu commands.

Preserving Outline Structure in a WordStar File

As mentioned in the previous chapter, when you port to a word processor file, all text and headlines will become flush left. If you have an extensive, indented outline, with or without paragraphs, you cannot preserve its organization while using this option, as you can't use the format option that numbers your headlines, and none of the headlines, no matter what their logical

PORT MENU COMMANDS

P	(PRINTER) Port file to printer.
T	(TEXTFILE) Port file to or from text file.
R	(RECEIVE) Receive text file into your outline.
L	(LINE-ORIENTED) Receive file in line-oriented form. (Hard carriage return at the end of each line)
W	(WORD-WRAPPED) Receive file in word-wrapped form. (Hard carriage returns only at ends of headlines, ends of ThinkTank paragraphs, and where you inserted them.)
S	(SEND) Send text file to disk.
S	(STRUCTURED) Send text file in structured form (compact file with enough information for ThinkTank to reconstruct your outline).
F	(FORMATTED) Send text file in formatted form. Format controlled by print formatting options.
W	(WORDPROCESSOR) Send text file in word processor form. All headlines will be flush left. Paragraphs will be flush left except where you started them with spaces, and will contain carriage returns only at the end, or where you have inserted them.

Table 9.1: PORT menu commands.

relationship, will be indented. But there are some tricks that may help.

If you have an outline with no paragraphs and you want to preserve its structure, try the following:

PRESERVING OUTLINE STRUCTURE IN A WORDSTAR FILE

KEYSTROKES	COMMANDS, ACTIONS, EFFECTS
cursor keys	1. Place the bar cursor on the highest-level headline of the section you want to port.

P T S F [filename]	2. Create a formatted text file. This allows you the same formatting options you have with the printer.
Y	3. Look at the format options. Choose either indented or numbered output, depending on your taste (one might argue for flush left and numbered, because even in a text file, ThinkTank will add an extra degree of indentation to the first level under the bar cursor, and you may want to avoid spending time deleting spaces to get the margins right).
Esc (N or S) **Space Bar**	4. Send the file to the disk.
P T R L [filename]	5. Port the text file back into your outline in line-oriented form.
	6. This will give you a ThinkTank paragraph consisting of the headlines of your previous outline, which will return under the headline **TEXT FROM [FILENAME.EXT]** The bar cursor will move to this dummy headline.
P T S W [filename]	7. Port the new paragraph to a word processor file.
Del O	8. You may then want to delete the temporary outline from your file, as you should have no further need for it.

Your new word processor file will now consist of the headlines from your outline, indented or numbered as you chose and separated by hard carriage returns.

If your outline contains paragraphs as well as headlines, you can port your whole outline (or any part of it) to a formatted text file, port it back to a new outline, and then port it to a word processor file. This will work only if your outline, including headlines and text, is less than 900 lines or 20,000 words, as porting the text file back into an outline will turn it into a single ThinkTank paragraph.

If none of this works, consider porting your outline to a series of word processor files in segments, so that no segment has so many levels of headlines that you can't figure out their relationship to each other. Then use WordStar's file-merging commands to reconstruct the document.

Combining Outlines

The PORT menu can be used to combine all or part of one outline with all or part of another. The key to doing so is using the structured type of text file.

Combining two complete outlines is probably the easiest of these alternatives, but if your outlines are large, there may not be enough room on disk to do so. This technique is especially helpful if you have started a number of small outlines in separate files and want to combine them into a single file. Here are the procedures:

COMBINING OUTLINE FILES

KEYSTROKES	COMMANDS, ACTIONS, EFFECTS
	1. If the two files you want to combine are not on the same disk, take the program disk out of drive A, and replace it with the disk the other file is on.
F C E	2. If the file you want to move into your main outline is not already up on your screen, close the currently open file.
B or E	3. Open the file you want to bring into your outline.
Ctrl-Home	4. Move the bar cursor to the summit.
P T S S [filename]	5. Create a structured text file of the entire outline.
F C E E [filename]	6. Close the currently open file and open the one you want to add it to.

cursor keys	7. Place the bar cursor on the headline below which you want the added text to appear.
P T R W [filename]	8. Port the new text file into your outline.
	9. The headline that was under your bar cursor when you created the text file will now appear in your outline, at the same level of indentation as the headline above it. Your text file will be in outline form, collapsed under this headline.
F1 cursor keys Esc	10. You may want to use the MOVE command to reposition this headline, so it is indented to the degree you want it to be (F1 cursor-left or -right Esc). If you wish, you can move it elsewhere in your outline at the same time.
	11. After you close ThinkTank, you may want to use the DOS **ERASE** command to erase the old outline from your disk, saving the structured text file as a backup.

If you want to combine *part* of one outline with another outline, the steps are essentially the same, except that you place the bar cursor on the headline superordinate to the part you want to move to another outline, rather than at the summit. If you have several sections at the same level that you wish to move to another outline, there are two ways to proceed. You can create a structured text file of each one separately, and then port them into your receiving outline separately; alternatively, you can create a dummy headline and nest all the parts you want to transfer under it, reconstructing the original form of your outline after you have finished porting.

Sometimes you may want to create an outline that has parts of two or more other outlines, but does not contain all of any of them. Again the procedure is basically the same:

COMBINING PARTS OF OUTLINES

KEYSTROKES	COMMANDS, ACTIONS, EFFECTS
P T S S	1. Create structured text files of all the parts you want to combine.
F C N [filename]	2. Close the file that is currently open and begin a new file.
P T R W	3. Port the structured text files that you want to combine into your new outline.
F10 F10 P	4. Promote the recreated outlines.
Del O	5. Delete the dummy headlines.
F4	6. Edit the **Home** line appropriately, and press ◄┘ when you are finished. You may want to save all the text files as backups.

Copying and Renaming Files

At times you may want to copy entire ThinkTank outlines. The quickest way to do that is to use the DOS **COPY** command. But there are times when you will want to make copies using ThinkTank either to have the outline available under two different names (although copying through DOS is easier), or to shrink your data base, the reason for which is discussed later under "What to Do When Your Disk is Full." The steps are essentially the same as those used to combine outlines:

COPYING A .DB FILE

KEYSTROKES	COMMANDS, ACTIONS, EFFECTS
	1. Open the file you want to copy.
Ctrl-Home	2. Place the bar cursor at the summit.
	3. If your file is long, you will probably want to place a fresh disk in drive A.
P T S S [filename]	4. Create a structured text file of the entire outline.

F C N [filename]   5. Create a new file on the disk you
                         have placed in drive A. Since it will be
                         on a separate disk, you can give it
                         either the same name as the original
                         file or a different one.

You will now have two identical files and a structured text file
backup. You can give them different names if you wish.

HOW TO SHRINK YOUR FILE

Sometimes you will notice that your .DB file is so large that
your disk is getting dangerously close to full. A double-sided
floppy disk will hold 354K, or 362496 bytes. With a .SAV file of
1024 bytes on the disk, you can expect to run out of room
quickly if your .DB file is over about 320K (327680 bytes, which
is the number that will show up on the disk directory), especially
if you plan to add some long paragraphs.

In this case, you do the obvious—port a chunk of your outline
to a structured text file on another disk, and delete that part of
the outline. When you check your directory, however, the file is
as large as it was before. What a pain!

This is an unfortunate characteristic of many data base systems,
and it is true of some early releases of ThinkTank, as well. When
you delete things from a data base file (including a ThinkTank outline file) as a rule, nothing is deleted. The program merely resets
some internal pointers so that the part you deleted becomes invis-
ible to you (and to the program). Incidentally, this is one reason
why you can undo a deletion.

There is a way to shrink your file in spite of this limitation. Basically, the procedure is exactly what you did when you copied a
file by way of a structured text file. The structured text file does
not contain anything that you deleted, so when you port it back
into a new outline, the outline will be considerably shorter than
the old one. To review briefly:

HOW TO SHRINK A .DB FILE

KEYSTROKES   COMMANDS, ACTIONS, EFFECTS

                      1. Place a data disk in drive A (if your
                      current outline is in drive B). This may

	be a disk on which you store your backup files, or a fresh, DOS-formatted disk. In any case, it must have at least 100K of space available on it.
P T S S [filename]	2. Port the **entire** data base to a structured text file on the disk in drive A.
F C N [b:filename]	3. Place a fresh, DOS-formatted disk in drive B. Create a new outline file with the old name, or a new name if you prefer.
P T R W [filename]	4. Port the structured text file you made in step 2 to the new outline file. You will find that the text file was around 100K, and the new outline file will be about 200K, which gives you a lot more room on the disk.

Preserving the Structure of an Outline

Before you go through the time and trouble of double-porting a long outline, you might want to take some steps to make your outline shorter, just to assure some extra head room. You may have numerous paragraphs in your outline which you don't need immediately, but will still want to be able to refer to. Here is a useful technique that will allow you to do this, and shrink your file considerably.

PRESERVING OUTLINE STRUCTURE WHILE ELIMINATING PARAGRAPHS

KEYSTROKES	COMMANDS, ACTIONS, EFFECTS
P T S S [filename]	1. Port the section you want to delete to a structured text file, so you can call it back when you need it.
P T S F Y	2. Port the **same** section to a formatted text file. (You must use a different file name, or a different extension.) When

setting up the format, you will send no paragraphs to the file, only the head-lines, and only to as deep a level as you need to refer to. Use the following format settings:

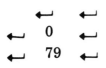

1. Single spacing.
2. Left margin at 0.
3. Right margin at 79.
4. As many lines to a page as there are headlines that you want to port. You can use any number here, as long as it's less than 900. You will probably have to delete some carriage returns later any-way, so you can use the default setting of 66.)
5. Indented.
6. To depth 3.
7. Headlines printed to whatever depth you want to preserve in your outline.
8. Paragraphs printed to depth 0.
9. Section numbers to depth 0
10. No table of contents.
11. No page headers.
12. No page footers.
13. Print without pausing.
14. One copy.
15. Automatic line feed.
16. No initialization message.

Del O   3. Delete from your outline the portion that you have just ported twice.

P T R L [filename]   4. Port the formatted text file back in the same place, in line-oriented form (i.e, leave your bar cursor where it is after the deletion is completed).

You will now have a ThinkTank paragraph with the following characteristics:

1. It will start with five carriage returns.

2. If there was a paragraph attached to the bar cursor headline (level 0), it will follow the carriage returns. It will be interrupted by groups of carriage returns in bizarre places. Ignore this fact for now.

3. Your headlines will follow, indented just as they were in your outline, but with three extra spaces at the left (it's that extra indentation after the header again), and without the plus and minus signs that tell you which outlines are empty and which are full. Each will be followed by a carriage return.

4. The headlines may be periodically interrupted by a group of carriage returns. This represents the page breaks that will be inserted after the number of lines you specified per page have been sent to the file.

5. There will probably be a large block of carriage returns at the end of the paragraph.

6. The headline will read **TEXT FROM FILE [FILE-NAME.EXT]**.

Now you will want to reformat this paragraph:

REFORMATTING A "PARAGRAPH" OF HEADLINES

KEYSTROKES	COMMANDS, ACTIONS, EFFECTS
Alt-S cursor-down Del Y	1. Mark and delete (Del Y) the leading carriage returns and the first paragraph (if there is one).
cursor-down Del	2. Move down to any interrupting blocks of carriage returns. Hold down the Del key until they are gone.

cursor-down Alt-S

Ctrl-End

3. Move to the carriage returns that follow your headlines and delete them.

Ctrl-Home

Del Del Del
cursor-down

4. Finally, you may want to realign the whole business so that it conforms to the rest of your outline. Press Ctrl-Home to get to the beginning of your paragraph, and then delete three spaces from the beginning of each line until you reach the bottom.

Except for the missing plus and minus signs, your paragraph now reproduces your outline exactly as it would appear if you had used F8 to expand it to the depth you wanted. It's still a ThinkTank paragraph, however, which means that you can't use the MOVE, INSERT, and DELETE commands on the headlines that are present. But this paragraph gives you a complete outline of the text that you removed. You have preserved the text in a structured text file, which allows you to port it back into an outline when you need it.

You may think that it's faster to go through the whole outline and delete all the paragraphs one at a time after porting the whole thing out, but believe me, it isn't. Once you get the feel for this process, it becomes very simple and fast, and saves a lot of trouble.

WHAT TO DO WHEN
YOUR DISK IS FULL

Sometimes, you'll be working away, totally absorbed, and won't know that your disk is full until you try to enter a headline, or exit the Paragraph Editor. Then you find out because ThinkTank sounds its alarm and the message **disk full!** appears on one of the menu lines. Unfortunately, this seems most likely to happen when you are in the Paragraph Editor, and have reached the end of a long paragraph that you want to save.

If you have version 1.000 of ThinkTank, your data base is almost sure to crash at this point. (See below on how to recover a crashed data base.) You can write to Living Videotext and ask for version 1.001, which doesn't have this problem. When you reach this point in version 1.001, you will be returned to the Paragraph Editor, so that you can delete some text and try again. If you watched the text scroll by in the space between the menu bars while you tried to save the paragraph, you will know how much you have to delete before going on, because the last line of text that flashed by is the last one that will fit on the disk.

Of course, you don't want to lose all your text, and since much of the paragraph you are working on may be new material, you don't want to delete it. There is a way out:

RECOVERING FROM A FULL DISK

KEYSTROKES	COMMANDS, ACTIONS, EFFECTS
	1. Turn on your printer. (If you have a serial printer that needs redirected output, and you didn't load the redirect, you're out of luck! Always load your redirect before loading ThinkTank. See the section in Appendix B on creating a .BAT file for a way to simplify the process.)
Ctrl-End	2. Move the cursor to the end of your paragraph.
⇧ -PrtSc	3. Dump the screen to the printer.
PgUp ⇧ -PrtSc	4. Move up a "page" (21 lines) and dump the next screen to the printer.
	5. Keep repeating step 4 until your collection of screen dumps includes the last line that will fit on the disk. Now you have hard copy of everything from your paragraph that won't fit on the disk, so you can reenter the text once you are out of the jam.

Alt-S Ctrl-End
Del Y

6. You will already be at the last line of text that will fit on the disk. You can then safely delete everything after that point and exit the Paragraph Editor.

Next, you must find a few other things that you can safely delete. If there is no text you can afford to lose, port some of it to a structured text file before you delete it from the outline. If you still don't have enough room for the end of your paragraph, you'll have to shrink your data base (see above) before proceeding. At least you won't have lost the fruits of your labors.

A FEW WORDS ABOUT FILE SIZE

The minimum size of a .DB file is 5120 bytes, which is supplemented by a .SAV file of either 512 or 1024 bytes. Storage is incremented in units of 512 bytes, so if your file is 5121 or 5630 bytes, 5120 + 512, or 5632, bytes of storage will be allocated on the disk.

Any headline in a file takes 128 bytes, regardless of the number of characters in the headline. Every time you indent a level, another 128 bytes are used. No additional bytes are used for moving to the left, however.

If your file consists of only headlines, and has an average amount of indentation, you can store about 1600 in a single file, whereas if your file consists mostly of paragraphs, you can store approximately 2,700 lines. This is because structured text files use considerably less storage than .DB files. A structured text file of a .DB file consisting primarily of headlines will take about one-fourth the storage space of the .DB file, while one consisting primarily of pararaphs will take about a third of the storage space of its source file. Word-processor files of outlines containing many paragraphs take about one-fourth the storage of the source file.

RECOVERING A CRASHED DATA BASE

ThinkTank is not crash-proof. In some situations, you will find that ThinkTank will not respond. For example, if you try to port to a printer that isn't there, or if you try to port to a printer that isn't properly interfaced, ThinkTank will do nothing. Also, in version 1.000 a **disk full!** message is generally an indicator of a crash. You can still crash version 1.001 when you get the **disk full!** message through dogged persistence. There may be a few other ways to crash the program, as well.

If the program crashes, your data base has probably crashed as well. Even if the program hasn't crashed, a **.DB** file will sometimes crash. You know that your data base has crashed if one or more of the following things happens:

1. You try to expand a bar cursor outline (most often one with a paragraph under it), and you hear a whirring or clicking that continues forever and nothing on the keyboard will make it stop.

2. You try to delete something and the same thing happens.

3. You see strange graphics characters or random letters on the screen.

Generally, this means that one of two things has happened. Either the window is not functioning, so that what you see on the screen is not accurate, or (worse) some internal pointers have been reset to point to the same line of text over and over again.

Since the computer is probably not responding to your keystrokes, the first thing you have to do is reboot, as just described. The screen will look as though you have just turned the computer on. Reload ThinkTank. When it opens your outline, press Ctrl-Home to get to the summit, close everything up (−), and expand it one level (+).

Continue to each first-level headline, systematically expanding and collapsing everything. If your text looks intact, including the section where you encountered the error, then the problem was that the window wasn't functioning, and you can safely continue.

However, if you try to expand the part where you had found the error, and you get the same bizarre result as before, your data base is seriously crashed. Follow these steps carefully:

RECOVERING A CRASHED DATA BASE

KEYSTROKES	COMMANDS, ACTIONS, EFFECTS
Ctrl-Alt-Del	1. Reboot the computer.
	2. Reload ThinkTank, if necessary.
cursor keys	3. Move the bar cursor to the headline under which the disaster is hidden.
F1 cursor keys	4. Try to move the headline under which the disaster is hidden to the very end of your outline, and place it at the first level of indentation. *Do not use DELETE-UNDO.* If problems arise, repeat steps 1 and 2, and skip to step 9.
Ins	5. Add a dummy headline directly below the summit.
F1 cursor-right F1 cursor right, etc.	6. Move all of your other first-level headlines one degree to the right, except for the one with the problem.
cursor keys T S S [filename]	7. Place your bar cursor on the dummy headline, and port to a structured text file.
F C N [filename]	8. Port the structured text file into a new outline on a fresh disk. You have now recovered all of your data base except for the one section or paragraph with the problem. You will have to reconstruct this section from your notes, your memory, or your backup files.
cursor keys	9. If you were unable to move the damaged portion of your data base out

of harm's way before porting, you must port everything out around it. Move your bar cursor to the first first-level headline below the damaged section.

Ins Esc

F1 cursor keys Esc
10. Insert a dummy headline, and move it above the one to which you had moved the bar cursor.

F1 cursor-right

F1 cursor-right, etc.
11. Move all the first-level headlines below the dummy headline one degree to the right.

cursor keys

P T S S [filename]
12. Place your bar cursor on the dummy headline, and port to a structured text file.

cursor keys
13. Move the bar cursor to the first first-level headline in your outline (unless that is where the problem occurred).

P T S S [filename]
14. Port that portion of your outline to a *different* structured text file.

15. Repeat steps 13 and 14 for each first-level headline up to the one containing the damage.

16. Port out any portions of the section in which the damage occured that you can without including the damaged portion.

F C N [filename]
17. Start a new outline on a fresh disk.

P T R L [filename]
18. Port all your text files from the old outline into the new one.

A crashed data base may also indicate damage to the disk. You should exit the program and use the DOS **COPY** command to copy any other files from the damaged disk to another disk. Next, run the DOS **CHKDSK** program to see whether your crashed disk has any bad sectors. If it does, throw it away. If it does not, you can reformat it using the DOS **FORMAT** program.

PROBLEMS AT THE SUMMIT

There are several sticky situations you can get into when you work at the summit of an outline. I'll describe them here, along with ways to get around problems.

How to "Do a 'Undo' at Home"

On occasion, you may have the unnerving experience of deleting text with the bar cursor at the summit, and discovering that you have in fact deleted your entire outline. When you press Del U to undo the deletion, you get the error message **can't do a "undo" at home!**. Well, fear not. All is not lost! Simply insert a dummy headline directly beneath the summit (the only place you can insert anything at such a juncture), perform the UNDO at the dummy headline, and presto! Your outline reappears. You can then do a PROMOTE (F10 F10 P) and delete the dummy headline.

You can use the same technique when you want to "do a 'undo' at home" and there is an outline present. Alternatively you can undo the deletion one headline below the summit and then move it.

A Paragraph at the Summit

If you place a paragraph under the summit, you will not be able to copy it, unless you want to make a copy of the whole outline. You will not be able to merge anything to it because you cannot place any other headline at the same level. And you cannot move it.

Obviously, the simplest solution is *not* to insert a paragraph under the headline at the summit. If you have already done so, however, and want to perform one of the above operations on it, your only recourse is to port the entire outline to a structured text file, and then port it back into another outline. The summit of your old outline will then be directly below, and one level indented from, the summit of your new outline. You can then treat the paragraph under your old summit line as you would any other paragraph.

However, you can delete a paragraph at the summit. Simply place the bar cursor at the summit and press Del P.

THE PHANTOM CARRIAGE RETURN

Sometimes when you are at the end of a ThinkTank paragraph, you will find that, having entered a carriage return, you cannot get the cursor to move past it. Every time you hit the cursor-movement keys to start a new line, the cursor bounces to the final carriage return and the computer beeps. If this happens, and you want to add text at the end of the paragraph, simply press the ←┘ key again, to insert an additional carriage return. That will bring you to the beginning of the next line. You can then insert text to the left of the carriage return, which will move along under the cursor as you type.

Once you have inserted at least one character (including a blank space), you can safely delete the carriage-return marker with the Del key. However, after you have done so, your screen might appear to go blank (except for the menu), and you will hear a continuous clicking noise. When it stops, and you try to type something in, you get the message **no room for last key-stroke!** What has happened is that the Paragraph Editor has inserted carriage returns on all the lines still available in your paragraph.

Although you can't prevent this from happening, there is an easy cure.

STALKING THE PHANTOM CARRIAGE RETURN

KEYSTROKES	COMMANDS, ACTIONS, EFFECTS
Ctrl-Home	1. Move the cursor to the beginning of your paragraph.
cursor-down	2. Use the cursor-down key to move down through the text you have

	entered until you get to the end of it. You will then find carriage-return markers at the beginning of each line.
Alt-S Ctrl-End	3. Enter SELECT mode, and press Ctrl-End. You will have selected all the carriage returns at the end of your paragraph.
Del Y	4. Delete the carriage returns.
	5. Your cursor will now be at the end of the text you have entered. Continue typing as if nothing had happened.

CANCELING A COPY

Although the lower menu bar says **press (esc) to cancel** when you use the COPY command, you can't cancel it. This can be a problem if you try to copy just the first paragraph of a long section, and don't realize that there's more text nested under the same headline. You won't realize this until you see all the other text whizzing by on the screen. It will continue until everything under the bar cursor is copied or the disk is full, whichever comes first. Sorry, but there's no way out of this one. Before you enter the COPY command, be sure that there is no more text than you want to copy under the bar cursor headline. Do this by pressing F8 twice. This will quickly expand and collapse the first-level headlines under the bar cursor. If more text is present, do a PROMOTE before copying, and then do a simulated DEMOTE after the copying process is finished.

TWO FINAL WORDS

Good luck!

10
THINKING
ABOUT
THINKING

In this book, we have gradually progressed from relatively simple forms of organization to forms of greater complexity. In Chapter 4, we began with a simple, unordered list, imposed order on it, and then transformed it into a different type of order—a calendar. Then we created a form to use for generating any number of calendars. In Chapter 5, we created more complex forms that could be used to impose order on complex tasks—keeping track of sales calls and maintaining a resume. In Chapter 6, we watched large masses of complex information being organized and reorganized for different purposes. Finally, in Chapters 7 and 8, we added the finest degree of detail—complete text—and looked at various ways to produce printed copies to share with others.

Underlying this development is a hidden theme. ThinkTank can accept your ideas *as* they arise, and then be used to build up complex structures from them, and finally, to reduce those structures into manageable form. In humans, the accretion of ideas and their organization into meaningful structures takes place in different parts of the brain. The left hemisphere controls the logical, linear processes, while the right hemisphere generates the type of thought involved in the creation and manipulation of patterns. Since both of these are fundamental but separate aspects of human thought, we could argue that ThinkTank mirrors the structure of human thought.

Furthermore, ThinkTank takes advantage of both modes of thinking. This is its greatest strength, and one of the characteristics that makes it such an innovation. On one hand, you can impose order from the top down, taking a big idea and breaking it down into smaller and more manageable components, following a linear structure generated by the right hemisphere. On the other hand, you can build up a big idea starting from fragments. And as the organization of your idea develops, ThinkTank represents it visually, so that it can be grasped through right-hemisphere thought processes. The indentations of a ThinkTank outline clearly indicate the relationships among various aspects of your ideas, thus giving you an overview of the pattern of your thought, one that the left-hemisphere processes can grasp intuitively. By fusing the logical and intuitive processes and externalizing both of them, ThinkTank makes explicit aspects of the creative process that are normally unconscious.

There are other ways ThinkTank can effectively increase the mind's capacity to deal with ideas and problems. Since only a limited amount of information can be kept in mind at one time, complex ideas must be broken down into smaller parts. The more complex the idea, the more parts it will have. However, as the number of parts increases, so does the number and complexity of the relationships among them. Because ThinkTank lets you move easily from one level of structure to another, and rearrange structures just as easily, you can use it to get a clear overview of your idea, and to rearrange its parts into meaningful systems of organization. By externalizing these aspects of thought for you, ThinkTank can thus actually increase your ability to develop ideas and to solve problems.

Indeed, people who have used the program regularly over six months or more say they have noticed a change in their way of thinking. When new ideas begin to arise, they fall into patterns more readily than they previously did. One user told me that he can more easily grasp the main points of any argument. He is so accustomed to generating hierarchical organization, that he now mentally organizes the various points automatically as he becomes aware of them. Other users have noted that they can more readily perceive the patterns inherent in their own thoughts. To them, ideas that once seemed disconnected now become parts of larger thought structures more readily.

This tendency may have profound implications for the future. Children who grow up using ThinkTank, or a program like it, may develop the capacity to handle large amounts of information, and to structure it at an early age. Thus, they may be able to solve problems more effectively than their elders. Since effective organization of information can help to anticipate problems, it may become more possible for people to anticipate and prevent problems *before* they have to solve them.

ThinkTank can thus be a powerfully liberating tool. Using such a tool, individuals now have the potential to deal with information on a level of complexity that could previously be handled only by organizations. Further, it allows the user to impose his or her own organization on the information, thus drawing directly on the intuitive powers of the imagination. Thus, creativity need no longer be restricted by hierarchical forms of organization imposed from without, but rather, may be permitted to flow freely from its own wellsprings.

A

ALPHABETICAL SUMMARY OF THINKTANK COMMANDS

ALL

Keystroke: Alt-A
Mode: Paragraph Editor SELECT Menu

Deletes all instances of a specified group of characters within a paragraph, moving forward or backward from the present cursor position, chosen by cursor-left or cursor-right key.

ALPHA

Keystrokes: F10 F10 A
Mode: Top Level

Alphabetizes all first-level headlines under current bar cursor headline. Displayed on Secondary Command Menu.

BACKGROUND CHARACTER TOGGLE

Keystrokes: Alt-F2
Mode: Top Level

Changes "background" character on screen display from period to space, and vice versa.

BACKSPACE

Keystroke: Backspace key
Mode: Headline Editor

Deletes characters to the left of the flashing cursor.

BACKSPACE

Keystroke: Backspace key
Mode: Paragraph Editor

Deletes characters to the left of the flashing cursor.

BACKUP

Keystroke: B
Mode: Paragraph Editor EXIT Menu

Saves the current form of a ThinkTank paragraph to disk, then returns you to the Paragraph Editor with the cursor in its previous position.

BROWSE

Keystrokes: Alt-X
Mode: Paragraph Editor SELECT Menu

Selectively replaces a specified group of characters within a paragraph moving forward or backward from the present cursor position. You choose the direction of movement with the cursor-left or cursor-right key. Highlights each instance of the specified group of characters, allowing you to choose to delete with the ← key or continue the search.

BROWSE

Keystroke: B
Mode: FILES

Displays file names and summit-level headlines of all outline files on disks in either drive.

CARRIAGE-RETURN DISPLAY TOGGLE

Keystrokes: Alt-F3
Mode: Top Level

Turns the display of carriage-return symbols on or off.

CLOSE

Keystroke: C
Mode: FILES

Closes currently open outline file.

COLLAPSE

Keystroke: −
Mode: Top Level

Hides all text (headlines and paragraphs) nested under current bar cursor headline.

COPY

Keystrokes: Alt-C
Mode: Paragraph Editor SELECT Menu

Copies all text that has been highlighted through use of Paragraph Editor SELECT command.

COPY

Keystroke: C
Mode: MERGE

When merging two paragraphs, copies the contents of the merge-from paragraph to the merge-to paragraph, so that the same text will appear in both places.

COPY

Keystrokes: F10 F10 C
Mode: Top Level

Copies all text (headlines and paragraphs) nested under, and including, current bar cursor headline.

DATE

Keystrokes: F10 F10 D
Mode: Top Level

Allows you to change the system date. Displayed on Secondary Command Menu.

DELETE

Keystroke: D
Mode: MERGE

When merging two paragraphs, copies the contents of the merge-from paragraph to the merge-to paragraph, deleting the merge-from paragraph from its current headline.

DELETE

Keystroke: Del
Mode: Headline Editor

Deletes the character on which the flashing cursor is resting, and subsequent characters to the right.

DELETE

Keystroke: Del
Mode: Paragraph Editor

Deletes the character on which the flashing cursor is resting, and subsequent characters to the right.

DELETE

Keystrokes: Del Y
Mode: Paragraph Editor SELECT Menu

Deletes text highlighted through Paragraph Editor SELECT command. To cancel DELETE command prior to deleting, press N instead of Y. To restore deletion at same location use EDIT-UNDO command. You cannot UNDO this type of deletion at another location.

DELETE OUTLINE

Keystrokes: Del O
Mode: Top Level

Deletes entire outline nested under, and including, current bar cursor headling. May be restored at the same or another location by the DELETE-UNDO command.

DELETE PARAGRAPH

Keystrokes: Del P
Mode: Top Level

Deletes paragraph attached to current bar cursor headline, without disturbing any headlines, or any other paragraphs. A paragraph deleted in this manner cannot be restored

DELETE-UNDO

Keystrokes: Del U
Mode: Top Level

Restores the most recently deleted outline directly beneath the current position of the bar cursor.

EDIT HEADLINE

Keystrokes: E H *or* F3
Mode: Top Level

Enters the Headline Editor, allowing you to edit existing headlines anywhere in an outline. To cancel changes, press Esc before moving the flashing cursor away from the current headline Press ⏎ to save all the changes you made since entering the Headline Editor.

EDIT PARAGRAPH

Keystrokes: E P *or* F5
Mode: Top Level

Enters the Paragraph Editor, allowing you to edit the ThinkTank paragraph under the current bar cursor headline. Entering this command is the only way you can move the cursor freely within a paragraph. To exit, press Esc.

ENTER

Keystrokes: E
Mode: FILES

Allows you to enter the name of an existing file to be opened.

ERASE HEADLINE

Keystrokes: F4
Mode: Top Level

Erases the current bar cursor headline. Press ↵ to save the new headline or Esc to restore the original one. You may continue in the Headline Editor after entering this command by moving the flashing cursor to another headline. If you do, Esc will not restore the original headline on which you entered the Headline Editor.

EXISTS

Keystrokes: E
Mode: FILES

Tells ThinkTank that you want to open an existing outline file, rather than create a new one.

EXIT

Keystrokes: Esc E
Mode: Paragraph Editor

Exits the Paragraph Editor and returns to the top level, saving any changes you made since entering the Paragraph Editor, or since the last time you saved changes.

EXIT

Keystrokes: Esc Y
Mode: Top Level

Exits ThinkTank and returns to the operating system (A> prompt).
If you press Esc by mistake at the top level, you can return to
ThinkTank either by pressing Esc again or by pressing N.

EXIT-UNDO

Keystrokes: ESC U
Mode: Paragraph Editor EXIT Menu

Exits the Paragraph Editor and returns to the top level, restoring
anything you changed since the last time you saved to its condition prior to editing.

EXPAND

Keystrokes: +
Mode: Top Level

Displays all first-level headlines under the current bar cursor
headline. If the bar cursor headline contains a paragraph, it will
also be displayed. This command may be amplified to include
additional levels through the use of command prefixes.

EXPAND/COLLAPSE HEADLINES

Keystrokes: F8
Mode: Top Level

Displays all first-level headlines under the current bar cursor
headline, keeping paragraphs hidden. This command may be
amplified to include additional levels through the use of command prefixes.

If headlines are currently displayed, this command collapses
them, and any paragraphs displayed under them.

EXPAND/COLLAPSE PARAGRAPH

Keystroke: F7
Mode: Top Level

Displays the paragraph, if any, under the current bar cursor headline. Command prefixes do not work with this command. If a paragraph is displayed, this command will collapse it.

EXTRA

Keystroke: F10
Mode: Top Level

Displays the Secondary Command Menu when the Main Command Menu is displayed.

FILES

Keystroke: F
Mode: Top Level

Enters the FILES mode, to close an existing outline, and open another or start a new one. If no outline is currently open, ThinkTank is in the FILES mode.

FIND

Keystrokes: Alt-F
Mode: Paragraph Editor SELECT Menu

Searches for a given group of characters within a paragraph. Will search forward or backward from the current position of the flashing cursor; direction of movement is determined by the cursor-left or cursor-right key.

FINISH

Keystrokes: Alt-S
Mode: Paragraph Editor SELECT Menu

Exits the Paragraph Editor SELECT mode to return to the Paragraph Editor, with the selected portion of the paragraph remaining highlighted. To return from the SELECT mode to the Paragraph Editor and turn off the highlight, press Esc.

FORMATTED

Keystroke: F
Mode: PORT

Selects the formatted type of text file to be ported, either to disk or to the printer. Format may be controlled by setting any or all of the 17 print formatting options.

FUNCTION KEY MENU

Keystroke: F9
Mode: Top Level

Displays a menu of the effects of function keys F1 through F8. Any of these keys may be selected from this menu by pressing ←┘ when the key is highlighted. To enter other top-level commands, you must press Esc first.

HELP

Keystroke: F10
Mode: MOVE

Displays a list of effects of various cursor keys when moving an outline.

HELP

Keystroke: F10
Mode: Paragraph Editor

Displays a menu of commands available in the Paragraph Editor, including a secondary SELECT Command Menu. Any of these commands may be selected by pressing ← when the key is highlighted. To return to normal Paragraph Editor cursor movement, you must press Esc.

INFINITY

Keystrokes: ⇧ -3
Mode: Top Level

A command prefix. When used with EXPAND or EXPAND HEAD-LINES, displays *all* headlines nested under current bar cursor headline. When used with End key, moves the bar cursor to the last visible headline in your outline.

INSERT

Keystroke: Ins
Mode: Top Level

Inserts a new headline beneath the current bar cursor headline. Position of insertion may be changed by using the cursor-moving keys. Press Esc to enter the current headline and return to the top level. Press ← to enter the current headline and return to INSERT mode. Press Del to delete the current headline and return to the top level.

KEYWORD SEARCH

Keystrokes: K S
Mode: Top Level

Searches for a specified group of characters anywhere in the outline under the current bar cursor headline. You have the option of continuing the search or not after each match. Will match characters regardless of case.

KEYWORD XCHANGE

Keystrokes: K X
Mode: Top Level

Automatically replaces all instances of a specified group of characters with a different specified group of characters anywhere in the outline under the current bar cursor headline. Will replace only if all characters are of the equivalent case.

LAST

Keystroke: L
Mode: FILES

Reopens the outline file that was most recently open.

LINE-ORIENTED

Keystroke: L
Mode: PORT

When receiving a text file, inserts hard carriage returns at the end of each line of text (headlines and paragraphs) as they appear in the disk file.

MAIN COMMAND MENU

Keystroke: F10
Mode: Top Level

Displays a menu of top-level commands, which may be selected from the menu by pressing ↵ when the command is highlighted. Does not include all top-level commands. To select top-level commands which are not displayed on this menu, and are not displayed on the Secondary Command Menu (displayed by pressing F10), press Esc first. Top-level commands that are displayed on neither of these menus are on the Function Key Menu, displayed by pressing F9 when at the top level.

MERGE

Keystrokes: F10 F10 M
Mode: Top Level

Appends text to the end of the paragraph under the current bar cursor headline from the next headline down at the same level of indentation. No headlines must be visible between the merge-from and merge-to paragraphs. If no paragraph is present under the bar cursor headline, will create a new paragraph of the material to be merged. The merge-from paragraph may be either deleted or copied.

MOVE

Keystroke: F1
Mode: Top Level

Allows you to move the entire outline nested under, and including, the current bar cursor headline to another position in the outline using the cursor-moving keys. Note that you cannot move a headline that is one of several at the same level to the *left* and have it retain its current vertical position. It will automatically drop below all the other headlines at its previous level.

You cannot undo a move, except by retracing your steps. Press Esc or F1 to record the new position and exit MOVE mode.

NEW

Keystroke: N
Mode: FILES

Starts a new outline file.

NEW PARAGRAPH

Keystroke: F6
Mode: Top Level

Starts a new paragraph under the current bar cursor headline. If a paragraph is present, deletes it. You can avoid deleting a current paragraph by pressing N, which returns you to the top level. Y deletes the paragraph and places you in the Paragraph Editor.

Exiting the Paragraph Editor with the UNDO option will delete the new paragraph, but will not restore the old one if one was present.

PORT

Keystroke: P
Mode: Top Level

Enters the PORT mode, from which you can elect to send text to the printer or create a text file.

PRINTER

Keystroke: P
Mode: PORT

Sends text to the printer when in the PORT mode. Generally text sent to the printer is formatted before sending, although you can send structured and word processor style files to the printer as well.

PROMOTE

Keystrokes: F10 F10 P
Mode: Top Level

Moves all headlines under the current bar cursor headline one level to the left. Generally used when you want to delete the current bar cursor headline, but do not want to delete the outline nested beneath it.

READ

Keystroke: ←
Mode: Top Level

Holding down the ← key at the top level moves the bar cursor down through all levels of the outline, expanding everything that is currently hidden.

RECALL

Keystroke: F4
Modes: FILES, KEYWORD, FIND

Reenters the last text string you entered when ThinkTank asks you for a text string, with a prompt such as **name of DOS textfile?** or **pattern to search for?** This is especially useful for recalling file names when you are porting, or when you have inadvertently performed a SEARCH or FIND on the wrong part of your outline.

RECEIVE

Keystroke: R
Mode: PORT

Merges a text file from disk to your outline file, directly beneath the current bar cursor position. Text file may be received in either word-wrapped or line-oriented form.

RETURN

Keystrokes: R or Esc
Mode: FILES

Returns you to currently displayed outline, in top-level mode, from FILES mode.

RETURN

Keystrokes: R or Esc
Mode: Paragraph Editor

Returns you to Paragraph Editor from the EXIT Menu without saving or changing anything.

SECONDARY COMMAND MENU

Keystrokes: F10 F10
Mode: Top Level

Displays menu of top-level commands not available in either the Main Command Menu or the Function Key Menu. Commands from this menu may be selected by pressing ↵ when the command is highlighted. Press Esc to return to the Main Command Menu. Press F10 to return to the top level.

SELECT

Keystrokes: Alt-S
Mode: Paragraph Editor SELECT Menu

Enters SELECT mode, to highlight text to be copied or deleted. Selection starts from the current position of the flashing cursor and may be expanded in any direction (or contracted, once it exists) using any of the cursor-moving keys on the numeric keypad, including Home, End, PgUp, and PgDn. Press Esc to cancel the selection and return to normal Paragraph Editor cursor movement.

SEND

Keystroke: S
Mode: PORT

Specifies that you want to send a file to the disk or printer, rather than receive on into your outline.

SOUND TOGGLE

Keystrokes: Alt-F1
Mode: Top Level

Turns the sounds made by ThinkTank on and off.

START

Keystroke: Alt-S
Mode: Paragraph Editor SELECT Menu

Begins marking a selection for copying or deleting.

STRUCTURED

Keystroke: S
Mode: PORT

When sending a text file, specifies that you want the file to be a compact version of your outline, containing enough information for ThinkTank to reconstruct the outline. Generally used to create backup files, or as an intermediate file when sending text from one outline file to another.

TEXTFILE

Keystroke: T
Mode: PORT

When in PORT mode, tells ThinkTank that you want to send or receive a text file to/from a disk file.

TYPEOVER

Keystrokes: Alt-T
Mode: Paragraph Editor

Replaces text instead of inserting. *Note:* The Paragraph Editor is normally in INSERT mode. That is, if you start typing within a paragraph, the text to the right of the flashing cursor will be moved to the right. When in TYPEOVER mode, ThinkTank will not type over a carriage return. When a carriage return is encountered, it will be pushed to the right, ahead of the flashing cursor. Return to INSERT mode by pressing Esc.

WINDOW

Keystrokes: F2 or Space Bar
Mode: Top Level

Allows you to adjust the portion of your outline currently visible on the screen. F2 allows you to scroll up, down, left, or right, using the arrow keys on the numeric keypad. Pressing Esc freezes the screen display at its current position unless the bar cursor is off the screen. If the bar cursor is off the screen, the portion of your outline displayed will have the bar cursor headline as its first or last line, depending on whether the bar cursor is above or below the currently displayed portion when you press Esc. The entire bar cursor headline will be displayed, including the plus or minus sign, so if the plus or minus sign was to the left of the left margin, the left-to-right position will change to accommodate it.

When at the top level, pressing the Space Bar will scroll the screen progressively three spaces to the right and then to the left, as far as it can go and still display the entire bar cursor headline.

WORD-WRAPPED

Keystroke: W
Mode: PORT

When receiving a text file, formats the text so that the only hard carriage returns included will be those already in the text file.

If the text file you are receiving was created by porting headlines to a formatted text file, receiving it word-wrapped will place all consecutive headlines in a single paragraph, separated by three spaces.

WORDPROCESSOR

Keystroke: W
Mode: PORT

When porting to a text file, creates a file in a format readable by WordStar, and some other word-processing programs. In this format, all headlines will be flush left and terminated by carriage returns. Paragraphs will be word-wrapped, with carriage returns only where they have been entered and at the end.

XCHANGE

Keystrokes: Alt-X
Mode: Paragraph Editor

Displays the Paragraph Editor eXCHANGE Menu, from which you can choose to search for a group of characters within the paragraph. Replaces all instances of a group of characters, or selectively replaces instances of a group of characters.

APPENDIX

B

INTRODUCTION
TO PC-DOS

Your computer's disk operating system (DOS) is a collection of files and programs that manage data in your computer, controlling every aspect of the flow of data between your disks and your computer. Over 40 commands are available in DOS. Although many of these commands are advanced, there are a few that every user of PC-DOS or MS-DOS based computers should know.

In many other applications programs, DOS is *transparent*. It is present, but you don't have to interact with it directly. With ThinkTank, however, unless you have made your disk self-loading, you must load the DOS system disk before loading ThinkTank. Also, you cannot perform DOS functions while ThinkTank is running.

Thus, you need to know something about DOS in order to use ThinkTank effectively. If you have not used DOS directly, this appendix will give you the information you need to get started.

DOS has a pool of some 40 commands. Some are loaded into the computer along with DOS. (These are called *internal* commands.) You know DOS is present when you see the A> prompt on your screen. It will remain in the computer's memory until you turn the computer off, or reset it with Ctrl-Alt-Del.

The remainder of the commands call up separate programs on the DOS System Disk. To use these commands, you must have the DOS System Disk in drive A. These are called *external* commands.

SEEING WHAT'S ON YOUR DISKS

To see what files are on your disks, simply type

    dir ←┘

(for "directory") when you see the A> prompt. The computer will display a variety of information about the files on the disk in drive A: the names of the programs and other files, their length in bytes, and the date and time they were last modified or saved on disk. It will also tell you how much space, in bytes, is still available on your disk.

You can see such a directory of the files on the ThinkTank disk as well. Figure B.1 shows the directory of the ThinkTank disk.

```
A>dir

   Volume in drive B has no label
   Directory of   B:\

   TANK      EXE     208512    4-29-84    9:18p
   TANKOPTS  DAT       4608    5-29-84    1:47p
   TANK      DB       10752    5-29-84    1:38p
   TANK      SAV        512    5-29-84    1:46p
   INSTALL   EXE      47488    2-08-84    5:07p
   AUTOEXEC  BAT          7    2-08-84    5:08p
           6 File(s)         37888 bytes free
```

Figure B.1: The directory of the ThinkTank Program Disk.

If you would like to see the directory of a disk in drive B, type

dir b: ↵

when you see the **A>** prompt. If you expect to be doing a lot of work with the disk in drive B, you may want to temporarily change the drive priority of your system by typing **b:** when you see the **A>** prompt.

It doesn't matter to DOS whether you use uppercase or lowercase letters—either is acceptable.

FORMATTING DISKS

To store anything on a disk, you must use a *formatted* disk. To format a disk, place it in drive B and the DOS System Disk in drive A. Be sure that there is nothing of value on the disk in drive B, because formatting erases it completely. Type:

format b: ↵

The computer will respond with:

Insert new diskette for drive B:
and strike any key when ready

When you strike a key, the computer will say:

Formatting . . .

The red light on drive B will come on and you will hear some whirring and groaning noises for about a minute. When the noises stop, the computer will add the message **Format complete** to the **Formatting . . .** message, and display the following, if all is well:

> 362496 bytes total disk space
> 362496 bytes available on disk
>
> Format another (Y/N)?_

Your disk is now ready to accept data. If you press Y, the process will repeat. If you press N, you will be returned to the A> prompt.

If you have a faulty disk, the message will say something like:

> 362496 bytes total disk space
> 2048 bytes in bad sectors
> 360448 bytes available on disk

In this case, take the disk back to the dealer or send it back to the manufacturer, and ask for a replacement.

NAMING FILES

Every file on any disk must have a name. DOS imposes certain limitations on file names: they must not be more than eight characters, and may include any combination of letters and numbers. Although DOS will allow you to use certain punctuation marks in file names, ThinkTank will not.

A file name may optionally have an *extension* of up to three characters (letters and/or numbers). The extension is separated from the file name by a period (.). Generally, they are used to indicate that a group of files are related, or to distinguish between different types of files. ThinkTank files normally have three types of extensions: outlines have the extension **.DB**, for *data base;* files that record what the screen looked like the last time you closed the outline have the extension **.SAV**, for *save;* and text files have the extension **.TXT**, for *text.*

Each of these extensions has certain effects. The .DB extension tells ThinkTank that the file is an outline. Since ThinkTank automatically appends this extension to any outline file you create, you don't need to include it in the file name.

When you browse through the disk directories from within ThinkTank, the only file names you will see are those with a .DB extension. However, ThinkTank won't treat a file as an outline if you simply add this extension because it also looks for the summit line of the outline. If it cannot display a summit line between the menu bars, it will skip that file when browsing. If you enter the name of such a file from the keyboard, you will simply get the error message, **can't open that outline!** On the other hand, you can hide an outline from ThinkTank by changing the extension from .DB to something else. (See the section on renaming files.) You must change the extension back to .DB if at a later time you wish ThinkTank to be able to open the file.

Whenever you close a .DB file, ThinkTank creates a .SAV file, to record where you left off. The file name of the .SAV file is the same as that of the .DB file.

Certain extensions are reserved for certain types of files. You should not use them for other types of files. .BAS is used for programs in the BASIC language, .EXE and .COM are used for other types of programs, and .BAT is used for *batch* files, which are files, or programs, consisting of a series of DOS commands, which will be executed sequentially when you enter the name of the file.

You may use your own extensions on text files, if you wish. For example, if you create many text files of different types, you might use .ST for structured text files, .FMT for formatted text files, and use the default .TXT for WordStar files, as WordStar also uses the .TXT extension.

Don't be too clever in naming your files. If you aren't careful, you won't remember what your files contain when you see their names.

RENAMING FILES

You may sometimes find it necessary to rename a file. For example, you may want to have two copies of a given file on the same disk. Since you cannot have two identical file names on a single disk, you have to give one of them a new name. Or, you may wish to change the extension of a file, to remind you that it is related to another file. In this case, you would also have to rename the file.

The DOS command for renaming files is **RENAME.** To rename a file, when you see an **A>** prompt, type:

rename oldname.ext newname.ext ←┘

where **oldname** is the old file name, **newname** is the new file name, and **.ext** is the extension. You can change the extension, the file name, or both at once. If the file you want to rename is on a disk in drive B, type:

rename b:oldname.ext newname.ext ←┘

Whether you use capital or lowercase letters, the disk directory will show all file names in uppercase. If the computer gives you the message **file not found,** check the disk directory to be sure you are spelling the old name correctly. If you get the message **bad command or filename,** or **illegal number of paramaters,** check what you have typed to be sure that you have spelled everything correctly, and that the spaces are in the right places.

You can rename a group of related files by using DOS's *wild card* symbol, **∗**. For example, suppose you have a set of ThinkTank files with the names, **OUTLINE.DB, OUTLINE.SAV,** and **OUTLINE.TXT.** Let's say you want to rename them all so that they keep their extensions, but are called **WORKLIST.** Type:

rename outline.∗ worklist.∗ ←┘

This tells DOS to rename all the files named **OUTLINE** to **WORKLIST,** while keeping the extensions.

Similarly, you may change the extension on a group of related files. If you have been letting ThinkTank give your word-processor files its default extension **.TXT,** for example, and now want to distinguish them from other types of text files, you could type

rename ∗.txt ∗.wp ←┘

Then all the files on the disk in drive A which have the extension **.TXT** will have their extensions changed to **.WP.**

DOS will not give you a message unless it detects an error, so check the directory after renaming files to ensure that all has gone as you intended.

COPYING FILES

Copying files is the easiest way of making sure that you have an extra copy available if something damages your disk. You can copy files to the same disk with a different name, to a different disk with the same name, or to a different disk with a different name. You cannot copy a file onto the disk on which it is presently located and give both copies the same name, because the computer won't know which of the two you want when you ask for it. To copy a file onto the same disk, type:

> **copy oldname.ext newname.ext** ↲

The new name must differ from the old by at least one character either the name or the extension. If the new file is a backup copy, you might use the extension **.BAK** or **.BKP.**

To copy a file from drive B to drive A without changing its name, type:

> **copy b:oldname.ext a:** ↲

To copy a file from drive A to drive B without changing its name, type:

> **copy a:oldname.ext b:** ↲

To copy a file from drive B to drive A, and give the copy a new name at the same time, type:

> **copy b:oldname.ext a:newname.ext** ↲

You can use the wild card character (*) to copy a group of files the same way you use it to rename a group of files. For example:

> **copy b:*.db a:** ↲

will copy all **.DB** files from the disk in drive B to the disk in drive A.

When you have made a successful copy, the computer displays:

> **1 file(s) copied**

If you have copied more than one file by using the wild card character, the number in the message will change to reflect the actual number of files copied. You should always use the **dir** command for the drive to which the copy is being sent, to verify the success of the operation.

ERASING FILES

There are several reasons you might want to erase a file. You might simply have no further use for a file. Or you may have copied something like a .DB file onto another disk because you started it on a disk full of other files, and now find that you have no more room in your outline to add things. You may then want to erase it from the original disk. You can erase a file from a disk, but once you do so it will be gone forever. Alternatively, you might copy all the other files from your original disk, and then erase the originals. You might also want to reorganize your disks: copy groups of related files onto a single disk, and then eliminate them from the various disks on which you had originally created them. The command to erase a file is:

> **erase filename.ext** ←┘

If your file name has an extension, it must be included in the command, even if only one file has that name. Otherwise the computer will display:

> **bad command or filename**

You can use the wild card character in erasing. For example, when you want to erase both a .DB file and its corresponding .SAV file, type:

> **erase outline.*** ←┘

If an erasure is successful, you will simply be returned to the A> prompt. Use the **dir** command to check on the results.

You can also erase an entire disk by using the wild card character in the **erase** command:

> **erase *.*** ←┘

or, if the disk is in drive B,

> **erase b:*.*** ↵

If you type this command, the computer will respond with:

> **Are you sure (Y/N)?_**

so you don't accidentally erase an entire disk. If you wish to pro-ceed, press Y ↵ . If a disk is completely erased, the computer will display the message

> **File not found**

when you enter the **dir** command.

BACKING UP DISKS

You can back up an entire disk simply by typing:

> **copy b:*.* a:** ↵

If the files on the source disk have been repeatedly changed, they may be scattered in bits and pieces all over the disk; this com-mand will regroup them so that each file is continuous.

But if your files are not scattered, there is a much faster way to copy an entire disk. It requires a DOS external command. Place the DOS System Disk in drive A and type:

> **diskcopy a: b:**

the computer will display the message:

> **Insert source disk in drive A**
>
> **Insert target disk in drive B**
>
> **then strike any key when ready**

The computer will then copy everything from drive A to drive B, in blocks as large as its memory can hold, formatting the target disk as it goes if necessary. When it is finished, the prompt:

> **Copy another (Y/N)?_**

will appear. If you don't want to copy another, type N, and you will be asked to reinsert your DOS System Disk before proceeding.

CHECKING MEMORY

Another external command you may find useful is the **CHKDSK** command. This will check the amounts of memory available both on your disk and in your computer. To use it, place the DOS System Disk in drive A and the disk you want to check in drive B. Then type:

> chkdsk b: ↵

After checking the disk, the computer will display any error messages, along with the following status report:

> NN disk files
> NNNNNN bytes total disk space
> NNNNNN bytes remain available
>
> NNNNNN bytes total memory
> NNNNNN bytes free

In place of the N's will be numbers telling you how much space is available on the disk, in the computer's memory, etc.

CREATING A .BAT FILE
FOR EASY LOADING

If you have a number of DOS housekeeping tasks to perform before you start using a program, you should consider creating a .BAT file to take the tedium out of setting up. You can create a .BAT file using any text editor, or a word processor such as WordStar in nondocument mode.

For working with a PC with 512K of memory, a RAMdisk, and a 1200-baud serial printer, I created the **BAT** file shown in Figure B.2 using EDLIN, the text editor on the DOS System Disk.

```
MODE LPT1:=COM1:
MODE COM1: 12,N,8,1,P
COPY TANK.EXE C:
C:TANK
```

Figure B.2: A .BAT File.

I replaced the **AUTOEXEC.BAT** file on the ThinkTank Program Disk with this file using the **copy** command, and I copied the **MODE.COM** program from the DOS System Disk onto the ThinkTank Program Disk by the same means. Here is what this short program does:

1. **MODE LPT1:=COM1:** loads the **MODE.COM** program, necessary for the printer's operation, into the computer from the ThinkTank disk, and redirects printed output from LPT1, the normal parallel output port, to the communications port.

2. **MODE COM1: 12,N,8,1,P** sets the baud rate to 1200, and establishes the communications protocols necessary for the printer.

3. **COPY TANK.EXE C:** copies the actual ThinkTank program into the RAMdisk.

4. **C:TANK** loads the program from the RAMdisk into the computer's working memory.

With this program, I simply insert the ThinkTank disk and turn the computer on. The computer will perform all the operations outlined above, just as if I had instructed it to do so by entering the commands from the keyboard.

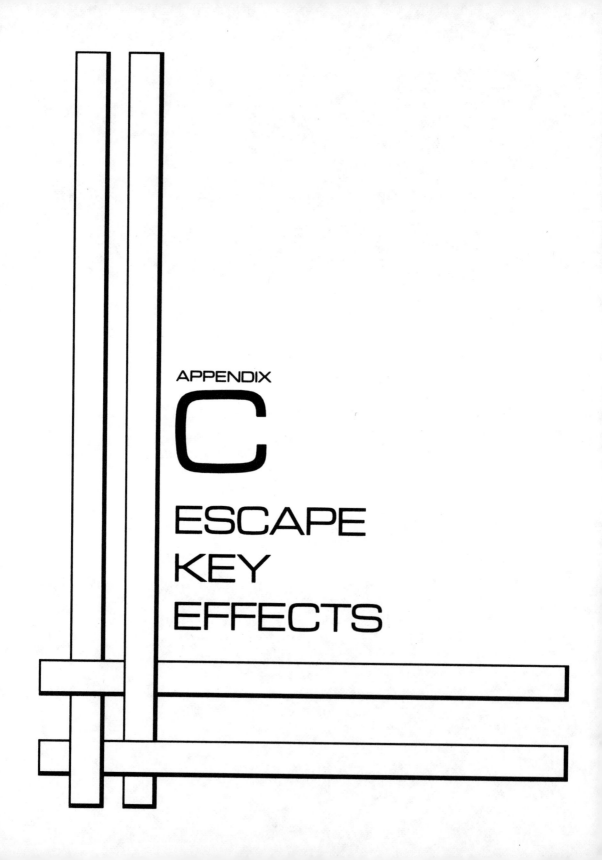

APPENDIX

C

ESCAPE KEY EFFECTS

The escape key has an effect in virtually every mode. The following table summarizes those effects. Commands are grouped by mode. Top-level commands are farthest to the left, with their subsidiary commands indented below them.

MODE/COMMAND	EFFECT
DELETE	If type of deletion has not yet been entered, cancels DELETE command, then returns to top level.
ERASE HEADLINE	Restores erased headline and returns to top level.
FILES mode	Returns to top level.
Function Key Menu	Returns to top level.
Headline Editor	Cancels any changes to current headline and returns to top level.
INSERT	Enters headline, then returns to top level.
KEYWORD mode	At any level of KEYWORD mode, returns to top level. If pressed *after* you have responded to the prompt **pattern to replace with?**, but *before* you press the ← key, returns you to the prompt **pattern to search for?**

Main Command Menu	Returns to top level.
MOVE	Enters current position of moved outline, then returns to top level.
Paragraph Editor	Enters EXIT mode.
EDIT Command Menu	Returns to normal cursor movement.
EXIT Menu	Returns to Paragraph Editor without saving or changing anything.
FIND command	Cancels command, returns to normal cursor movement. If pressed *after* entering a set of characters to be found, but *before* pressing ← , cancels the entry. This allows a different set of characters to be entered.
SELECT Menu	Cancels SELECT command, returning to normal cursor movement. After an operation has been completed, returns to normal cursor movement without highlighting selected portion.
TYPEOVER mode	Returns to normal INSERT mode.
XCHANGE command	Cancels command, returns to normal cursor movement. If pressed *after* entering a set of characters to be found or replaced but

before pressing ↵ , cancels the entry. This allows a different set of characters to be entered.

PORT mode	Returns to top level. At every level in the PORT Command Menu, returns to previous level. When sending or receiving a text file, interrupts the transmission process. When printing, interrupts the printing operation.
FORMAT settings	Cancels new entry, restores previous settings.
Secondary Command Menu	Returns to Main Command Menu.
WINDOW	Enters current window position, unless bar cursor headline is not fully displayed; otherwise displays nearest full window including bar cursor headline.

INDEX

Selections from The SYBEX Library

Computer Books for Kids

THE COMPUTER ABC'S
by Daniel Le Noury and Rodnay Zaks
64 pp., illustr., Ref. 0-167
This beautifully illustrated, colorful book for parents and children takes you alphabetically through the world of computers, explaining each concept in simple language.

MONICA THE COMPUTER MOUSE
by Donna Bearden, illustrated by Brad W. Foster
64 pp., illustr., Hardcover, Ref. 0-214
Lavishly illustrated in color, this book tells the story of Monica the mouse, as she travels around to learn about several different kids of computers and the jobs they can do. For ages 5–8.

POWER UP! KIDS' GUIDE TO THE APPLE IIe® /IIc™
by Marty DeJonghe and Caroline Earhart
200 pp., illustr., Ref. 0-212
Colorful illustrations and a friendly robot highlight this guide to the Apple IIe/IIc for kids 8–11.

BANK STREET WRITING WITH YOUR APPLE®
by Stanley Schatt, Ph.D. and Jane Abrams Schatt, M.A.
150 pp., illustr., Ref. 0-189
These engaging exercises show children aged 10–13 how to use Bank Street Writer for fun, profit, and school work.

POWER UP! KIDS' GUIDE TO THE COMMODORE 64™
by Marty DeJonghe and Caroline Earhart
192 pp., illustr., Ref. 0-188
Colorful illustrations and a friendly robot highlight this guide to the Commodore 64 for kids 8–11.

Humor

COMPUTER CRAZY
by Daniel Le Noury
100 pp., illustr., Ref. 0-173
No matter how you feel about computers, these cartoons will have you laughing about them.

MOTHER GOOSE YOUR COMPUTER: A GROWNUP'S GARDEN OF SILICON SATIRE
by Paul Panish and Anna Belle Panish, illustrated by Terry Small
96 pp., illustr., Ref. 0-198
This richly illustrated hardcover book uses parodies of familiar Mother Goose rhymes to satirize the world of high technology.

Special Interest

COMPUTER POWER FOR YOUR LAW OFFICE
by Daniel Remer
142 pp., Ref. 0-109
How to use computers to reach peak productivity in your law office, simply and inexpensively.

THE COLLEGE STUDENT'S PERSONAL COMPUTER HANDBOOK

by Bryan Pfaffenberger

210 pp., illustr., Ref. 0-170

This friendly guide will aid students in selecting a computer system for college study, managing information in a college course, and writing research papers.

CELESTIAL BASIC

by Eric Burgess

300 pp., 65 illustr., Ref. 0-087

A collection of BASIC programs that rapidly complete the chores of typical astronomical computations. It's like having a planetarium in your own home! Displays apparent movement of stars, planets and meteor showers.

COMPUTER POWER FOR YOUR ACCOUNTING FIRM

by James Morgan, C.P.A.

250 pp., illustr., Ref. 0-164

This book is a convenient source of information about computerizing your accounting office, with an emphasis on hardware and software options.

PERSONAL COMPUTERS AND SPECIAL NEEDS

by Frank G. Bowe

175 pp., illustr., Ref. 0-193

Learn how people are overcoming problems with hearing, vision, mobility, and learning, through the use of computer technology.

ESPIONAGE IN THE SILICON VALLEY

by John D. Halamka

200 pp., illustr., Ref. 0-225

Discover the behind-the-scenes stories of famous high-tech spy cases you've seen in the headlines.

ASTROLOGY ON YOUR PERSONAL COMPUTER

by Hank Friedman

225 pp., illustr., Ref. 0-226

An invaluable aid for astrologers who want to streamline their calculation and data management chores with the right combination of hardware and software.

Computer Specific

Apple II—Macintosh

THE EASY GUIDE TO YOUR APPLE II®

by Joseph Kascmer

147 pp., illustr., Ref. 0-122

A friendly introduction to the Apple II, II plus and the IIe.

APPLE II® BASIC PROGRAMS IN MINUTES

by Stanley R. Trost

150 pp., illustr., Ref. 0-121

A collection of ready-to-run programs for financial calculations, investment analysis, record keeping, and many more home and office applications. These programs can be entered on your Apple II plus or IIe in minutes!

THE APPLE IIc™: A PRACTICAL GUIDE

by Thomas Blackadar

175 pp., illustr., Ref. 0-241

Learn all you need to know about the Apple IIc! This jargon-free companion gives you a guided tour of Apple's new machine.

THE BEST OF EDUCATIONAL SOFTWARE FOR APPLE II® COMPUTERS

by Gary G. Bitter, Ph.D. and Kay Gore

300 pp., Ref. 0-206

Here is a handy guide for parents and an invaluable reference for educators who must make decisions about software purchases.

THE EASY GUIDE TO YOUR MACINTOSH™

by Joseph Caggiano

280 pp., illustr., Ref. 0-216

This easy-to-read guide takes you all the way from set-up to more advanced activities such as using Macwrite, Macpaint, and Multiplan.

Commodore 64/VIC-20

THE BEST OF COMMODORE 64™ SOFTWARE

by Thomas Blackadar

150 pp., illustr., Ref. 0-194

Save yourself time and frustration with this buyer's guide to Commodore 64 software. Find the best game, music, education, and home management programs on the market today.

GRAPHICS GUIDE TO THE COMMODORE 64™

by Charles Platt

261 pp., illustr., Ref. 0-138

This easy-to-understand book will appeal to anyone who wants to master the Commodore 64's powerful graphics features.

PARENTS, KIDS, AND THE COMMODORE 64™

by Lynne Alper and Meg Holmberg

110 pp., illustr., Ref. 0-234

This book answers parents' questions about the educational possibilities of the Commodore 64.

THE EASY GUIDE TO YOUR COMMODORE 64™

by Joseph Kascmer

126 pp., illustr., Ref. 0-126

A friendly introduction to the Commodore 64.

CP/M Systems

THE CP/M® HANDBOOK

by Rodnay Zaks

320 pp., 100 illustr., Ref 0-048

An indispensable reference and guide to CP/M—the most widely-used operating system for small computers.

MASTERING CP/M®

by Alan R. Miller

398 pp., illustr., Ref. 0-068

For advanced CP/M users or systems programmers who want maximum use of the CP/M operating system . . . takes up where our *CP/M Handbook* leaves off.

THE BEST OF CP/M® SOFTWARE

by John D. Halamka

250 pp., Ref. 0-100

This book reviews tried-and-tested, commercially available software for your CP/M system.

INSTANT CP/M:® A KEYSTROKE GUIDE

by Robert Levine

250 pp., illustr., Ref. 0-132

This novice's guide includes a complete explanation of terms and commands, showing how they appear on the screen and what they do—a quick, foolproof way to gain proficiency with CP/M.

IBM PC and Compatibles

THE ABC'S OF THE IBM® PC

by Joan Lasselle and Carol Ramsay

143 pp., illustr., Ref. 0-102

This book will take you through the first crucial steps in learning to use the IBM PC.

THE BEST OF IBM® PC SOFTWARE

by Stanley R. Trost

351 pp., Ref. 0-104

Separates the wheat from the chaff in the world of IBM PC software. Tells you what to expect from the best available IBM PC programs.

THE IBM® PC-DOS HANDBOOK

by Richard Allen King

296 pp., Ref. 0-103

Explains the PC disk operating system.

Get the most out of your PC by adapting its capabilities to your specific needs.

BUSINESS GRAPHICS FOR THE IBM® PC
by Nelson Ford
259 pp., illustr., Ref. 0-124
Ready-to-run programs for creating line graphs, multiple bar graphs, pie charts, and more. An ideal way to use your PC's business capabilities!

DATA FILE PROGRAMMING ON YOUR IBM® PC
by Alan Simpson
219 pp., illustr., Ref. 0-146
This book provides instructions and examples for managing data files in BASIC. Programming design and development are extensively discussed.

SELECTING THE RIGHT DATA BASE SOFTWARE FOR THE IBM® PC

SELECTING THE RIGHT WORD PROCESSING SOFTWARE FOR THE IBM® PC

SELECTING THE RIGHT SPREADSHEET SOFTWARE FOR THE IBM® PC
by Kathleen McHugh and Veronica Corchado
100 pp., illustr., Ref. 0-174, 0-177, 0-178
This series on selecting the right business software offers the busy professional concise, informative reviews of the best available software packages.

IBM PCjr

IBM® PCjr™ BASIC PROGRAMS IN MINUTES
by Stanley R. Trost
175 pp., illustr., Ref. 0-205
Here is a practical set of BASIC programs for business, financial, real estate, data analysis, record keeping, and educational applications, ready to enter on your PCjr.

Software Specific

Spreadsheets

THE COMPLETE GUIDE TO YOUR IBM® PCjr™
by Douglas Herbert
625 pp., illustr., Ref. 0-179
Learn to master the new hardware and DOS features that IBM has introduced with the PCjr. A fold-out reference poster is included.

DOING BUSINESS WITH MULTIPLAN™
by Richard Allen King and Stanley R. Trost
250 pp., illustr., Ref. 0-148
This book will show you how using Multiplan can be nearly as easy as learning to use a pocket calculator. It presents a collection of templates for business applications.

MASTERING VISICALC®
by Douglas Hergert
217 pp., 140 illustr., Ref. 0-090
Explains how to use the VisiCalc "electronic spreadsheet" functions and provides examples of each. Makes using this powerful program simple.

DOING BUSINESS WITH VISICALC®
by Stanley R. Trost
260 pp., illustr., Ref. 0-086
Presents accounting and management planning applications—from financial statements to master budgets; from pricing models to investment strategies.

DOING BUSINESS WITH SUPERCALC™
by Stanley R. Trost
248 pp., illustr., Ref. 0-095
Presents accounting and management planning applications—from financial statements to master budgets; from pricing models to investment strategies.

MULTIPLAN™ ON THE COMMODORE 64™

by Richard Allen King

260 pp., illustr., Ref. 0-231

This clear, straighforward guide will give you a firm grasp on Multiplan's functions, as well as provide a collection of useful template programs.

Word Processing

INTRODUCTION TO WORDSTAR®

by Arthur Naiman

202 pp., 30 illustr., Ref. 0-134

Makes it easy to learn WordStar, a powerful word processing program for personal computers.

PRACTICAL WORDSTAR® USES

by Julie Anne Arca

303 pp., illustr., Ref. 0-107

Pick your most time-consuming office tasks and this book will show you how to streamline them with WordStar.

THE COMPLETE GUIDE TO MULTIMATE™

by Carol Holcomb Dreger

250 pp., illustr., Ref. 0-229

A concise introduction to the many practical applications of this powerful word processing program.

Data Base Management Systems

UNDERSTANDING dBASE II™

by Alan Simpson

260 pp., illustr., Ref. 0-147

Learn programming techniques for mailing label systems, bookkeeping, and data management, as well as ways to interface dBASE II with other software systems.

THE ABC'S OF 1-2-3™

by Chris Gilbert and Laurie Williams

225 pp., illustr., Ref. 0-168

For those new to the LOTUS 1-2-3 program, this book offers step-by-step

instructions in mastering its spreadsheet, data base, and graphing capabilities.

MASTERING APPLEWORKS™

by Elna Tymes

250 pp., illustr., Ref. 0-240

Here is a business-oriented introduction to AppleWorks, the new integrated software package from Apple. No experience with computers is assumed.

Languages

BASIC

YOUR FIRST BASIC PROGRAM

by Rodnay Zaks

182 pp., illustr. in color, Ref. 0-092

A "how-to-program" book for the first time computer user, aged 8 to 88.

BASIC FOR BUSINESS

by Douglas Hergert

224 pp., 15 illustr., Ref. 0-080

A logically organized, no-nonsense introduction to BASIC programming for business applications. Includes many fully-explained accounting programs, and shows you how to write your own.

EXECUTIVE PLANNING WITH BASIC

by X. T. Bui

196 pp., 19 illustr., Ref. 0-083

An important collection of business management decision models in BASIC, including inventory management (EOQ), critical path analysis and PERT, financial ratio analysis, portfolio management, and much more.

Pascal

INTRODUCTION TO PASCAL (Including UCSD Pascal™)

by Rodnay Zaks

420 pp., 130 illustr., Ref. 0-066

A step-by-step introduction for anyone

who wants to learn the Pascal language. Describes UCSD and Standard Pascals. No technical background is assumed.

THE PASCAL HANDBOOK
by Jacques Tiberghien
486 pp., 270 illustr., Ref. 0-053
A dictionary of the Pascal language, defining every reserved word, operator, procedure, and function found in all major versions of Pascal.

DOING BUSINESS WITH PASCAL
by Richard Hergert and Douglas Hergert
371 pp., illustr., Ref. 0-091
Practical tips for using Pascal programming in business. Covers design considerations, language extensions, and applications examples.

Other Languages

UNDERSTANDING C
by Bruce H. Hunter
320 pp., Ref 0-123
Explains how to program in powerful C language for a variety of applications. Some programming experience assumed.

FIFTY PASCAL PROGRAMS
by Bruce H. Hunter
338 pp., illustr., Ref. 0-110
More than just a collection of useful programs! Structured programming techniques are emphasized and concepts such as data type creation and array manipulation are clearly illustrated.

Technical

Assembly Language

PROGRAMMING THE 6502
by Rodnay Zaks
386 pp., 160 illustr., Ref. 0-135
Assembly language programming for the 6502, from basic concepts to advanced data structures.

PROGRAMMING THE Z80®
by Rodnay Zaks
624 pp., 200 illustr., Ref. 0-069
A complete course in programming the Z80 microprocessor and a thorough introduction to assembly language.

Hardware

FROM CHIPS TO SYSTEMS: AN INTRODUCTION TO MICROPROCESSORS
by Rodnay Zaks
552 pp., 400 illustr., Ref. 0-063
A simple and comprehensive introduction to microprocessors from both a hardware and software standpoint: what they are, how they operate, how to assemble them into a complete system.

THE RS-232 SOLUTION
by Joe Campbell
194 pp., illustr., Ref. 0-140
Finally, a book that will show you how to correctly interface your computer to any RS-232-C peripheral.

Operating Systems

REAL WORLD UNIX™
by John D. Halamka
209 pp., Ref. 0-093
This book is written for the beginning and intermediate UNIX user in a practical, straightforward manner, with specific instructions given for many business applications.

SYBEX COMPUTER BOOKS

are different.
Here is why . . .

At SYBEX, each book is designed with you in mind. Every manuscript is carefully selected and supervised by our editors, who are themselves computer experts. We publish the best authors, whose technical expertise is matched by an ability to write clearly and to communicate effectively. Programs are thoroughly tested for accuracy by our technical staff. Our computerized production department goes to great lengths to make sure that each book is well-designed.

In the pursuit of timeliness, SYBEX has achieved many publishing firsts. SYBEX was among the first to integrate personal computers used by authors and staff into the publishing process. SYBEX was the first to publish books on the CP/M operating system, microprocessor interfacing techniques, word processing, and many more topics.

Expertise in computers and dedication to the highest quality product have made SYBEX a world leader in computer book publishing. Translated into fourteen languages, SYBEX books have helped millions of people around the world to get the most from their computers. We hope we have helped you, too.

For a complete catalog of our publications please contact:

U.S.A.	FRANCE	GERMANY	UNITED KINGDOM
SYBEX, Inc.	SYBEX	SYBEX-Verlag GmbH	SYBEX, Ltd.
2344 Sixth Street	6–8 Impasse du Curé	Vogelsanger Weg 111	Unit 4–Bourne Industrial
Berkeley,	75018 Paris	4000 Düsseldorf 30	Park
California 94710	France	West Germany	Bourne Road, Crayford
Tel: (800) 227-2346	Tel: 01/203–9595	Tel: (0211) 626441	Kent DA1 4BZ England
(415) 848-8233	Telex: 211801	Telex: 8588163	Tel: (0322) 57717
Telex: 336311			Telex: 896939